LIVING AWARENESS

Awakening to the Roots of Learning and Perception

PETER WRYCZA, PhD

LIVING AWARENESS

Awakening to the Roots of Learning and Perception

PETER WRYCZA, PhD

GATEWAY BOOKS, BATH, UK

First published 1997 by
GATEWAY BOOKS,
The Hollies, Wellow,
Bath, BA2 8QJ, U.K.

Copyright (c) 1997 Peter Wrycza

Distributed in the U.S.A. by
National Book Network
4720 Boston Way, Lanham, MD 20706

Cover design by The Design Studio, Bristol

Text set in Goudy OlSt 10½ on 12pt

by Oak Press, Castleton
Printed and bound by
Redwood Books of Trowbridge

British Library Cataloguing-in Publication Data:
A catalogue record for this book is
available from the British Library

ISBN 1-85860-045-6

Contents

1. Awareness — Life's Secret Seam of Plenty 1
2. Levels of Life 24
3. Awareness, Relationship and Maturation 35
4. From Time to Timelessness 53
5. Unity in Diversity: Living in Wholeness 61
6. Pathways to Awareness: From Movement to Stillness 71
7. Moving Being 80
8. From Sensing to Transcending 96
9. Awareness-with-Feeling; Freeing the Emotions 115
10. Language and Awareness: The Syntax of Self 126
11. Open Heart Learning: Updating Personal Patterns and Beliefs 153
12. Role, Identity and Personal Purpose 178
13. Living Awareness in Groups 197
14. From Personal to Planetary Transformation 212
15. The Way in Wisdom 224
Afterword: A Personal Quest 230
Appendices: Living Awareness in Practice 239
Glossary 241
Reading Around Living Awareness 244
Addresses 246
Index 247

Acknowledgements

I would like to thank the many teachers and friends, but for whom this book would have remained undreamt and unwritten. In particular, to select a few key figures, I was deeply nourished at important moments by the inspiration of Robert Dilts and Gene Early from the world of NLP, Natalie Rogers of PCETI, Gabrielle Roth of the Moving Centre, and Marharishi Mahesh Yogi, founder of TM.

I am deeply grateful also to Peter and Martine Winnington and Jan Ardui for their warmth, hospitality and support throughout this work's long gestation. Thanks, too, to Lynn Bell, Huntley Dent, Jude Elsen, Barry Hesketh, Jim Manske and my mother and brothers who provided valuable, timely and sometimes painful feedback; to Madeleine de Joly and Jeanette Berson who believed when I doubted; and to Dinah who doubted when I believed.

That this book is in your hands is also thanks in large measure to Cecelia Albert, Joyce Collin-Smith and, of course, Alick Bartholomew, my publisher, who were so sure that what I had written deserved a wider audience.

CHAPTER ONE

Awareness — Life's Secret Seam of Plenty

Summary
Living a life of quality — the issue in times of plenty — calls for a journey into our inner selves. There we can find the keys of love and wisdom contained in our own essence, our awareness. Active awareness of life's varied elements depends on an underlying simple 'pure awareness'. This is our most significant and underused resource. Greater openness to it transforms every facet of our personal and professional lives in a positive way. Resolution of the collective problems that plague our times depend upon it.

Know that by which everything is known. Upanishads

Changing times

We live in times that are both amazing and impossible. Science and technology have given us untold abundance, particularly in the so-called developed world. We are physically larger, generally healthier, and live longer. If you are reading this book, you probably already have the wherewithal to enjoy what for many of the poorest people on our planet would be a life of luxury. Yet in your heart you may well be no better off. You may have much to appreciate in your life, and yet still be uneasy about the kind of world we are creating for ourselves and our children. Quality of life is now a key issue — both for individuals and for whole cultures.

Rapidly accelerating change means that developments, which previously might have taken a generation of two, happen within a few years. This acceleration of time has mixed effects. On the one hand we discover incredible possibilities as our world shrinks with ever-new ways of global communication — satellites, computer networks, multi-media, and so on. But we also find our traditions eroding, cutting us off from our past, destabilising our present, and making the future uncertain.

With accelerated electronic sophistication comes increasing alienation from the natural world. Whereas our ancestors measured the change of times with sensitivity to the phases of the Moon, shifts in the seasons, and patterns in the weather, we rely on the digital watch. We live and work in environments increasingly divorced from nature. Environmental illness, allergies, and the sick-building syndrome remind us that we are out of kilter with the natural world.

Our solutions always seem to carry a price tag. We boost food production with the aid of pesticides and fertilisers that deplete the soil and upset the balance of nature. We enjoy ease of movement with expanded transport, while contributing to air pollution. We know that the economics of ever-increasing growth fit ill with the finite resources on our planet, but find that the present system has a momentum of its own.

Our age is one of relativity. Our media and urbanised sophistication easily make as blasé — 'been there; done that', as the saying goes. In our great cities, people from the diverse cultures of the world rub shoulders. Mass tourism and TV have shown us how many different ways there are to live. We are increasingly aware that meaning is a function of personal and time-bound interpretation; whereas previously people had faith, we have comparative religion.

With old traditions and values in meltdown, we are unsure how to replace them. Many people — and perhaps you are among them — sense a need for deep renewal. The challenges and opportunities of our times suggest that there are no easy solutions. Our leaders offer little solace, for they share the same dilemmas as ourselves.

Yet possibilities for renewal are ever-present. Our societies form large scale living systems, of which each of us is part. And living systems intrinsically seek the creative edge between order and chaos. Individually and collectively we can be more in harmony with a way of living in which we adjust appropriately to changing conditions. Each of us can begin to reclaim a life of quality, and in so doing contribute to renewal in the whole.

The great cultures and traditions of the world have been inspired by those who, like Aeneas, mythic founder of Rome, or Dante, one of the fathers of the Renaissance, went into the underworld or wilderness, to emerge with answers for their times. We may not see ourselves as a new Aeneas or Orpheus. But each of us can undertake a voyage of discovery within our own hearts and minds. This book is an invitation to such a journey.

Towards a Life of Quality

The secret of a life of quality doesn't lie in what we do, nor in what we own. It is not to be found in where we live, nor even in who we have in our lives. For we all know of those who have plenty, appear to do more interesting things, live in more beautiful places than we do, or have more engaging partners, but still aren't satisfied.

It is so easy to fall into thinking that the key to a life of quality lies in what we have or do in our life that we forget that these are by no means the whole answer. Satisfaction doesn't lie in the content of life. It is not to be found in the world, but in some deeper, more elusive quality. And if we are to discover this and have it present in our lives, we need to know more about the nature of experience itself.

REPRESENTATIONS OF REALITY

Most people who have visited an old school or childhood haunt years later are surprised at how small things seem to the adult eye. The places themselves may have changed little, but our perception of them has altered.

Most of the time, we act as if there is a real world 'out there'. But the real world is always interpreted by our machinery of experience. We don't experience things directly. We create representations of what might be out there in the world. What we see and hear are interpretations of reality through our minds and bodies. Our senses do not replicate the world, they invent it for us.

And that applies when we are engaged directly with the world, looking, listening, and touching in the present moment. But a lot of the time we are involved not only with our representations of the world, but with our representations of those representations. Whenever we dip into memory and, say, relive a pleasant moment with a friend or imagine how we will spend our next holiday, we are experiencing our mind's creations of what happened or what might happen.

In that sense, we don't live in the real world, but in our own private version of it. If we don't like the quality of our life, we may have to take some responsibility. And if we do shape our own realities, we may also discover ways to experience things differently so that what we encounter in life matches our hopes and dreams more closely. If all reality is virtual reality, we can create virtually anything. We can make changes.

ATTENTION

Since the key to a life of quality lies in part in how we think about and perceive our world, our attention is vital. For instance, a friend of mine, Jane, often finds that she worries a lot about things that never actually happen. She learns that an awkward aunt plans to come and visit. She makes pictures in her head of previous times when that aunt has visited and scolded her children. She imagines the same things happening again. She says to herself "It will be awful, what can I do?" She feels she must receive the aunt, and complains about it to her husband and neighbours. They commiserate, or offer the usual "Why don't you . . ." advice, to which Jane replies, "You don't understand, I can't do that. . .", and continues to complain.

When the aunt actually arrives, it turns out she has just fallen in love and is sweet and happy with everyone, or perhaps she has 'flu and doesn't come at all. Jane has spent weeks with her attention firmly focused on what would go wrong and made herself miserable, perhaps others too. All for something that never happened.

There is a place for downside planning; but the question is, overall, where and how are we directing our attention? Is it serving the quality of our lives? Or is it making us miserable?

Take a moment to make a brief inventory of where you habitually direct your attention, or perhaps more accurately, where it directs you. You may like to use a blank notebook as a personal journal in which to record your thoughts as you progress through the book. For now, consider whether you attend appropriately to:

* yourself
* other people.
* your work and to things such as your home, hobbies, and interests.

Are these balanced, or do you neglect your needs for other people's, or theirs for yours? Do you give too much attention to your career or possessions or collecting information, reading even the backs of cereal packets? What feedback do others give you about how you direct your attention in life?

Do you dwell too much on the past? Or neglect the past, failing to learn from mistakes and repeating the same old patterns over and over again?

Are you too much in the future, worrying or dreaming about what next week, next year, or even years down the road might bring? Or do you neglect the future, finding, say, that your radiator has cracked, because you forgot to put in anti-freeze before the frosts came?

How do you relate to the present? What parts of your world do you emphasise? Do you 'count your blessings'? Do you see beauty, even in the ugly? Or are you for ever noticing what's wrong with other people and what's missing in your life? Does your attention lean towards criticism or appreciation of what you experience in daily life? Is the balance right?

Does your attention get turned enough to the things that you really care about in ways that match your sense of what is truly important in your life? What do you neglect that you regret now, or sense you might regret later on? (For instance, it's a constant comment of parents that their children grow up so quickly and they didn't really enjoy them enough while they were little.)

How might you need to reorient your attention to have a better balance in life, and find yourself more truly attentive in ways that support a life of quality?

In a sense, making an inventory of where we direct our attention is the easy bit. What is more challenging is to reorient the attention, so that it works for us in more delightful ways. For this we may need to understand a little more about the nature of attention and what influences it.

Attention is the directing of the machinery of experience towards certain kinds of experience. The Latin roots *ad-tendere* mean 'holding towards'.

There are four primary modes of attention — according to whether we direct it towards inner or outer experience, and whether we focus our attention broadly or narrowly. We exercise each of these four modes in relation to the main channels of sensory experience. We can orient our attention more to what we see, hear, or feel and touch.[1]

Where do you direct your attention — more towards what you experience in the world around you or in your own internal world? Are you action-oriented or a dreamer?

Which of the sensory modalities do you seem to favour? Do you favour what you see or hear or do you attend a lot to language, talking to yourself in your head, reading, or conversing with others?

Do you direct your attention broadly or narrowly in each of the different sensory systems? Notice how it is to shift your visual focus from narrow — perhaps to a single hair on the back of your hand — to broad, taking in as wide a view as possible of the place where you are. Switch backwards and forwards; how does this instantly affect the quality of your experience?

Listen to the sounds in your environment. Pick one and notice all the possible nuances within that one sound — qualities and fluctuations of location, volume, tempo, rhythm, tone, and pitch. Now allow yourself to notice all the sounds in your environment at once.

Notice one small part of your skin, where you can feel something, a warm or cold patch, or a place where your skin is in contact with your clothing or the chair where you are sitting.

Now allow yourself to be aware of the whole surface of your body at once. Repeat the above processes for your inner experience. Close your eyes and let yourself be aware of a small part of your visual field or some detail in your memory of a favourite place. Then let the focus of your inner eye expand to include the whole field of vision containing your memory image.

Listen to a memory of a piece of music or the voice of a loved one. Focus narrowly on some aspect of the inner sound, then imagine that your inner ear is attuned broadly, listen to your inner field of sound as a whole, even if it is just the sound of silence.

Be aware of some small sensation inside your body. Now have a sense of your whole body, feeling every part of it at once.

What mix of the four modes of attention in relation to the various sensory channels do you favour? How might you redirect your attention to enhance the quality of your experience?

FILLING ONE'S PERSONAL SPACE — WALKING WITH ATTENTION

Attention tends by nature to be selective. Turning our attention towards one point of focus can be valuable — as when listening to a piece of music or a lecture on a challenging subject for instance. But when we get excessively focused, we can lose the richness of our other modes of experience, such as the simple delight in feeling alive. At the same time, we may find that our attention is not only selective, but sometimes oriented towards noticing what's missing, rather than what's actually there. This can be useful when we work as quality control on a chocolate factory production line and can see at once that the caramel fudge is missing. But it can also impoverish our life and be unpleasant for others, if we are always noticing what's been left undone — like the parent who demolishes a child that is proud for having got nine out of ten in maths by asking, "How come you didn't get ten?" Orienting the attention to include appreciatively what is actually there augments peace and fulfilment in ourselves, and increases harmony in our relationships. The following practice helps develop appreciation of what's there.

Space is common to all sensory modes. We exist within space. As the character from the Goons radio series put it when asked what he was doing in the coal cellar, "Everybody's got to be somewhere". Whatever we hear, see, or feel always has some kind of location in space. All our experience occurs in some part of our personal mind-space. Allow yourself to recognise the full extent of that space. How far can you imagine yourself extending above you, beneath you, around you? Imagine that you extend far in all directions, allow yourself to feel every part inside of your body, to be aware of the space in which occurs everything that you see, hear, or feel.

Imagine walking with full, open attention. Imagine that you are filling space with your attention at once fully inside and out. Let your attention be in all the three main sensory channels, and include smell too. Imagine experiencing all three systems at once, within your expanded personal space, breathing fully. Now walk in that way.

Most of us have to walk somewhere each day. It may be to a bus stop or train station or from a car park to the office. You can use that time to walk with this full multi-modality attentiveness, and notice what happens to the quality of your experience. Open your attention for a while in this way every day to the full range of possible experience.

INTENTION

I remember a little girl, her face grim on a hot summer's afternoon in France. She's perhaps two or three years old and angry with her parents, because they've woken her up. The family stop to buy ice-cream. Her brother and sister are enjoying theirs. So angry is she that, although she loves ice-cream, she refuses one for herself. She is firmly set on responding in a way that she thinks will punish her parents, even though it hurts herself too. This is the power of intention.

Intention orients our attention. Through it, we select one set of possibilities from all the possible choices that we have at any instant. Intention sets the direction of both perception and action. It influences the quality of our experience profoundly.

Intention works through both our conscious and unconscious mind. We may intend to have a cup of tea and initiate and complete the project right away, carefully and consciously putting water to boil, sorting cups and saucers, finding tea, and so on.

Equally, we may set an intention and forget it, for our unconscious mind to remind us promptly. Maybe we have a letter to post. We put it in our pocket, forget it for a while, until we pass a post office or letterbox, and something whispers, "Remember that letter you needed to post".

At any moment, we may have more than one intention competing for our attention, perhaps one conscious and the other unconscious. For instance we may 'intend' to clean the house or to study, yet find that another part of us has had a different idea and distracted us, taking us to the telephone or to meet some friends.

This happens because some of our intentions are part of our natural inclinations (to play and have fun, for instance), others are part of our socialized self, that has learned what it must, ought, or should do for a good life. The two intentions may both be important but conflict.

Intentions may also be set in the moment and when realised, as with our letter, promptly forgotten, or they may be set to remain active throughout our lives. A distraught American parent of a street urchin, adopted from poverty in Korea, once told me how the child, although now living in abundance, compulsively steals and hoards food. Deep inside her, there is still a part of her that is worried that she may once more have not have enough to eat. We all have programmes like that of past intentions which recur in our lives. They may be as general as, 'seek approval from others' or as specific as 'avoid persimmons; they pucker your mouth.'

Intention supports the myriad goals large and small that give coherence and direction to our lives. How we manage our intent determines to a very large extent what we get in life. Fortunately, we can begin to set intention deliberately, so that it works for us. We can learn how to revise some of our old intents that no longer serve (the theme of a later chapter). And by gently and repetitively seeding the conscious mind with current intent, we can direct our unconscious mind to help us move more quickly towards the realisation of what we truly want and need. We can become our own wishing well or our own fairy god-mother.

In many cultures, prayer has traditionally been a way of setting intent. A young Balinese woman explained to me that she always prays before going to sleep, using the customary flower offerings and mantras. One of her requests is that she may be free to choose in life what is good for her, but if she is about to choose something that is bad for her, may God let her know.

When I asked whether and how he lets her know, she described a number of feelings in her body that tell her something is amiss. She also told me that before she sleeps as part of her night prayer she asks God to show her the future in her dreams. She said she notes her dreams and finds that things she dreams subsequently happen in her life. People she may not have seen in a long while will appear in her dreams and then suddenly return in real life, dressed exactly as she had seen them in her dreams.

Setting intention does not require formal prayer or belief in God. It simply requires us to know clearly and accurately what we need for our overall welfare. Identifying, asking for, and releasing the desire sets all parts of ourselves to respond. We do not need to hang on to the intent with the conscious mind; this only puts obstacles in the way of our openness to what is happening. It obstructs the space in which solutions can emerge. For instance, if we are trying to learn or understand something, we can ask our conscious and unconscious mind to help, and then let the request go. It is surprising how quickly we can make progress in this way, when we are stuck.

And it is not just our own mind that seems to be involved. At times it seems as if the world also conspires to support our desires. It's as if there is a larger pattern in which all minds occur, what Bateson called "the pattern that connects" — the Mind of nature itself — and when we are in tune with ourselves and with that larger pattern, our intentions manifest in surprising ways.

You may have felt this on days when things have gone well for you — it's as if you only have to think 'Parking Space' and one opens up, even in the busiest part of town. It's as if for a period you are in deep harmony with a larger pattern, you are in synchrony with the dance of life itself. Once, when working with a charitable foundation in Bali, I needed to meet a fellow director from Australia. Arriving in the village of Ubud, I asked where he was. I was told he had gone to Sri Lanka with his wife some months earlier. As I settled in for a cup of tea on the veranda of the bungalow where I was staying, he walks up. I'd been in town twenty minutes; he also had just arrived.

Sometimes there is a time delay in the manifestation of intent, sometimes short, sometimes long. Anyone who has written will recognise that one may intend to write, but it may be some while before the ideas come together in a way that is reasonably satisfying. With larger projects, it may take months or years before our intent seems to gather momentum and things happen in surprising ways.

If we are our own wishing well, it is important to wish wisely. For what we truly wish for may well happen. When I wanted to do a PhD, I applied for a grant. Somehow, I just knew I would get one; I wanted it very much. On the day the letter confirming it came, I knew it was there in the letterbox, and so it was. Later on, I found that writing a thesis involved a lot of personal commitment and was often a lonely process. It was easy to get distracted. I set my intention to complete it, by imagining my thesis with my name on it finished and bound on the library shelf, along with all the others. Somehow this kept my purpose firm. Even when the grant had expired, I did what was necessary to finish. But was this really the best use of two or three years of my life? I learned a lot and acquired valuable skills, but as my external examiner wryly inquired when I arrived for the final viva, "Well, Mr Wrycza was it really worth doing all this work for something that will be read by just two people?"

We cannot not set intent, for even not to do so requires some intent, but we can learn to set intent with discrimination.

A WAY TO SET INTENT
1. Identify what you want to set your intent for. Specify it as precisely as possible and write it down.
2. Check that what you want is acceptable and welcome to all parts of you. Ask yourself "Do I truly want this?" If you notice some objection, adjust your intent so that you take into account any inner concerns (e.g. so that you maintain balance between work and play, or your needs and those of your family, whatever the issue). If there are no objections, allow yourself to sense your feeling of wanting in all parts of your body. This is a key step.
3. Let yourself relax as fully as possible. Thank your conscious and unconscious mind warmly for its past service to you and ask it to help you to realise your intention.
4. Imagine your intention is already in the process of coming to realisation. Enjoy the feeling of this happening, fully and completely.
5. Let these thoughts and feelings go, and thank your conscious and unconscious mind for its cooperation.

Some extra points:
* When you first set a new intention, also have the intention to reset your intention on a daily or twice daily basis until your desired result manifests. You can do this by imagining yourself setting your intention, perhaps every morning or every evening, for a couple of weeks or until your intention manifests.
* An external reminder to reset your intention may also help. For instance, consider keeping a note to yourself close to your bed.
* Have the intention to review your life periodically and identify where you need to set new intent. This can make personal development a continuing, self-renewing process.

INTUITION AND INTENT — AT THE EDGE OF THE BEAM
If a life of quality resides not in the world itself — for we know this only

indirectly through our representations — but in ourselves and our relationship with those representations, then attention and intent are very important. But they are not the whole story.

The question remains, for a life of quality, what ultimately are we to set our attention towards? Of all the possible intents, which ones do we choose? And how do we deal with those intents that we have wittingly or unwittingly set up in the past, which are creating habitual responses in our lives now?

You may have noticed: we don't really know where our thoughts come from. Suddenly a thought appears in the mind. We can think that thought, and we may choose to attend further to it or to related thoughts. Perhaps we think 'I wonder what to have for dinner tonight'. We can choose to plan a menu, and imagine making a certain kind of meal. But at some point that train of thought was a gift from another part of ourselves.

When we set our intent consciously, we are very much dependent on what options come to the conscious mind. The wise setting of intent depends on something deeper than intent, something we might call intuition or the creative ground of thought. It is this part of ourselves which offers us the intentions from which we choose and which helps us to choose wisely. Perhaps the most important kind of intent we can have, then, is to move into a deeper relationship with this shadowy part of ourselves, inviting greater wisdom and creativity into our everyday life.

We need to harness our attention to accomplish practical tasks in life, but when we harness it too tightly we separate ourselves from the unexpected gifts lurking at the edge of attention. To write these words, I direct my attention to the task at hand, and I am alert to pick up the words as they arise in my conscious mind. At the same time, if I am too focused, I get lost in the individual letters and words of what I am writing; I lose the connection with the larger meaning I am trying to express, I lose the helpful hints and ideas lurking at the edge of my field of attention.

I call this opening of attention to include the fringes of conscious awareness, being at the edge of the beam, attentive to the twilight zone between what is within the beam of the light of conscious awareness and what is almost or not quite conscious, in the zone of obscurity beyond. A Balinese healer friend of mine calls it "living with your shadow". One day, while talking about this he leaps up, legs akimbo, sending chickens and dogs flying, points his finger and exclaims: "Walk with your shadow, talk with your shadow, sit with your shadow, eat with your shadow!" For it is from the shadow that we get the early warning signals of changes in the world around us or in our internal needs. We can then respond more quickly and appropriately. Once situations have developed they are much harder to influence. This may mean being sensitive and responsive to a change in another's attitude towards our proposal in a business meeting. Or knowing, as a friend of mine puts it, when to go to the toilet. It may mean respecting our inner needs so that we don't abuse our bodies and make them sick over a long period of time. The Scottish psychotherapist Winifred Rushforth attributed her vital longevity to just this principle. "I never go against my unconscious", she writes.[2]

EARLY WARNING SIGNALS

Take a moment to review a situation that became difficult in your life, perhaps in your communication with another person. Perhaps you made a mistaken purchase or took an unfruitful path of action in your career or work. Review in your mind the events leading up to the difficulty you encountered. What was the very earliest signal that let you know that something was amiss? Was it something you saw or heard, something you said to yourself, or a feeling inside you?

Review three more awkward situations in this way. Is there a pattern to the early warning signals you get and override?

If you had noticed and responded to those signals at the time, how might events have been different? Imagine responding differently to those early signals, what were some other choices that were open to you in each instance?

Imagine two or three future situations where you might encounter those same early warning signals. In each case, imagine two or three possible ways of responding to them instead of overriding them.[3]

One of the most valuable intentions we can set is to be more receptive to the creative intuitions arising at the edge of the beam. As we do so the energy and quality of our life changes. We come to have the sense that the current of life is carrying us. We are surfing on the ocean of existence, rafting on the white-water of life. We are flowing with it, dancing. Heaviness and lethargy are sure indicators that we have lost the connection with this creative current of life flowing in and around us; we have let ourselves be fixed, nailed to an old mould. Life abhors this.

When we set our intent to function at the edge of the beam, we are in a way turning the whole machinery of experience back onto itself. If we are attending to the intuitive source from which our creativity emerges, if we are learning to function at the edge of the beam, we are starting to open to the nature of awareness itself.

AWARENESS

Attention, intention, and the subtle source of intuition all depend on awareness. To recognise the options for intention, which in turn orients our attention, requires awareness. Without awareness, there is no experience. Awareness is implicit in every experience we have. As such, awareness is the ultimate prerequisite of a life of quality.

Sometimes we take awareness to mean understanding a problem or situation. Thus we might say that a television programme on the plight of the homeless gives us an awareness of the issues involved. Such a notion of awareness comes close to equating it with being informed or having knowledge about. Such awareness can be more of a burden than a blessing, particularly if we are left with a sense of serious but intractable problems. In this book, the term 'awareness' is used more generally as our simple ability to entertain and recognise experience. (As such, it is also virtually interchangeable with 'consciousness').[4]

Typically, awareness is bound up with what we are aware of. I remember as a child running down an avenue of flowers my own height, feeling the energy and enthusiasm in my own body, the smells, and dappled colours, reds, greens, and mauves, and orange of the golden rod, the warmth of the sun on my back, the sight of cabbage-white butterflies beating their wings. In such moments of heightened awareness we are not only aware of whatever is in our field of experience, we are also aware that we are aware. In privileged moments, we not only find that we have more awareness of the qualities of what we are aware of — the beauty of a forest, the delicacy of a flower, or the presence of a loved one — but in that moment of knowing and recognition there is implicit a heightening and an awakening of something inside ourselves. Together with whatever we perceive, our own knowingness comes to our attention.

One of the tragedies of our flight into the past or the future is that we miss the richness of the present moment. However, being oriented to the present moment doesn't guarantee full awareness. Even when we are aware of the current contents of consciousness, too often our enjoyment is muted, for what we see, hear, and feel overtakes our awareness and overshadows our experiencing Self. Each morning we return miraculously from the annihilation of sleep, but all too often we don't really wake up. We lose ourselves continuously in thoughts, media chatter, and chores to which we may barely attend. We suffer a double loss, half-conscious of what we see, hear, or feel, and oblivious of that glimmering peace and joy-tinged awareness of our own nature.

PURE AWARENESS

Our awareness, then, is like Janus, two-faced. On the one hand, it can be turned to the possible contents of our life; on the other, it can simply be aware of itself. When this is the case, we may find it hard to ascribe any qualities to it. Awareness has no shape, or sound, or smell. Any associated feelings are very subtle. We could say that when we have awareness by and in itself we have 'pure awareness' and when we are full of content we are 'aware of'. In everyday life, we usually forget pure awareness, and experience what we are aware of.

One may wonder if something so abstract is worth the time of day. Yet in a sense pure awareness is the subtle secret of life itself. There is nothing more important than it, for everything else depends on it. Without it we would not be able to experience anything at all. Awakening to it enhances the quality and accuracy of our perceptions, guaranteeing greater 'awareness of'. In cleaning the mirror of consciousness, reflections in it reveal brighter colours and sharper contours. To invest in pure awareness is to invest in gold, securing us from the fluctuations of any particular currency of experience. In it we recover a long-lost buried treasure. Pure awareness is our own essence. It is what we ultimately are.

Many poets, philosophers, saints, and sages have described pure awareness and its importance for them. Paul Valéry, the French poet-philosopher, who spent an hour or two every morning exploring the nature of his own mind, described how he became increasingly aware, at a deeper level of experience than his personality and personal history, of "a profound note of existence" which formed a kind of permanent background to the changing patterns of personal experience. He called it "la conscience pure", "pure consciousness" or "le Moi pur", "the pure Self". To miss the time of communion with it, he notes, was like missing a morning bath. Proust also discovered this 'pure Self', but in his case by probing memory. He found that certain stimuli, such as the taste of a Madeleine tea-cake dunked in lime-flower tea, triggered old memories, such as his childhood holidays in the village of Combray, in a very deep way. In such 'involuntary memories' (so-called because they cannot be reached consciously) he reported the presence of something deeply rewarding and fulfilling. This he identified as a kind of extra-temporal sense of being, unnoticed in the original experience and common to both present and past, but usually overlain by the contents of the present moment. This, he concluded was the only worthwhile and reliable element in life, and what he had really been seeking through friends, relationships, and travel. Tennyson, too, encountered a valuable state of clarity and certainty, "utterly beyond words". This deathless state seemed to both extinguish the personal self and to fulfil it, "the loss of personality (if it were so) seeming no extinction but the only true life." He reached this state by repeating his own name inwardly, until it faded away and he "passed into the Nameless as a cloud melts into heaven".

If pure awareness is usually obscured by the contents of consciousness, one simple way to begin to know it, a number of writers suggest, is to be curious as to what lies between the various contents of consciousness. As with T.S.Eliot's stillness "half-heard between two waves of the sea", we can sense pure awareness in the gaps between thoughts and between perceptions. As Sogyal Rinpoche puts it. "When one past thought has ceased and a future thought has not yet risen, in that gap, in between, isn't there a consciousness of the present moment; fresh, virgin, unaltered by even a hair's breadth of concept, a luminous, naked awareness?"[5] To quote another teacher, "When your attention is off a thing and not yet fixed on another, in the interval you are pure being."[6]

Try this little experiment. Notice how your attention normally appears to slide effortlessly from one thing to another. If your mind seems to be racing, let yourself breathe a little more fully and deeply than usual, allowing a little lull between the out and in breaths. Take a moment to look around you. Notice where your attention falls. Allow your attention to rest there as long as it does, notice where it shifts to next, whether to some other aspect of your field of vision or to something you might be saying to yourself. Let yourself catch the transition point between the two focuses of attention. What do you find there?

Nothing much, perhaps. Such an endeavour may be new and strange for you, but that gap is the creative source of all that is fresh and new in our lives. To become familiar with it is to escape from our usual rutted thinking into a place from which the unexpected can arise. This next experiment may give you some experience of that creative gap and also demonstrate a little of its creative power and usefulness. Again, don't worry if this proves a little challenging. You may be unused to exploring these subtle aspects of experience. There will be other opportunities!

THE CREATIVE GAP AND PRACTICAL PROBLEM-SOLVING

1. Identify a manageable issue — some aspect of your life where you would like more understanding or new choices. Notice how you picture that issue.

2. Take a moment to breathe deeply and fully, releasing any physical tension. Sit in a poised and alert posture, feet on the ground, legs and arms uncrossed, spine upright.

3. Let yourself identify the state that occurs between two moments of attention, as in the experiment described just above. Alternatively, you may find it helpful to let your attention move between the two ways of seeing the cube below. Once you catch the transition state in-between, let go of the cubes and rest in that state. If you find that you see both at once, simply relax into that double state.

4.   Enter and prolong that in-between state for a moment or two, without focusing on anything in particular, gently returning to the state if you notice that you have lost it.

5.   Staying in that state, reintroduce a sense of the problem-issue, and notice what happens to your sense of the problem. How does you perception of the problem or your relationship with it change?

The Power and Value of Awareness

Pure awareness, although both subtle and abstract, has immense practical value. It is the inexhaustible source from which all our thoughts and images arise and against which they are perceived. As such it is the creative ground of intention and intuition, silently computing and containing the infinite complexities and irreconcilable opposites of our life.

At the same time, it is the source of the sparkle, joy, and vitality which we enjoy when we are in touch with of our own being. It is gentle, soothing the wounds and hurts of whoever bathes in its calm waters. It is utterly delightful, easing peace and contentment into every cell of our body. It is patient, never grumbling at our unmindful neglect as we pursue the lesser prizes of our obsessions in the world of 'awareness of'. It is infinitely tolerant, unflinchingly accepting whatever is reflected in it. It is always there to return to like our very own best friend, never absent, always comforting.

Above all, pure awareness provides us with the security of a settled sense of self in the midst of the ups and downs of everyday life. Through it, like Paul Valéry, we come to enjoy a solid sense of being who we are, whatever happens on the surface of life. We may be buffeted by strong feelings as we deal with some upheaval in life — perhaps a financial shock or a bereavement — but deep within there is a layer of unshakeable security. In short it is a resource that is always ours and always ready to serve in countless practical ways.

Pure awareness passes beyond the boundaries of our personal existence. It is a common denominator to all experiencing selves. Without taste or colour or sound, there is nothing to personalise it. As such, it is that undercurrent of intelligence and life that inspired minds in every culture and age have sensed we all share. Paul Valéry compares it to "this precious zero of mathematical writing to which all algebraic expressions are equal". In experiencing it, we come to something like a ground state, not only of ourselves, but of all things.[7] We apprehend — poets, philosophers, and mystics from around the world remind us — the very essence of existence itself.

Awareness is thus our bridge to the creative ground in which all things abide and from which they spring. When we enter into a deep relation with our own awareness we go to the heart of 'the pattern than connects'. Our perspective shifts. We find ourselves part of a set of relationships in which whatever happens is connected to everything else. Chance events of all kinds — perhaps, a swooping hawk or trotting coyote that cross our paths — speak of this pattern. When I left Lancashire after 11 years at a major transition point in my life, as I closed the van doors, and turned the ignition to start my journey, a sudden storm squalled for a few minutes, showering great drops of rain. A rainbow glowed across the grey sky, arcing across the road I was to take to new life. Two and a half years later, as that journey appeared to end, with my first ever purchase of some land, in Bali, a new rainbow punctuated my transaction.

In such magical moments, there is not necessarily a relation of cause and effect. Only an impeccable timing in which events are correlated in a deep and powerful pattern. In the simple field of consciousness-existence dwell the subtle strings, the invisible nerves and arteries of the universe. Entering that field aligns us with the streams and currents of life itself. To align ourselves with it, is to align ourselves with the power of the universe. As our experience of it deepens, our needs seem effortlessly to be met. Synchronous and serendipitous events and encounters mark like milestones our growing alignment both with ourselves and our world. For instance, with the land purchase, only apparent chance meant I bumped into the person with the piece of land that first spoke to my soul and said: make a home and centre here.

Pure awareness is thus the ground of intuition. It helps us discriminate in every aspect of our life — from where to live, what career to follow, or who to have as friend or partner, to what to eat or when to sleep or wake. With greater awareness, we make better choices, picking options that genuinely enrich our life rather than those which impoverish it. If we are confused as to what to do, thinking more about the various options, may just take us through another circle. Letting go of all the thoughts, settling into inner quietness, letting the mind become like a still lake, allows the right answer to come. As Wordsworth, poet of such experiences puts it "with an eye made quiet, we see into the life of things".

Our intellects are valuable, but ultimately limited. We cannot possibly know the ultimate effects of the choices we make. The variables are too numerous and too tentacular, reaching out far beyond our present moment into a future we do not know, interacting with elements we cannot even imagine. Weighing up the variables, as far as we can, is important, but the limits of our conscious minds means they can only take us so far. Awareness takes us into a deeper relation with the underlying pattern of life itself. It takes us beyond the limitations of linear mental thinking to a place of greater wisdom that can compute everything at once, a place which effortlessly and automatically and implicitly holds the strands of life. From there, we are not only better able to solve problems, but they seem to solve themselves, just as the worst situations are magically more manageable after a decent night's sleep.

Awareness brings into balance the conflicting needs of the different parts of our life — mind, emotions, body, and spirit. When these are in conflict, we tend to think in a circular way, going from one point of view to a qualifying 'yes but'. Pure awareness aligns all parts of ourselves and takes us to a place in which we jump outside the closed circuits of contradiction to discover with absolute certainty exactly what is appropriate for a given situation.

Once our choices are made, awareness helps in the achievement of our goals. It offers a fail-safe navigation aid in the journey to fulfilment, helping us gauge the progress we are making. It helps us monitor and adjust our course so that we are more likely to reach our outcomes with least strain on ourselves and most harmony with our environment. It lets us know if and when we need to update our goals or modify our destination. Through the early warning signals in our body or mind, mentioned earlier, it helps us recognise the instant and on-going feedback present at every level of our life, enabling us to do the right thing at the right time.

AWARENESS AND LIFE-LONG LEARNING
When we are open to pure awareness, everything we experience is fresh and full with new possibilities. We can draw on past experience without being hide-bound by it. Any sight or sound, a passing cloud or bird, can trigger hints and help with unanswered questions. You've probably noticed that often when you have struggled to understand or assimilate some new learning, it takes a fallow period, a pause or break — whether a hot drink, a walk in the woods, or a simple time of silence — before integration and understanding can occur. In letting go of what we are trying to learn, we come closer to the creative gap, creating a space in our own awareness, in which the answers to our unresolved questions can emerge. With the moment of discovery, when a problem is solved, excitement, satisfaction, and awareness explode in our bodies and minds.

Learning and living are inextricably interwoven. Through learning, past experience is available to help us in the future. Whether in formal education or in the school of life itself, awareness helps us become our own best teacher. It enables us to recognise quickly what the 'lesson' is and to check how we are doing with it. It lets us adjust our response and monitor the effectiveness of that. It allows us to recognise when we need to learn a new way to learn and to discover and use that. It helps us know when we need to practise to integrate something. It lets us know when we are complete and are ready to move on to something else, so that we don't have to learn the same things over and over again. In short, it helps us make the transition from learners to knowers, while remaining innocently open to the unknown.

AWARENESS AND RELATIONSHIPS

Awareness also eases the smooth working of any partnership. If one partner of a couple has been at work — making phone calls, scribbling memos and reports, and rushing to meetings all day — the other may be in a very different state when they meet in the evening. Perhaps he or she has been caring for children and home. The one who has been working returns, perhaps after a stressful drive in rush-hour traffic or sardined in a commuter train, fatigued and word-numb. He/she fails to notice the bouquet of flowers on the table, the fresh cake, the clean windows, and with a grimace and a grunt, silently collapses into an armchair. Meanwhile the one at home, starved of companionship and over-eager to share, has failed to register and allow for the blanched skin colour and slight tightness of expression of the face, suggesting the need for some recovery time. Each senses the unspoken demands of the other and feels the enormous pressure of their own needs. The home becomes a forest in drought that any little spark can set alight. The quality of awareness in either or both partners can mean the difference between adjusting easily to each other's needs and a conflagration.

In our deepest experiences of intimacy, we may marvel at our difference or delight in shared interests and responses, but we do so through a mutually enlivened sense of being. We love others for their own sakes, yes, but also because they help us open to a deeply satisfying quality of feeling more alive and full in ourselves. Awareness is ultimately our common ground and bond.

AWARENESS AND ORGANIZATIONS

Awareness can also make the difference between the first and second-rate organisation. A company may do all the right things — careful product design, production, and marketing. But it requires awareness to coordinate all phases, to recognise the steps that will be needed, and to ensure the sensitivity of tone and timing that ultimately determines success in the market place. Awareness is the essence of entrepreneurial flair, the ability to seize the moment.

The climate or atmosphere in an organisation has a powerful impact on people's readiness to make a contribution. Climate can easily sour. It only takes a few crass decisions or a failure to recognise the early warning signals that something is amiss. Awareness on the part of all concerned, but particularly management, can mean the difference between an organisation that people want to give their all to and one where a poisoned atmosphere saps the energy, good will, and unity of purpose essential for an enjoyable and effortless pursuit of success. Awareness helps people to recognise the wider implications of policies and decisions so that better decisions are made in the first place and that they are implemented sensitively.

Awareness is the *sine qua non* of effective leadership. It enables the leader to be aware of his or her own strengths and weaknesses and to recognise when to act and when to pause. It helps organisational leaders pick up the subtle early warning signals that all is not well and to respond to them accordingly.

Perhaps even more important, growth in awareness among employees can help create leaders among those not in official positions of leadership. With greater awareness, people recognise more quickly and accurately what is happening in their lives and respond more appropriately, saying and doing what is right in a given situation — not just from their own point of view, but in relation to the larger whole.

Awareness thus also helps an organisation to remember its relationship to the wider system that includes other organisations, countries, and our physical environment. With awareness an organisation is more likely to steer a course that balances short and long term needs. It will choose a pathway that ensures its own survival, while respecting the wider environment.

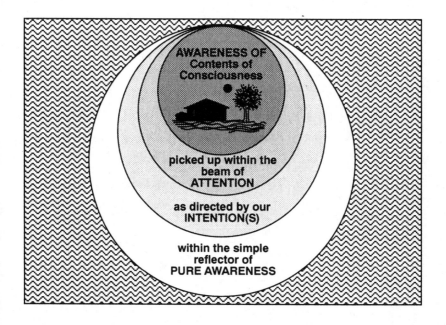

STRUCTURE OF EXPERIENCE

New Thinking for a New Era

Awareness is not only the hidden resource that can transform individual and organisational life. It is the key to the survival and well-being of our planet as a whole.

In theory, we have everything we need to solve any problem in the world. Yet, things never happen quite as planned and so our major problems — whether economic, political, or social — remain unsolved. For instance, we send aid, but it ends up in the wrong hands, fuelling corruption and repression, making people rely on hand-outs. We finance new dams or factories in far off places, and they disrupt the old fabric of life. As with individual action, the possibilities are too numerous and varied, subject to what Bateson called the unpredictable nature of "collateral energy". No super-computer in the world can anticipate the full consequences of a given policy. But greater awareness can help us use our resources in ways that alleviate problems rather than acerbate them or create new ones.

You've probably noticed that to think clearly of complex things, you need a degree of calm and quiet. When individuals are aware, they are more calm and responsive to what is happening; they are not over-committed to any one course of action. Pure awareness induces orderliness, just as a lake becomes calm and still when the wind drops. Such awareness is a pressing need not only for our leaders, who are making the key decisions affecting the lives of all on our planet, but for those that they lead. When the population as a whole is calm and aware, it helps our leaders make wiser decisions. When there is a high level of collective awareness, the right solutions and resources surface, and mistakes are quickly corrected.

Our current challenges as a civilisation result from our underlying assumptions about ourselves and our relationship to the larger whole. These are deeply dualistic. We tend to think in terms of opposites and polarities, dialectic and disputes — Republicans or Democrats, Government or Opposition, right or left. We behave as if we consider ourselves separate from nature, lords over it. Our dominant scientific paradigm reinforces this dualism. We place ourselves outside nature in order to examine its workings and understand and isolate its laws, putting them to work for our benefit. Nature represents a reservoir of resources to exploit, a set of forces and obstacles to channel and tame.

But now we need a more unified way of thinking and being. For we are faced with the effects of how we conceive and relate to the world. Runaway materialism has created such pressure on our environment that we know that we must balance our needs and actions with those of the larger whole. If we forget we are part of a web of forces far larger and more powerful than ourselves, we will find ourselves swept away by those forces. This we know, even if the changes in our way of life are as yet cosmetic.

The dominant scientific paradigm has already begun to deconstruct itself. We now know that objectivity has limits. Physics, the bastion of objectivity, admits that the observer influences the observation. Once we leave the sensory surface of life, what we find depends on how we measure — particle or wave according to the process used. Our understandings of the infinitesimal and the infinitely big depend on metaphors, images, and constructs — billiard balls and curved surfaces — derived from sensory experience in the here and now. Physicists' analogies reflect the minds that make them. We can no longer leave ourselves out of the equation. Our maps and models speak too much of us. Our intelligence is implicated in the order of things. What are we? How do we fit into our understanding of reality? These questions of poets and philosophers, suspended while the objective order was dissected, are now the new frontier. Our physicists have become like poets and philosophers talking in symbols and paradoxes. Their description of the subtle realms of matter edges closer to the visionary and unitary insights of mystics through the ages.

Dualistic thinking is under challenge, yet it is still influential. We value its hard-won practical pragmatism after millennia of mystery. We don't want to go back to the dark ages, nor do we want to go forward to another darkness by destroying ourselves. We find ourselves in between, conscious of the limitations of the old and needing a new paradigm, new images and symbols, that can transcend and contain the old, be larger than it, but have space for it.

We need new thinking, so that we include ourselves as part of a larger picture, so that we operate from fresh assumptions about our relationship to each other, to the larger whole, and all that is in it. Yet, we cannot create new ways of thinking just with thinking. Our very reliance on thinking has been one of our weaknesses, leading us to rely excessively on the constructs of the conscious mind.

A new philosophy of wholeness must ultimately come from a living experience of wholeness. By opening fully to our own pure awareness, we can become grounded in that which is intrinsically unifying, so that we eat, breathe, sleep, wake, love, work, and play with a sense of oneness suffusing and sustaining difference.

In this context, this book, then, develops a simple thesis: *The unifying ground of pure awareness is our simplest, most valuable and inexhaustible resource. Through appropriate understanding, practice, and experience, we can awaken to it. Doing so resolves difficulties and unfolds fulfilment in our daily lives, in our relationships, and in our societies.* These pages provide a practical and comprehensive handbook for its awakening and integration into a more enjoyable and productive daily life. Using this book, you can discover and own more of the rich territory that you truly are. The opening chapters outline a map of the psyche that shows the relationship of our hearts and minds to each other and to our inner being; subsequent chapters outline a pathway to its realisation — through a deeper relationship with ourselves and others; through the stillness of meditation; by using movement to promote dynamic being in body and mind; by using the different layers of the psyche, from senses to self, to unfold rather than submerge awareness; by piercing the veil of language and neutralising restrictive beliefs; by transcending and fulfilling identity to live with a deep sense of personal purpose; by helping the groups we are in become more cohesive; and by spiritual renewal through heightened consciousness as a potential unifying factor among the diverse cultures and traditions of our world.

As we awaken to our own deepest nature, the images, symbols, and new thinking for our times will appear — as happened in the past, in the dreams and inspiration that come to individuals and inspire whole cultures. As we open to our essence, everything unfolds naturally.

AWARENESS AND ULTIMATE QUESTIONS

In this sense, awareness, wordless and innocent, can also help us with the ultimate questions of meaning that we and every generation face.

From time to time, most of us raise our heads from our daily concerns. As we peer into the night sky at the stars strewn like gleaming grains of sand on rich black velvet, we may ponder the mystery of our existence on this little planet in a corner of an endless universe, wondering how it all came to be, what it all means, and whether we are alone.

However we try to explain it, the miracle of our life defies comprehension. To suggest that consciousness has emerged from the self-combining possibilities inherent in matter itself, like smoke from a chimney, does not really satisfy. It merely raises new questions as to how the elements of the universe came to contain the possibility of sustaining greater complexity. Equally imponderable to the conscious mind is the idea of some creating consciousness that has manifested it all. Where did it come from? When did it come to be? Was it there forever? How long is forever? What was there before forever?

Such questions can easily take us into black holes of uncertainty or simplistic resolution. Only our awareness can hold us on the edge of the wonder, awe, and inexplicable majesty of a starry sky, a sunset behind desert mountains, ocean waves rolling on a sandy beach, or a single bluebell in spring. With awareness, what we cannot understand, we can acknowledge with reverent presence and enter into with lyrical delight. With awareness we may not understand, but we can know — as the ecstatic dance of our own being takes us like a burning brand into the universal fire, smouldering in the depths of all things.

Postscript: and You?

What is awareness for you now? Let yourself be aware, for a moment, of your own awareness. Notice briefly that part of you which is experiencing. Where does it seem to be located? In or outside your body? Where is its centre, if it has one? How far does it seem to extend in space? What have you not yet noticed about this awareness?

NOTES

1.   These distinctions were inspired by Nelson Zink, "Twelve Modes of Attention", *Anchor Point*, July, 1994. And the *Structure of Delight*, pp.96-102.

2.   *Something Is Happening*, p.157

3.   Chris Hall calls this a "method of earlier detection".

4.   For me there is a slight difference of flavour. 'Awareness' has a more self-contained sense of the presence of my own knowing-beingness. 'Consciousness' leans more in the direction of taking cognizance of. The key difference is between awareness/consciousness-with-contents and pure awareness/consciousness, what Franklin Merrell-Wolff calls "consciousness-without-an object".

5.   *The Tibetan Book of Living and Dying*, p.160

6.   Swami Nisargadatta Mataraj, *I Am That*, p.90

7.   *Oeuvres*, Gallimard, Paris, 1957, I, 1228.

CHAPTER TWO

Levels of Life

Summary

In Chapter One, we considered how the quest for quality calls for a journey into our own experience. This journey involves a gentle aligning of intent so that our attention can be awake to the subtle intuitions 'at the edge of the beam' and ultimately can open to its own nature as pure awareness itself. This chapter goes deeper into the relationship of our various forms of 'awareness of' to pure awareness. How is it that pure awareness is so easily obscured? Is this inevitable? To answer these questions, we consider the structure of our experience in a number of discrete and interlocking layers.

On Having No Head

Some years ago, I visited a headless man. Let me explain. When I began writing this, I interviewed a number of people who seemed to have clear experiences of pure awareness — among them, the author Douglas Harding, originator of a homespun philosophy and some ingenious 'experiments' in consciousness which he calls the 'headless way'. Douglas, whom I found living peacefully in a wrinkle in the Suffolk countryside, a few miles from where I had gone to secondary school, maintains that our embroilment with 'awareness of' begins with our erroneous identification as a child with the 'meatball' on our shoulders. Once we take on a name and face, he suggests, we lose our pristine openness, and our problems begin. Like many who have had clear experiences of transcendence, Douglas is so convinced of its importance that he makes teasing people to this new way of perceiving the world his top priority. He suspects that pandering to 'awareness of' is a distracting waste of time.

Douglas' position raises difficult questions. If the key to a life of quality is ultimately enhanced openness to our own pure awareness, and attending to the myriad forms of 'awareness of' a side-show, then what is the right relationship between pure awareness and 'awareness of'? An extreme pre-occupation with pure awareness implies turning away from the contents of consciousness, the facts and phenomena that fill our daily lives, towards an asceticism that is likely to appeal to few. One might justifiably ask, where is the quality in a life that appears to reject all the avenues through which we usually enjoy quality — nature, art, music, intellectual exchange, relationships, good food, to name just a few?[1] The other extreme, rejection of pure awareness and a seeking of quality in the contents of consciousness alone is equally unsatisfactory, since without the animating element of expanded awareness we can find ourselves mired in a morass of porcine sensation.

One way to reconcile these two extremes is through an understanding of how our inner worlds are organized in a number of discrete but interacting layers or levels of experience.[2]

Levels

Part of my childhood experience can illustrate this. When I was growing up in Norwich, still at primary school, I used to love fishing. A kindly Catholic priest, knowing my family was struggling financially, gave me a brand new fishing rod and reel. At every opportunity, I was off to the river Wensum, walking along the banks to find spots where perch or roach would swim suspended in the light current, a few feet down, not far from the weeds.

At first I had to learn the basics of how to put a hook on the line, weights to make it sink and the float stand up, so that it could indicate what was going on in places where the water was murky.

Eventually, I could cast the line without getting the hook caught in the willows, or the line snarled round rod and reel, to a spot in the river where, carried by the current, it could drift between weedbeds.

While the line was out in the water, there was a moment of quiet, as the float drifted with the ripple-furrowed current. Sometimes the float trembled or bobbed momentarily, before streaking away at an angle, and I thrilled to the rush of fish.

Where the river became broad and shallow, the current slowed. On days when there was no wind, I'd put the rod down and find myself floating on the surface, like a reflected cloud. With an eye on the float, I was somehow watchfully awake, yet resting on a bed of silence and peace, tickled only by the drifting fuzz of a falling feather or dandelion seed.

In this little account, most of the levels of experience are present. The world in which we find ourselves, firstly as children, then later as adults, creates a context in which we are shaped by forces larger than ourselves. Our **environment** teaches us about the kind of world we are in and what expectations others have of us in our interactions. Unfortunately my world denied me the river for whole swathes of time, and I was consigned to sitting at a school desk, wearing a blazer and tie.

We communicate with our world through our **body** and **senses**, our 'doors of perception', which bring us 'news of the universe' — the colour of the sky, the sounds of leaves caught in the wind, the weight of the rod in the hand, the texture of little pellets of bread-bait, rolled between finger tips.

Through the body, we act on the world that is influencing us, cutting forked twigs to support the rod, wearing down the grass, on the path by the river bank.

Our **mind** monitors and filters our sensory experience, labelling what we encounter. Whether in images or in words that we hear in our head, the mind codes and comments on experience. Mind stores memory for future reference. It removes the innocence of the present. The names of what we knew influence what we encounter.

Mind provides the raw material for a deeper part of our ourselves, our intellect, to organize and interpret. If mind knows the names of perch and pike, **intellect** knows how to sort them into the world of fish. It knows how to gather the experiences of the hours and days spent by the river to find the deeper patterns of how the river changes with the seasons, and the fishes' habits change with it, breeding at times, sometimes sluggish, some-times quick, now feeding, now fasting. Mind and intellect together structure our sensory experience, knowledge, and actions into the skills and **capa-bilities** that we eventually take for granted. Thus we learn how to handle the weight of the rod, and the lightness of the line, sensing the weight of the tackle, and to cast accurately, allowing for the wind and trees. These and other sub-skills, such as anticipating the way a fish thinks, eventually make up the capability of 'fishing'.

If the mind is responsible for rote learning, the intellect opens under-standing and hence choice. It evaluates the merits and demerits of a course of action: whether to go to school or take off for the river, for instance. But choosing is never innocent. The head decides in the light of deeper feel-ings. **Feeling** creates biases, leaning us towards options that we enjoy and anticipate benefiting from, or moving us away from ones that we dislike. Feeling guides the intellect in determining our **values,** what we hold to be important. Our values in turn set the criteria we use to determine what we will move towards or away from — the freedom to roam by the river with the sky and birds and the opportunity for respite from the pressures of school and home.

In shaping our values, feeling and intellect also form our **beliefs,** or what we hold to be possible or impossible, necessary or inevitable, or simply true. Beliefs and values set the course for action, mapping the boundaries we create or accept in our personal worlds. For instance, I knew I could learn to fish, although sometimes it felt as if I might never succeed. I also never really doubted that I had to follow the adult assumption that school was a necessary, important, and unavoidable part of life. I assumed I had to go to school. So I never played truant.

Over time beliefs and values shift. I treasure my memories of lakes and rivers; I love to be near water, but I have no desire for an activity that might inflict unnecessary pain on another creature.

Together the things we do in the world that is familiar to us, with the capabilities they form and the beliefs and values that make them possible shape our sense of who we are, our **identity.** Part of my identity as a child was being a fisherman. Now I am no longer. But the memories are still part of me, and my relationship with rivers and fishing continues to shape who I am.

Although identity has continuity, like a river, it is changing as the river changes on its course to the sea. What is constant is the peg of 'I' to which my changing sense of self remains attached. The River Wensum in Norfolk keeps its name till it merges with the Yare. Sometimes it is a quiet rural stream and sometimes a concrete-banked city waterway, yet it remains Wensum. In the same way the sense of 'I' gives continuity to experience. Yet we are usually virtually unaware of our 'I'. The word may appear in every sentence we say about ourselves, as in 'I am reading these words', but we pass so quickly to the actions and objects we speak of — in this instance, reading and writing — that we are barely conscious of what this 'I' refers to.

Deep in the 'I' we discover its essence in the river of life. Sometimes on a quiet day, I used to become aware of my seeing, feeling self. That is the secret of the real magic of fishing. In awakening in riverside stillness to the perceiving 'I', I go beyond it to a kind of peace in which my personal boundaries seem to melt and I am part of a summer's afternoon, reflecting the hum of flies and bees, sky and sun in the silence of a silvered sheet of river. In such moments, when our self expands to include the world, our awareness reveals itself as not only that which takes cognisance of any level of experience, but that which is able to find itself in it. Pure awareness, is both compleletely vulnerable to the contents of consciousness and potentially present at any level to which we give full attention.

Just as a river presents surface and depth, so our experience offers parts that are now conscious, now unconscious. When the surface is calm, it offers, like our minds, a relatively honest reflection of the world, matching cloud for cloud, tree for tree. In the rush to recognize reflection, we forget the reflector. Yet, sometimes in the right light, we catch a glimpse of that reflecting surface, like a hint of our own awareness.

Sometimes, too, we may seek to discover what lies hidden in the depths of ourselves, and the unconscious may become conscious. I remember being frustrated with the usual methods and lying on the river bank, staring straight down into the water to find a family of perch. Dispensing with the float, I simply dangled my baited line before their noses. It's one way to catch some of the secrets of awareness — lying in wait for the emerging impulses of creative thought. And beyond them, in the depths, lie the rotting leaves of a decomposing past, ready to form a peaty mulch which will give new life to plants and flowers. And sometimes, we can only cast our line into the darkness and wait for the fishes of our dreams to respond to our waiting attentiveness.

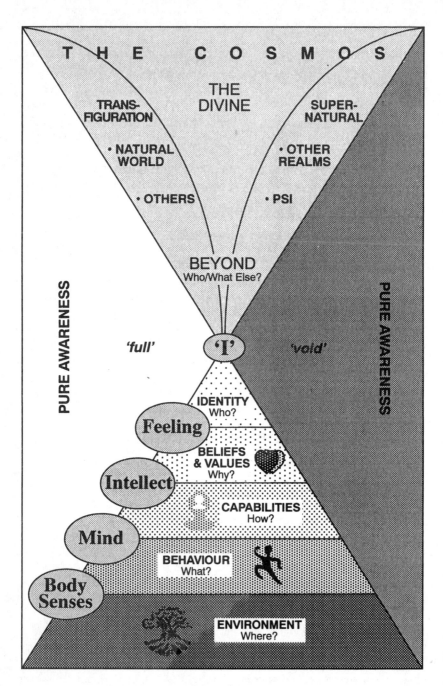

LEVELS OF EXPERIENCE

The Edge of Beyond

This fishy tale takes us to the edge of beyond. For many people, their most meaningful experiences are those which seem to break the boundaries of their personal self and put them into contact with aspects of experience that seem somehow of another order or in another realm. Such experience can be quite varied.

For instance, we may find that the there is a kind of **transfiguration of the natural world,** as we awaken to a heightened sense of the harmony and wonder inherent in the world around us — the ocean at sunset, a wheat field sewn with poppies, or the pattern of frost on a windowpane. We may sense a deep beauty and coherence in things and we may feel at one with that beauty.

Sometimes **others** take us to the edge of beyond. At the major transition points of birth and death, or in a meeting of hearts and minds in the crucible of love, we may sense the depths and mystery of life implicit in the very existence of another being. They may help us reach deeper aspects of ourselves. We may even sense that our differences touch in a shared ground. At those special times our personal boundaries seem to soften and we have a sense of connecting with another's essence and through that with the essence of life itself.[3]

Often artists, writers, and musicians try to perpetuate such experiences and make them available to others. Art then becomes a means for awakening to a sense of the wonder of the beauty of existence itself.

Sometimes it is if a crack opens in the material world to reveal a glimpse of the **supernatural.** We sense that there may be much more to life than meets the usual senses, that various extrasensory or '**psi**' experiences are possible, that we can communicate across time and distance with other beings from other places, even other worlds. The world becomes a place of magic, of unseen presences, of beings from other realms — of fairies, trolls, and angels — living at the edges of our ordinary perception. We enter a mythic realm in which archetypes enact deep aspects of our psyche.

When such experiences are particularly intense, people may even describe, like Dante or Virgil, journeying to **other realms** or planes of existence — heavens, hells, other planets — which set our own in creative tension between forces of light and dark.

Beside or beyond such experiences, we may also sense a connection with the **Divine** source of life itself. We can encounter such experiences through the transfiguration of the natural world or in opening to other realms. We may also find ourselves awakening to it in prayer or meditation. Or we may encounter it in moments of apparently God-given or God-filled grace that arrive unannounced, as when clouds part and a shaft of sunlight hangs silently in a darkened room.

One may wonder whether any of these experiences are 'real' or 'true'. In a sense this is an inappropriate question. Irrespective of their objective reality, many people have such experiences and consider them of great importance. Such experiences may radically reshape the meaning given to the mundane levels of life. In them, we are reminded of the mystery and wonder of the larger pattern. It is fascinating to note that experiences like those briefly mentioned here are described in quite different cultures around the world. They reflect important shared aspects of our human heritage.

Beyond the Edge of Beyond

All the experiences of the different levels we have described so far in this chapter involve some form of 'awareness of'. There is some content within consciousness, even if it appears most divine and heavenly. The heightened quality of the contents of consciousness naturally draws us to them — whether it be nature, art, another person, or even a sense of the Divine. Glimpses of pure awareness may be present in such experiences, but they are often so intertwined with the contents of consciousness that awareness itself may be ignored.

In the *Divina Commedia*, in the deepest part of hell, Dante has to squeeze through a narrow passageway between two worlds. He clambers past Lucifer who is lodged at the junction between hell, where the soul is permanently turned away from God and consumed by various forms of materialism, and the upper worlds of purgatory and paradise in which the soul is oriented to the One Source.

Lucifer, the hairy beast, trapped in a kind of funnel between two orders of existence, symbolizes our ego, our sense of a separate selfhood, which effectively severs us from our natural connectedness with the larger whole. Our 'I' forms a pivotal junction between our personal world and that which is beyond, between the mundane and the supra mundane.

But at that point of intersection, between time and timelessness, between self and the larger whole, a further dramatic possibility presents itself, and that is to jump altogether outside the dualistic constraints of 'awareness of' into the simple unity of pure being-awarenesss.

When our infant awareness identifies with our body, located in a point in time and space, we create the conditions for identifying with the label 'I' and all that accrues to it. Then everything is ripe for confusing what we truly are with what we are aware of. As Swami Nisargadatta, a simple shopkeeper, who in the space of three years deeply explored his own nature, puts it,

In the great mirror of consciousness images arise and disappear and only memory gives them continuity. On such flimsy foundations we build a sense of personal existence — vague, intermittent, dreamlike. This vague persuasion: 'I-am-so-

and-so' obscures the changeless state of pure awareness and makes us believe that we are born to die and suffer. (I Am That, p. 113)

Nisargadatta, along with many other inspired teachers, suggests that one way 'home', towards knowing our own essence, is to go deep into the nature of the pivotal 'I am'. There entering fully into an experience of our own existence, we can re-cognize the core of our own being, consciousness itself. It may take time (three years in his own case), but entering into the sense of our own existence eventually yields a deep and freeing return to that pure awareness we have never really lost.

Typically, people describe pure awareness as 'flat', 'void', 'dark', 'absent', or else 'lively', 'full', 'light' and 'present'. These descriptions reflect two ways of apprehending it. If it is pure unexpressed possibility, it requires only a small shift for us to recognize more the absence of manifestion or more the utter openness to possibility. Which facet we recognize depends a little on the depth and familiarity of our experience. As Rilke put it, "Even in the becoming silent, there were new beginnings, sparks and transformations coming forth." It may take a while to begin recognizing the fullness present in empiness.

If our Being is outside the frame, it is beyond all the levels, and hence utterly transcendent. Commentators throughout the ages suggest that it cannot really be known by words nor by the mind. It can only be known by a kind of gnosis in which we become it.

Eventually such experience leads to a profound reordering of the person in which one ceases to identify with the machinations of our usual individual self, and identifies instead with the pure field of consciousness itself. As Nisargadatta again puts it:

One thing is quite clear to me: all that is, lives and moves and has its being in consciousness and I am in and beyond that consciousness. I am in it as the witness. I am beyond it as Being. (p. 92)

Pure awareness is thus not only transcendent, it is immanent within every level as that which permits knowing to take place. Pure awareness is both outside the frame and within it. It is both beyond our 'awarenesses of' and interpenetrates the interlocking levels that make up our lives. Any mode of experience can either conceal or reveal it.

Thus, returning to the dilemma posed by Douglas Harding as to whether, given the importance of pure awareness, it is necessary to attend to 'awareness of', my present answer is yes. 'Awareness of' does obscure pure awareness, but particularly when we know nothing of the latter. We have no reason then to lend it any importance. Clear experience of pure awareness quickly brings a radically new way of relating to oneself and the world. And as we become familiar with it, 'awareness of' is also enhanced. 'Awareness of' is part of our human condition. Most people find it important for a full life. Bringing attention fully into any experience, at any level — physical, sensory, mental, emotional, identity, and even those touching the edge of beyond — can also reveal the full essence of the knower. Any moment of 'awareness of' can reveal pure awareness. Full realization actually involves realizing the presence of Being not only behind, but within all our experience. Our challenge is thus not one of choosing between 'either or', but of how to enjoy 'both and'. This becomes much easier when we begin to recognize our own pure awareness and its subtle and peaceful zestfulness.

The aim in this book, then, is to make full use of the potential synergy of the two modes of awareness. In later chapters, we consider ways to enhance 'awareness of' at each level, while indicating how each level can help ground us more fully in pure awareness. The next chapter goes more deeply into the subtle relationship between singularity and difference that make 'awareness of' and pure awareness actually facets of each other. Later chapters return to the layers of experience discussed here, one by one, exploring their relationship to awareness in more detail. Thus Chapters Six and Seven deal with awareness in the body and its experience through stillness and movement; Chapter Eight with the senses, mind, intellect, and values; Chapter Nine with the emotions; Chapter Ten with one of the key vehicles of the mind and intellect, language; Chapter Eleven with deep-seated beliefs and assumptions that shape our world; Twelve with identity; and Thirteen with one part of the 'who else', awareness in groups. Chapter Fourteen returns to the relationship of pure awareness and spirituality, and the possibility of planetary renewal through an understanding of consciousness.

RESTING BETWEEN WORLDS

Before going to sleep, take a while, either sitting or lying to allow your attention very gently to rest in the body, with the faint intention of letting go of any knots or wrinkles. Allow yourself to release the sense of being a person you may have been holding during the day. Luxuriate innocently for a while in your own being-awareness and without trying to hold on to it, do not resist the slide into sleep.

On waking, wait a while, before plunging into action. Let yourself drift into waking, by resting in the in-between state, no longer asleep, but not yet fully awake, and as thoughts begin, let them come and go with out trying to follow them. Simply remain in a bed of resting-awareness.

If any questions concern you and come to your awareness, notice them and let them go, allowing a space in your awareness for any answers to emerge. Only when this in-between state appears to be fading and you sense that you are ready to move to action, gently rise allowing that peaceful inter-regnum to pervade your beginning day.

EXPERENCING DIFFERENT LAYERS

How does the map of different levels presented in this chapter match your experience? What layers or levels are part of your own experience? Do you identify other levels that we have ignored?

Relax as fully as you can and allow yourself to settle into a state of gentle reverie, rather than analytical thought. Before you begin, read these questions carefully. Allow the questions to guide your reflection, without following them attentively or slavishly. It doesn't matter if you give some questions more attention than others or if you forget some. You may choose to explore only some of the questions at one time and come back to the others. You may reflect inwardly or you might put each question at the top of a new page in your journal and let your thoughts flow onto the page. If you choose to reflect inwardly, you may like to have someone read the questions to you slowly and quietly with plenty of pauses, so you have time to reflect.

How do you experience the wider environment of our vast universe? Of our planet?

What are your immediate work and home environments like?

What key people are in your life? How are your relationships with them?

What activities fill your day? Are there regular patterns, occurring every day or week? How do you relate to what you do — with indifference, with enthusiasm, or some other response?

How does your body feel? What is your relationship with it? Does it serve you well? Do you take care good of it?

How about your mind and memory? How do you use them? What are their strengths and weaknesses?

What capabilities have you developed in your life? What are some you would still like to develop?

What is of great importance in your life? What do you value highly?

What do you hold to be true? What is at is if you believe about people in general? About the world? About yourself? Do you function as if you have a bedrock of trust or as if you exist in a frame of fear and anxiety?

What feelings do you frequently experience that you like? What feelings do you experience that you'd rather were less?

What kind of person are you? Who are you? Who or what is thinking these thoughts?

Who or what else are you connected to? Do you have a very deep personal connection with anyone that seems to involve something deeper than your individual selves?

Do you sometimes have a sense of connection with the wider pattern of nature or of some divine energy or presence. What is that like?

What would still be there if your thoughts ceased and there were no images or feelings? What is your experience of your own awareness?

BALANCING THE DIFFERENT LEVELS

The following little practice offers a gentle way of balancing the different levels of experience, relaxing and refreshing one ready for renewed activity.

Sitting quietly and calmly, breathing gently and fully, poised with your back upright, but not strained, take a few moments to become fully aware of your environment. Notice fully what you can see and hear around you. What are you feeling in and around your body?

Beware of what is happening in your mind. Are you aware of any thoughts and images arising and subsiding?

Allow yourself to have a sense of what you hold to be of fundamental importance in your life.

Let yourself be aware of the person who you are.

Notice what is there when you gently introduce the thought 'I am' and let it go.

Have a sense of the forces and energies that seem to flow through you, connecting you at a very deep level with the larger pattern of life, with the earth below, with the sky above.

Let yourself be aware, as much as you comfortably can, of your aware-ness, underlying and suffusing all this experience. Let that awareness expand to include your sense of who you are . . . what you hold to be deeply impor-tant . . . your mind with its thoughts that come and go . . . your feelings in your body . . . your senses . . . and the environment around you.

Take a few moments to enjoy this sense of awareness suffusing and per-vading all levels of your experience, then gently stretch and, if you like, record your experiences in your journal, before continuing with whatever you are doing.

NOTES

1.   This is my extrapolation, not that of Douglas.

2.   This chapter offers a personal mix of traditional oriental maps of the psyche and the map of levels of experience developed by Robert Dilts in the 1980s from the work of Gregory Bateson. It presents developments of that model, described at greater length in an article I wrote for *NLP World*, March, 1995, "Maps Beyond the Mind, NLP and Spir-ituality".

3.   According to one survey, 68% of Americans sense the sacred at the birth of a child; 26% during sex. *Newsweek*, December, 1994, p.40.

CHAPTER THREE

Awareness, Relationship and Maturity

Summary
The key levels of experience outlined in the previous chapter each mark a phase of a long process of maturation in which we discover what we truly are. One stage in this process involves mastering multiple roles and perspectives in life. This ability, so necessary for healthy relationships, opens the way to becoming fully ourselves, and thence to discovering that subtle essence which underlies all standpoints. From there we can awaken to that wholeness in which we live, knowing our awareness as the ground of all that is.

Ripeness is all.

Introduction

Have you ever wondered why you get on with some people like a house on fire, but with others you don't? One explanation is that we find ourselves at different phases of development. Each phase of our self-unfolding affects the way we understand ourselves. It influences our outlook on the world, how we view others, and our relationships.

In Chapter One you were invited to undertake a hero's journey to discover the ground of quality in yourself — your own pure awareness. In Chapter Two, we considered how different kinds of contents of consciousness now obscure, now reveal this awareness. Here we consider how the principal levels of experience also influence key phases in our unfolding. We consider a map of maturation which helps us situate ourselves on the path to self-knowledge. It indicates how our gradual awakening to awareness affects our relations with others.

In each phase of our life we identify with parts of our experience — perhaps our work, our feelings, our role as a parent, or our community — as we try to make sense of ourselves and our world. Each identification limits our wholeness. The contradictions that arise with each identification place us in opposition to important parts of our own experience. There is a pattern to these mis-identifications that most of us follow. Each level has its own outlook on life, its own drives, and its own often hidden agenda. Resolution of the challenges of each level requires a more comprehensive way of understanding the world, which leads to a new set of oppositions. Eventually, we reach an accommodation in which the contradictions disappear, in which all parts of our experience are integrated in one unified wholeness. This is a journey we all begin, but few complete. It has seven major phases or levels.[1]

Levels of Development — Personal

As a new-born baby, we are completely dependent on our environment to nourish us physically and emotionally, to shelter and care for us. Unable to move independently, we can only react to our experience. We live in a world that is emotional and instinctual, with little control over our bodily functions.

Eventually, we become aware that we are a separate, sentient being. As a toddler, we begin to move around more freely and to influence our environment. In the 'terrible twos' we strengthen and test our own power in relation to others.

Meanwhile, those around us are working hard to cement our identification with a name and face in the mirror. They teach us to identify others in the same way, dividing the world into discrete objects each with its own name. Parts of our behaviour are endorsed and encouraged, others are disapproved of. We discover that 'if you want to get along, you've got to go along.' We learn the value of compromise and giving. We begin to relate to ourselves and others through the collective filters of language and custom. We discover that social life includes rights and duties. We develop the notion of 'fairness'.

These three phases, emotive or instinctual, seeking power and control, and conforming socially, return over an even longer period as we mature into adults.

Adolescence throws us back into the first level of development, the emotive and instinctual. Life can be tempestuous and impulsive. Many teenagers oscillate between chronic dependence on others and attempts to assert a separate identity. Sensitive to peer pressure, we are concerned with how we appear to others and unsure which aspects of self are acceptable. We refine our public mask or persona, pushing unacceptable parts of ourselves into the 'shadow'. We monitor ourselves; strengthening what is sometimes called the 'meta position', the ability to notice what we are doing, looking over our own shoulder, as our own coach or critic. We may find ourselves talking to ourselves, commenting on what we are doing critically, "You shouldn't have said that" or favourably, "That was a nice move".

As we move into adulthood, our challenge is to establish our own independence. This requires a strong sense of self or 'ego' with our personal will directing the conscious mind. We develop new skills and capabilities and an assertive first position. We grow in confidence, but find that our drive for security through power and control often conflicts with others. Once again we have to learn to take others into account.

One of the several ways we confront the independent existence of others is when we fall in love. Falling in love can be intense. In one sense, this intensity is in ourselves, as we experience a heightening of consciousness, which colours our view of friends, family, and life as a whole. We identify the other as the source of that intensity, and also find that they have become an unpredictable extension of ourselves. Discovering that the other person really does have a separate existence with their own needs and interests can be painful. If the relationship is to flourish, 'I' have to find a way to understand and accept you as 'you'. As love matures, we understand the other person, intuitively sensing their atmosphere, habits, and patterns. We can anticipate how they will respond to situations. We develop second position, the ability to enter imaginatively into another's world and identify empathetically with their experience.

Sometimes, to figure out what's going on in a relationship, we need even more distance, so that we are not just looking over our own shoulder, but are objective about what is happening between ourselves and another. To be objective means taking the stance of a detached observer, that is, as if at a fair distance from both parties. This is a third 'perceptual position'.

We may also experience that our relationship seems to have a life of its own. Things happen between us that are different from what happens with others. Together we create a 'we' that has its own atmosphere and personality. The ability to identify with a relationship, almost to embody it and become it, so that we can sense what is happening in it as a whole, gives a fourth position.[2]

Having a family strengthens and develops the sense of 'we'. Our welfare is tied up with that of others. Others depend on us. If we have children, understanding them requires the ability to empathize. Not only are we concerned with the needs of our immediate family, we become increasingly aware of the interdependence of our family with the larger social fabric. The oughts and shoulds, passed on to us from our own parents, become part of a framework for viewing social relations as a whole. We realize that our well-being depends on mutual respect. We are in a phase of mutuality and conformity, caring for and contributing to the collective endeavour. We are immersed in the values and codes of our community.

The four perceptual positions — 'I', 'You', 'We', 'He/She/They' — plus the 'meta' ability to look over our own shoulders, detached from our own thoughts and actions, are the key to this third level of maturation, the cooperative or social. If in the first, instinctual phase of development, 'things affect me', in the second phase of seeking to exercise power and control, 'I affect things'. In the third, social phase, we discover that 'I affect you, you affect me', and thus that 'we affect each other'. Most of us consciously or

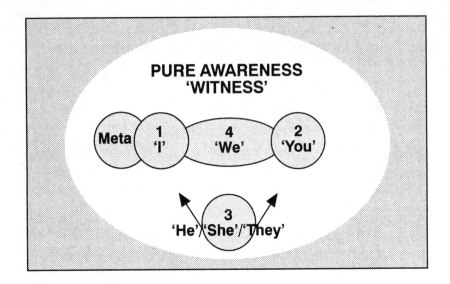

PERCEPTUAL POSITIONS

unconsciously learn to take the various perceptual positions, but generally we are more comfortable with, and spend more time in, some positions than others. Perhaps we tend to be a bit of an onlooker or perhaps we are always empathizing with others, neglecting ourselves, or disregarding others to care for ourselves. Maturation requires a balance among the different perceptual positions. That requires some awareness of our patterns and preferences. Can you identify your current biases among the positions?

Most people in most societies will enter and perhaps advance through the first two or three levels of development, with a considerable amount of individual and cultural variance. For instance, American children are encouraged to express themselves independently, while Japanese parents strongly condition their children not to interfere with others. This affects the cultural bias among perceptual positions, making Americans generally more individualistic. But in any society few go beyond level three, to establish a deeper level of personal integration.

INDIVIDUATION

In the third level of development, we can shift roles, we can adjust perceptual positions among the elements of a system, from first position, to second and third positions, and eventually to the fourth we-position. But we have not made the leap to recognizing that all positions and identities are in a sense arbitrary. We are still caught in the game of identifying with one position or another. We are not yet wise to the game itself. Roles and positions are like the clothes we happens to wear. We are not the various clothes we pick, but that which is wearing them. As we enter the next phase of development, we recognize how social life anchors us in the social constructs of selfhood. These are essentially mental and emotional. We find that the land of 'ought' and 'should', or being nice, places us in opposition to our own body. Psyche and soma are divorced.

At some point, to pass to the next level of development, we must become an individual, a person, in our own right. Jung and Maslow called this individuation or self-actualization. It often occurs in a period of readjustment in mid-life. Like Dante "In the midst of our path through life", we may go into "the dark forest where the right path is unclear" to achieve a deeper level of integration of parts of ourselves that were unconscious — particularly the body, which looks after our life as a whole in a way that the conscious mind cannot. Individuation involves accepting ourselves as an incarnate whole. We are more at home in the bodymind — freer of conventions, freer to choose and let creativity flow, perhaps for the first time, as we let go of derivative influences and flow with the stream of life.

Because men and women are physically different, a fact which social conditioning reinforces, they tend to identify consciously with different modes of being — masculine or feminine, respectively. Before passing to the fourth level of development, women may have to integrate more unconscious masculine aspects of themselves. For instance the kind of independent assertiveness that many men pass through in the second level of development. On the other hand, men may need to accommodate more of the receptive, sensitive, and intuitive feminine qualities necessary for mastery of the third social level of development.

Both may also have to accept and integrate repressed parts of the shadow. A woman who has quickly gone from the family home to marriage may be terrified when facing separation in her early forties. She may have spent a large part of her life creating a nice atmosphere for others. She has never fully faced the need to establish independence and survival. To do so may involve confronting very real and intense fears that have lain dormant.

Levels of Development — Transpersonal

However, in coming to a new level of integration as a person, we face a new dichotomy: between life and death. We come into our prime as our body begins to show signs of wear and tear, hints of its own mortality.

Resolution of this pair of contraries requires a deeper level of realization — that we are actually something beyond the bodymind. As Jean Klein puts it: "It is the body-mind which wakes up in the morning, but what you are already fundamentally is. The body-mind wakes up in your 'isness', in your beingness."[3]

This state of awareness transcends both life and death. It may be that we had been experiencing glimpses of pure awareness, either spontaneously or through following some meditative discipline. Individuation makes it easier for pure awareness to become not only something we dip into intermittently, between thoughts, but something that forms the backdrop to all experience. At the fifth level or stage of development, we realize fully that

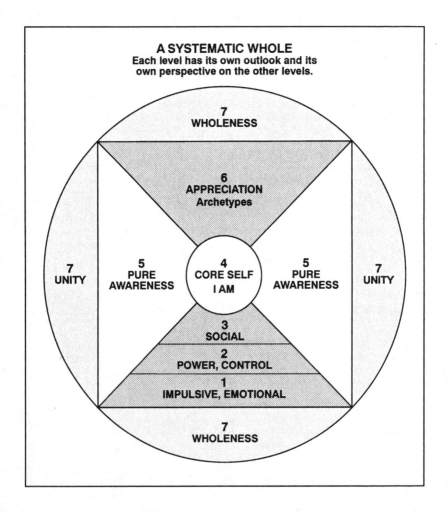

LEVELS OF DEVELOPMENT

we are this pure awareness. This transpersonal state ends our identification with the mortal and offers a new level of freedom: "To be a living being is not the ultimate state; there is something beyond, much more wonderful, which is neither being nor not-being, neither living nor not living. It is a state of pure awareness beyond the limitations of space and time. Once the illusion that the body-mind is oneself is abandoned, death loses its terror, it becomes a part of living."[4]

One of the characteristics of this fifth level of development is that we are as a witness to all the contents of consciousness including the activities and antics of our mind. Witnessing consciousness is pure, silent, uninvolved, and non-judgmental. It is peaceful, unbounded, changeless, self-aware beingness. Like a clear, still lake, it silently reflects within itself the margin of grass, trees, sky, and mountains. We notice not only the reflections, but that we are the reflector itself. Witnessing consciousness offers a perspective outside the first four levels of development, as spaces 5 in figure on p.40 suggest. It is the basis and backdrop of all perceptual positions. The active phases of experience continue, but we are an uninvolved observer, or rather an unmoved observingness, since there is really no active observer or observing, although these are happening.

At first, we may experience witnessing awareness intermittently. Perhaps, you have already had glimpses of this state. Or it may become continuous. Even sleep may be witnessed, for inner wakefulness eventually continues while the body lies relaxed in the physiological state of sleep. The Upanishads call this state of pure awareness *turya*, literally, fourth, the state that underlies the three states of waking, dreaming, and sleep.

With this fifth level of development, our relationships acquire a quality of clarity and objectivity. However we also experience some distance. In a sense, the world is now split into two, self and non-self, the non-changing impersonal field of our own being awareness, and the changing contents of consciousness. At the fifth level of development, there is a gap between ourselves and others. We may for a while wonder what has happened to our feelings.

However, the fifth level also opens the way to heal the dualism it engenders. Full experience of pure awareness frees us to love. Before individuation, we accept ourselves incompletely. And self-acceptance is a precondition for accepting others. The quality of our relationships is restricted up to level three or four, because we always have some personal needs and demands, often driven by our own lack of self-acceptance. We love according to what comes back. This is the graveyard of many relationships. Only the dissolving of our identification with the personal self permits truly unconditional love. "When all the false self-identifications are thrown away, what remains is all-embracing love", says Swami Nisargadatta.[5] This love is the ground of the universal compassion of Buddhism "for all sentient beings." It is the driving force in healing the final duality between self and non-self.

It manifests externally in a growing appreciation of the beauty, pattern and connectedness in the natural world. Our sense of the interconnectedness of all things grows, and with it our recognition of our part in that pattern.

It grows internally, as we recognize that the archetypes and symbols, which we previously thought had a separate existence, are manifestations and expressions of our own self. If previously we had worshipped a God or Gods, which from the lower levels would have appeared separate from ourselves, Other, dwelling above us, in Heaven, now we find that they are an intimate part of ourselves, almost our own essence.

Eileen Caddy (co-founder of the Findhorn Community in Scotland) describes this switch from considering the divine as other and realizing it as oneself. In the early days of Findhorn she reports hearing a voice of divine guidance, which over the years gradually changed. At first it addressed her as "My child", then "My beloved child". Later still she realized that she was separating herself from God: "There is no separation between ourselves and God, there is only 'I am'. I am the guidance. It took me many years to realize this. . . . About three or four years ago, it all suddenly changed and I realized that if I accept the God within, then 'I am' is the highest source. . .

Yes, I still listen to the voice, and we all have that voice inside us. . . . It is now in the first person."[6]

The growing closeness of Self and non-self, welded by our love and appreciation of all we experience, culminates in a new level of integration, symbolized by the mysterium conjunctionem, the union of opposites, in which self and non-self are realized as one. The lover and divine beloved — evoked by Sufi and Christian mystics, such as Rumi and St John of the Cross — who had been in a relationship of subtle and sensual intimacy, merge. This is the seventh phase of development. We live as that pure awareness which we now find interpenetrates and contains all that is.

In unity or wholeness, we recognize fully that we are not, as we had imagined, a small part of something larger, but we are that something larger. We discover that everything is part of us. The world occurs within our own Self. "I may perceive the world just like you, but you believe to be in it, while I see it as an iridescent drop in the vast expanse of consciousness."[7] This state resolves all contraries. There is no further conflict between Self and non-self, because everything is recognized as ourselves. Everything, as Bateson puts it "proposes a view of the whole". And we are that whole.

Rapport

Levels of development suggest in part why some of our relationships work much better than others. We relate most comfortably to those who share the same overall level, with its issues and outlook, as ourselves. If we find that we have to drop a level and talk down to people, that does not make for the most satisfying communication. Similarly, if we sense the person we are talking to has a more comprehensive frame than ourselves for approaching life, we may be impressed or uneasy, but not really in a position of full equality.

This has practical consequences throughout the levels. For instance, companies with a strong technical bent may have many well-qualified engineering and scientific staff, who are far more comfortable working to control parts of their physical world (level 2), than social relations (level 3). Promotion to management requires a fresh set of competencies and a willingness to relate to others in a new and more feeling way. The company may try to assist the required change with a training programme, but participants easily find the ideas, values, even the person of the trainers promoting the new level of development, unattractive and threatening.

Discerning with the Levels

A map of the different levels of development can help you identify areas that may need attention for your personal unfolding to progress. The following question will help you identify some of your current underlying concerns: Overall, what determines your well-being? Note your answer, and ask "What determines that?" Continue till you have a sense of your deep underlying concerns. Are you the source and origin of what happens to you or is your well-being bound up with people and things external to you? This will give you some idea of the level you might primarily be addressing in your life.

We do fluctuate somewhat among the levels. For instance, under pressure, we may drop a level or two, becoming controlling or emotional, like frustrated parents, who snap at their children. Most people have residual unfinished business with the lower levels. Much of this must be taken care of before we can easily enter into the transpersonal realms, without the distorting filters of the lower levels. The following questions will help you identify where you might need to give some attention:

Level 1: In what contexts or situations do you inappropriately depend on others or react in an unreasonably strong emotional way?

Level 2: Do you ever try to control the behaviour of others inappropriately? In what contexts are you manipulative? Or intolerant?

Level 3: Do you avoid conflict for fear of offending others? In what situations do you accept others' needs over your own?

Level 4: To what extent do you feel responsible for your own lot? To what extent are you content and at ease with yourself? To what extent are you relaxed, comfortable, and at home in your own body? If you knew you might soon die, how would you respond?

Exploring Perceptual Positions

Mastering perceptual positions is one of the keys to mastering the personal levels of development. Conscious familiarity with the different perceptual positions paves the way for the transpersonal levels, as we recognize the arbitrary nature of our identification with roles and positions. It frees us to be ourselves and recognize that our own pure awareness is the ground and backdrop to all positions. We easily forget how provisional are the patterns of personality and behaviour we take for ourselves. These simply cover core awareness. Recognizing their provisional nature allows us more choice, and gives a greater chance for our true immaculate Self, the ultimate wearer of our many masks and modifications, to shine through. The following activities will help you explore and master perceptual positions. Take you time and return to them occasionally.

FIRST POSITION
First position is the home base and starting point for the various positions. Take some moments to experience a strong first position, such as when you feel at home in your body, you know who you are and what you want and value, and are at ease with, and present to, your environment. You might recall and enter into a memory of a time when you felt this way. Allow your body to take the posture and breathing of that first-position you. How does it feel? How is your world in that centred first person point of view?

Does first position come easily and naturally to you? Do you know what you want, easily expressing and taking care of your needs? Are you comfortable and at home in your own body? Are you aware of your own feelings and fully connected to your senses?

When and where are you at ease in first position? Where do you lose first position inappropriately (e.g. when you don't assert your needs and others exploit you)? Do you sometimes hold first position inappropriately (perhaps when you could usefully take a more objective stance or be more empathic, considering others more)? Do you need to develop first position? How might you do so?

SECOND POSITION
Everyday life presents many opportunities for practising second position — for instance, travelling to work, eating out, or watching TV and film. Dance and sport also provide wonderful opportunities for imaginative insight into other ways of being. Noticing how taking second position with great athletes or dancers affects the feeling in your body.

When exploring second position, allow yourself to become inwardly quiet and settled. First find your own first position, then imagine setting it aside. After exploring second position, reassume your own first position.

You can explore second position while you are with others or from memory. In either case there are two key approaches: you can imagine you leave your own body to become them. Or take a mental snapshot or movie of them and imagine that they are now in you and you are experiencing and functioning as they would. Notice which approach suits you. How do the results of each approach differ for you? For most people, the latter gives a fuller sense of the other person.

Think of someone you know and love dearly. It may help to picture them with you and to hear their voice. Imagine for a moment that you are seeing the world through their eyes. Assume their posture and gestures, think and talk as they do. Imagine being them in two or three everyday situations — for instance, walking down the road, relating to people you know, responding to good or bad news, or doing a chore such as cooking, cleaning, or driving.

What seems to be different in their experience of the world from yours? What does second position teach you about them? How does your usual experience contrast with your sense of being them?

Can you easily put yourself in another's shoes? With whom is it easiest? With certain family members? Friends? Colleagues? With whom is it most difficult? In what contexts is it more difficult for you to take second position? When people are sick or well? Happy or sad? Aggressive or wounded? Independent or needy?

With whom do you *not* take second position? Allow yourself to take second position with them. What do you discover, as you imagine being them? Imagine being a beggar or a tramp. Someone from a different race or culture. What do you learn in each case?

It is not only with people that we can take second position. Second position allows us to know the universe we are in from the inside. It helps reduce the illusory separation from the world around us that our sense of 'I' has created. Deep and extended second position with our world is a precondition for, and means to, the recovery of the awareness of our ultimate unity with all.

Imagine taking second position with an animal or bird. Choose one, assume its stance, as best you can for a while. Try moving as this creature. How does it feel to be it? What does the world look like through its eyes? What does it sound like? How is the sense of movement? Of touch? Of smell? Of taste?

Become a favourite tree for a while. Imagine going to second position with familiar buildings — from cottages to cathedrals. How is it to be a teacup or a tangerine, a pebble or a rock? Imagine you are the sea. The sky. A slow meandering river. A fast mountain stream. The desert. A green field. A breeze. A strong wind. A gale. Imagine you are a favourite land-scape. Imagine you are our planet, our galaxy, or the universe as a whole. How does that feel?

Many writers, artists, and actors use second position as part of their crea-tive process. Keats' 'negative capability', Rilke's 'einsehen' ('seeing into'), and Hopkins' experience of 'inscape' all involve identifying with, and be-coming the object of perception. Keats mentions doing this with birds, Rilke with a dog. Hopkins spent hours contemplating stones and flowers. Balzac described following beggars and becoming them, feeling their tatters on his own back. Such identification gave these writers an inner knowledge, a felt sense, of whatever they contemplated. It helped them capture that experi-ence more accurately in writing.

Actors often assume the posture, gestures, and vocal mannerisms of people they meet. These provide models for the various characters they play. The neuro-psychologist Oliver Sacks, an occasional consultant to Hollywood, noted the ease with which Robin Williams observed and mastered his man-nerisms, and assumed a similar personality to his own. He considered De Niro's portrayal of Parkinsonian symptoms in the character Leonard (in *Awakenings*) so accurate he wished he'd recorded his EEG. He was con-vinced De Niro had become Parkinsonian at a neurological level.

Second position gives valuable insight into another's world, but should not be prolonged. Particularly if the other person is unhealthy or disturbed in some way. Second position can help us learn from others, as we 'model' them and their behaviour. Children learn this way, going to second position with parents and other significant people in their lives. Role models can inspire and teach, but their influence is often mixed, as most people have both strengths and weaknesses. It is important to choose models with cau-tion, as not everything we pick up in second position is positive. At times, we can take in 'negative' influences. Set intent to retain only what is useful. After second position, put the model aside and return to you own first po-sition.

MENTORS

Many people use friends or colleagues to help solve problems. Talking a difficulty over with someone else can help us discover solutions. With sec-ond position, we have a source of wisdom and insight, even if there is no one external to turn to.

Proust's housekeeper, Céleste, described how helpful she found his ad-vice. After his death, whenever she had a problem, she would ask herself, "Now what would M. Proust advise?" And invariably she would get a good answer. Céleste's question led her to imagine being him for a moment.

We store in our minds the patterns of those we know, particularly those we know intimately. When we become inwardly quiet, and access our records of the other person, we can allow our bodymind to suspend our own personal patterns, and adjust to a different way of being. Once we have adjusted to that different way of being, the resources enmeshed in that way of being are available to us.

Can you identify three or four people who have been sources of wisdom and insight, or practical help for you? (For some people nature or parts of nature can function in this way; for others, figures from literature or from religious scriptures fulfil this role.) Think of a problem or issue in your life that is unresolved. If you can't recall anything like that, think of something of importance to you that you would like to understand better. Who could help you with this? Settle into yourself, and imagine your inner helpers. What advice or answers to your question or problem does each give as you imagine being them? Do they offer they same or different insights? Return to first position and evaluate what you discovered.

META POSITION

When we are unsure whether to have another chocolate, or some other little indulgence, we can be aware of the dilemma, the hesitations in our self-talk, the hand reaching out and maybe drawing back, perhaps the congratulations of successful resistance. Part of our mind is evaluating other parts of itself. This doubling up on ourselves helps us adjust how we respond to people and situations. Meta position lets us step back a little from our first position self, to identify with a facet of self that observes, evaluates, and provides feedback. We are less caught up in what we are doing, and can recognize how to modify or improve it. Permanent meta position would detach us from the juice of life; absence of meta position could make us hasty, neglectful of the bigger picture.

Meta position is a 'disassociated' perspective. Pure awareness is both its own subject and object. As we localize ourselves in the body, we split the world into self and non-self, associating with the former. Subsequently, we separate ourselves into mind and body, often dissociating from the latter. We also dissociate from parts of our own mind, sifting and controlling our spontaneity, making parts become unconscious altogether. Passage through the levels of development involves the gradual healing of these various dissociations and recovery of wholeness, which is neither associated nor dissociated, but contains both. As we grow in understanding, we do not lose the ability to take multiple perspectives, but they become part of our conscious resources, rather than semi-unconscious habits that use us.

Conscious familiarity with our meta positions helps this process. There are many forms of meta position. Some people sense that they are slightly behind themselves, as if looking over their own shoulder. Others sense that they are in some other part of the room looking on, perhaps even high up. What seems true for you?

To consciously explore some of these options, first sit in full associated first position. Now leave your seat and walk slowly about the room, imagining you are still seated where you were. Walk around observing the seated you, noticing how you perceive your imagined self from different angles. Take a few moments to sample each position fully — from behind yourself, to the side, from in front, from high up (if you can, stand on another chair), from down below.

Now return to your seat and project part of yourself out into the room, to those places you just looked at yourself from. Imagine for a few moments that you are behind yourself, to the side, up in front, down below, looking at yourself. What do you notice from each position? Which seems most comfortable and helpful?

Practice using meta position in situations where you are not under pressure. Allow yourself to enter a fully associated first position, then for short periods imagine that you are slightly behind yourself, or in whichever location is comfortable. Notice what your experience is like.

Can you identify a number of challenging situations where meta position could help you adjust your responses? Imagine yourself in a number of those situations appropriately dipping into meta position.

THIRD POSITION

As our meta-position distances itself from our usual first position, till we are perceiving another as dispassionately as ourselves, it becomes third position. Usually this is equidistant between first and second position and off to one side (see pg.38). Third position helps us notice the patterns occurring in a relationship as a neutral observer might. It offers a complementary perspective to first position or empathic identification with 'other'. Third position balances the information we have gathered in first and second positions. We can look dispassionately at the 'dance' the two people create together.

In a public context, where you can discreetly observe others, such as a cafe, notice what is happening between two people or among a small group. Let yourself be an impassive observer. Take second position with each of the protagonists. Then return to the neutral observer position. Notice what this position feels like to mind and body. What do you gather about the individuals and the pattern of their relationship with each other?

When you are interacting with others, find out which mental vantage point in a room helps you observe in a neutral way what is happening between you and them.

Think of a close relationship that you have. Notice how you respond to the other person from your normal first position. Notice how you experience second position. What is it like to be them? How do you seem seen through their eyes?

Now take a neutral third position. What does this relationship look like from the outside? What's happening between you? What would an on-looker, as a fly on the wall, make of it?

The differences between these three points of view may stand out even more clearly when you physically move to a different place for each perspective. Try this, being sure to be the appropriate person in each spot, i.e. be fully associated as your present self in first position, associated into the other in second position, and off to one side for the third, onlooker's point of view.

In each place, notice and describe to yourself or a partner how you experience each position. What shifts in your understanding of the relationship in each place?

FOURTH POSITION

Fourth position gives a visceral, felt knowledge of what is happening in a relationship. In fourth position we are not observing but sensing through direct identification what is happening among the couples and groups of which we are part. Fourth position provides a sensitive barometer of the changes in climate in our relationships. It builds a caring, loving, inclusive approach to relationships, for true fourth position implies both 'I' and 'you', but together as one. From this place, we are motivated to appreciate and care for the whole, which includes both others and ourselves.

Think of a relationship you are in. Imagine stepping into the space between yourself and the other(s), so that you 'become' the relationship. You become a 'we' that includes both yourself and others. What do you experience in your body in this place? What do you feel? What images come to mind? (Information in fourth position will often come in some metaphoric or symbolic form, translating feeling into a condensed holistic representation.) Step back to a third or meta position. How do you experience the connections between the people involved and yourself? What is strong and what is weak in the relationship?

In your daily dealings with others, take moments here and there to experience your relationship as 'we'. Notice how your responses shift.

Notice what happens if you are sitting quietly and you allow your 'we' to include the environment you are in. What happens to any sense of separation? How inclusive can your 'we' become? Your family, your business, your community? Your nation? Humanity? The cosmos?

BECOMING YOUR OWN CONSULTANT

Now that you are familiar with the various perceptual positions, take some time to review a problematic relationship from all angles. Move physically from position to position.

1. Begin with first position, imagining yourself in a typical awkward situ-

ation with the other person. Notice your own experience and how you regard the other person. What sums up their attitude or behaviour towards you?

2. Step back a pace or two to consider your perspective from meta-position. How does the relationship look from here? How well are you handling it?

3. Go to second position. What do you experience as you imagine being the other person interacting with you? What do you find happening inside them. How do you come across through their eyes? What would sum up your attitude and behaviour, perceived from here?

4. From third position, how do you perceive your interaction as a dispassionate observer. How does your behaviour contribute to the other's response to you (and vice versa)? What is your relationship with yourself? How is your meta self relating to your first position self? Helpful? Supportive? Critical? Passive? What could help this relationship? How would that affect your interaction with the other person?

5. Step into the space between yourself and the other. Imagine becoming the relationship (fourth position). What do you experience as 'we'? What feelings and images come to mind? As the relationship, what advice do you have for the first position you?

6. Return to third position and evaluate what you have learned. Revisit, as desired, any of the positions to check intuitions and understandings, until you are satisfied that you have learned what you need for now.

7. Briefly pass through all the positions in reverse order (4, 3, 2, meta, 1), allowing a moment to assimilate the learnings from each place, and drawing them back into yourself. Notice how this moment of integration feels and how relations with others are in this state of awareness.[8]

SWITCHING PERCEPTUAL POSITIONS

How comfortable are you now with the different perceptual positions? What positions do you still find difficult? Which perceptual position do you neglect? In which contexts does this limit your effectiveness?

Whenever you are with others, switching quickly and freely among perceptual positions helps relationship. In your personal and professional communication, consider consciously using different perceptual positions for a while, including positions you neglect. Some internal questions will help this become natural:

What am I experiencing right now?

How is this situation for them?

What is happening between us?

What is the right point of view for this person or situation?

What point of view have I neglected?

Witnessing, Beyond all Positions

Briefly re-experience the various perceptual positions in regard to one of your relationships — take a first position, a second position, a third or meta position, and a fourth, 'we' position.

Ask yourself, What is present in all these positions? If necessary, experience the different positions again, once slowly and once quickly shifting among them.

You will probably notice that a very subtle aspect of yourself is there in all positions, though colourless, tasteless, and without smell or sound. This is that awareness which enables you to shift among all the different points of view. It is the witness and container of them all. Whatever we experience depends on this subtle awareness, even if we don't always notice it in the hurly-burly.

What happens when you identify with that unexpressed awareness which underlies every perceptual position? Notice how your breathing shifts a little lower in the chest and your eyes relax a bit, their focus softening. Now without losing that state, allow yourself to take this as the ground of a first position. This is the Self, the reason 'I' is always written with a capital letter. As this awareness, be aware of what is within your visual field, notice the sounds that fall within that silence, and the sensations within your body also within that awareness. You are simply experiencing with your senses, yet subtly aware of that field within which your experience falls.

Notice how this state brings peace and tranquillity, and yet you savour the beauty of what you behold. This is living with awareness. What happens if you briefly consider an issue that is current in your life as you rest in this state?

It would be a mistake to try to hold onto this state all the time. That could create strain. But this state can be lived naturally. This book explores a number of practices to help it occur.

For now, set your intent so that the deeper wisdom within helps you spontaneously take the appropriate perceptual positions for effective functioning in daily life. And have the intention to take some moments each day to turn your attention to that subtle source.

Closing Parable

The scholar Chu wandered into a strange town with a friend, where they were greeted by an old monk. The town was decorated with paintings, in one of which there was a pretty girl whose hair was down (signifying her unwedded status). She caught Chu's attention. The old monk thought to teach him a thing or two and suddenly Chu was in the painting, whose world had come alive, engaging the pretty girl in conversation. Soon the two were lovers. Within days it was plain, the girl had to put her hair up.

But then the sound of soldiers was heard, searching for unregistered outsiders. "Quick — hide", said the girl, and in the confusion, Chu found himself floating out of the painting, back down to the monk and his astonished friend. The monk pointed to the painting. There was the pretty girl. Her hair was up.

NOTES

1.   The model outlined here was developed by N. Zink and myself, synthesizing a number of sources. See "Levels of Development", N. Zink and P. Wrycza, *NLP World*, Vol. 2, 3, 1995.

2.   The notion of Perceptual Positions was originally developed by John Grinder and Robert Dilts. For the version here, including the fourth, 'we' position identified by J. Ardui and myself, see our article "Unravelling Perceptual Positions", *NLP World*, Vol. 1, 2, 1994, pp. 5-22.

3.   *Transmission of the Flame*, p. 75.

4.   *I Am That*, p. 122.

5.   *I Am That*, p. 195

6.   "Willing to Change", interview in *One Earth*, 12, pp. 8-11 (Findhorn Community), 1993-4, p. 9.

7.   *I Am That*, p. 179.

8.   This process is adapted from Dilts' Meta-Mirror, and the Core Consulting Process, developed by Jan Ardui and myself.

CHAPTER FOUR

From Time to Timelessness

Summary

In the two previous chapters, we explored the relationship of awareness to the various 'levels' of life and to perceptual positions. Here we consider how our experience ranges through time. The ability to access and sort experience pertaining to past, present, or future is a practical necessity. But true creativity and contentment depend on our ability to return to that simple awareness, which simply is, outside of time.

> *There is really no before and after for Mind . . .*
> *The present is the only thing that has no end.* Schroedinger

Awareness and Time

Awareness in its essence is outside of time. Pure and uninvolved, it is simply present to itself and whatever falls within it. Yet, just as it animates the different levels of experience and perceptual positions, so it appears to move through time.

Remarkably, from any vantage point in time we can attend to any other point, past, present, or future, focusing on any level of experience or perceptual position. For instance, if you pause now, you might remember when you began reading this book. You could even imagine yourself wondering, back then, what you might derive from reading it. Or you can imagine yourself six months from now, looking back at this moment, noticing what happened in your life in the months after reading these words. You can consider the possible impact of this book on your behaviour, capabilities, sense of self, relationships or indeed any other aspect of life.

Such mobility in time has practical value. It means we can revisit, re-evaluate, and learn from our past. Without it, we would need to continually reinvent ourselves and almost everything else. The accumulation of knowledge would be impossible. We would be forever rediscovering everything, from the wheel to wisdom. We would not be able to share and interact with others with any coherence, as we would not have any stability in our personal identity. We would be forever forgetting who we are.

Similarly, without the ability to conceive what has not yet happened, our actions would become random and aimless. The mobility of our awareness through time means we can plan for the future and be creative. It means we can determine and achieve goals. We can set intention.

But our very mobility in time carries a price: in entertaining images of the past or future, we become dislocated from the present moment, lost in 'awareness of'. We need to be far-sighted, but often we are reaching toward future plans and goals, anticipating disasters or delights that never happen in quite the way we expected. Similarly, we are often replaying mental tapes of past events, stewing over what has happened or trying to forestall recurrences. Perhaps we jump between recalling an uncomfortable exchange with a boss, and or working out what to do next time. Yet, in reality the past has already happened and cannot be changed, except by altering our memory and understanding of it. The future is not yet here and can only be prepared for, but not truly created. In between we risk overlooking a treasure — now.

For core awareness, there is only this now. Memories and imaginations, we forget, really only happen in a present moment, the eternal now, changeless bed to the river of transformation. Our apparent wanderings through time are in many respects so much mental froth. But this froth often obscures the clear creative well-spring of now, from which could otherwise bubble forth a fresh, immediate, and immaculately appropriate response to whatever is happening.

TIME PREFERENCES

What is your relationship to time? Are you often turning over old events, whether pleasant or unpleasant? Are you often in the future making plans and dreaming about what you want to create or experience, or worrying about what might happen?

Are you often under time pressure? Or do you live as if you have plenty of time? Are you able to relax and enjoy the present? How does your relationship with time change in different contexts — work, home, play, holidays? How is your relationship with time when you are most comfortable? When you are least comfortable? What makes the difference between comfort and discomfort?

Take two hours when you will not be disturbed by others to simply do nothing. During this time, don't read, write, or engage in any tasks or chores. Simply allow yourself to be. Notice what happens in your awareness, during this time. What patterns occur?

Does the time go quickly or slowly? Where is your attention most? In the past, future, or present? Is it internal or external? What kinds of 'awareness of' seem to mask pure awareness? You might want to record these observations in your workbook.

BOREDOM

In states such as doubt, disappointment, anxiety, worry, boredom, and fretting over spilt milk, we accentuate facets of the past, present, or future inappropriately. Unhelpful images and inner voices obscure pure awareness in time-bound mirages. With anxiety and worry, we lose ourselves in the not yet; with doubt we undermine our confidence in present or future choices; in fretting over spilt milk, we are haunted by the past; and with disappointment, our sense of what might have been rides roughshod over what is.

Yet each of these states can be a portal back to pure awareness. For instance, boredom implies that we judge what we are experiencing now to be unsatisfactory. It is not stimulating or rewarding enough in itself. Something better or more exciting is expected. Such judgement implies that we hold the ideal state to be one in which we are absorbed in something — dominated by experience, caught up in it, gripped by it. Thus our usual cure for boredom is a change of activity. We forget that the boredom is not outside in the thing judged, but in our judging.

Yet boredom can remind us that our attention is misplaced, directed away from the essence of the present moment. It offers an opportunity to reconnect ourselves with our self and with the present moment. It is a cue to ask inwardly: What is happening now? What am I not paying attention to, whether inside myself or in my environment?

Often it turns out that I am not appreciating what could be potentially fascinating in my field of experience. I am probably also not acknowledging some uncomfortable, restless feelings in my body. As I allow myself to acknowledge and be with them for a while, I allow them to dissolve and for my bodymind to settle into a deeper sense of oneness and being. I can then also apprehend and enjoy more fully what is in and around me now.

The Balinese are rarely bored, they hardly ever use the word. The Balinese are mostly still relaxed inside, not yet caught up in the culture of craving. Whatever they do, they do with quiet attentiveness, whether sweeping the floor, folding napkins, ironing, or creating some beautiful offering from fruits and sweetmeats, learning a dance, or carving an image of the divine. Everything becomes a kind of meditation in which inwardness is balanced with outwardness. I rest in myself, yet I engage in action. I am quiet inside, yet I do what needs doing at a relaxed pace. Actions are their own reward. Thus the Balinese happily put much creative energy into things that are intrinsically impermanent — such as little palm leaf designs for a momentary religious offering or exquisitely decorated animals and towers that will go up in smoke at a cremation.

Equally, the Balinese are comfortable doing nothing, simply sitting, chatting, or being quiet for long periods. If the present moment is its own reward, whatever needs to happens, happens with its own rhythm, in its own time, sometimes, slowly, sometimes fast, but with a rhythm dictated organically from within, rather than from a clock. As such the Balinese rarely look dissociated and harassed in the way that Westerners do. In visiting Bali, one of the first things a Westerner learns is to relax and flow in time more gracefully, enjoying what is, rather than trying to dominate and fill time like an exploitable commodity.

BEYOND THE BORING
Consider what routine activities you currently find frustrating, distasteful or boring — perhaps washing up or ironing or similar chores. What is implicit in your impatience with these tasks? What is it you seem to hold true about yourself or your time. Given that the tasks are part of your activities, how might you approach them differently? How can you attempt them with grace, simplicity, and presence? What state of body and mind do you need to be in? What kind of attitude towards the tasks might be more helpful?

BEING PRESENT — LETTING GO
In boredom and the related states of anxiety, worry, doubt, disappointment, and fretting over the past, we no longer flow deeply with the present moment. We contract the bodymind in some way, reducing our openness in the present. Yet presence is never far away. This next process makes it ever accessible.[1]

1. The first step to opening awareness, is to be present to not being present. For instance, you might check inside how open your field of experience is right now. Notice where there is any tension or tightness in the bodymind.

2. Allow yourself to breathe more slowly and deeply, and as the stream of preoccupations settles, ask inwardly: "What am I holding on to right now?" Notice what comes to your attention in answer to this question. Notice what states of mind you might be maintaining; notice what is 'tight' or 'blocked' in your body.

3. Then ask "Am I ready to let go of this?" If you are, let it go. Allow any tension to release so that the channels of your energy open up. You may repeat the process several times, allowing greater and greater openness.

4. This process can also help when you are experiencing strong uncomfortable emotions or reactions, such as anxiety, fear, resentment, or anger. If when you ask whether you are ready to let go, you find that a part of you wants to hold on to the emotion — perhaps you feel justifiably wronged — ask "What do I want through holding on to this?" Then ask of the answer, "Do I want to hold on to this? Am I ready to let it go?" Continue till you find the deeper level of underlying need that you can let go of. Consider you are complete when you return to a level of ease and openness.

You can use this little format, frequently in quiet moments, when in between events, perhaps waiting for a bus or train, or at moments of tension in difficult situations, such as challenging meetings, where you may be getting tense or losing confidence.

From time to time check how you tend to contract awareness. Ask "How have I restricted my awareness today?" Review the day briefly, noticing when and how you 'closed' your awareness down. Notice how this happened physically and mentally.

FREEWRITING
Writing, especially freewriting, can be a valuable way to open into present awareness. To freewrite, you don't have to know what you want to say; just write whatever comes. Don't analyse or edit, simply write swiftly and without censoring what comes to your attention. If things dry up, you might notice what you are experiencing in the moment and write about that — even if that means saying you're stuck or blocked.

Noticing and acknowledging fully and completely what is at the conscious level admits truthful and accurate awareness of the now. It lifts the dampening weight of repression and denial, allowing the great sun of being to shine through.

Freewriting helps you discover what is lurking just beneath the surface of the awareness. You tune into the edge of the conscious and unconscious minds. It lets you draw your attention to what is, yet allowing what is not yet in consciousness but 'wants' to be to come through. This opens the circle of consciousness to include more fullness-in-now.

Freewriting about the recent past can also be valuable. It reveals more of the being-awareness potentially present in the present moment. Our true Self, as Proust recognized, is always potentially present, like a continuing current of being, but it is often masked by everyday concerns or the condition of the body, which come between us and being fully in the now. Freewriting can peel away from memories their original present-moment shrink-wrapping, revealing their hidden immediacy.

It can be rewarding to use your journal to record your adventures into the mystery of now. Take a few minutes each day for a period to let yourself write yourself into being. Settle for a moment into what is happening in your now, and let your pen pick up more and more of what is going on. No expectation, no censoring, a simple conduit for whatever your bodymind presents to you in this present moment.

LEARNING FROM EXPERIENCE WITH AN IMAGINARY OUTER 'TIME LINE'
Much of our meandering through time in memory and imagination happens in a spontaneous and unconscious way. We can also valuably travel through time more systematically to reorient our experience.

1. Find a place with plenty of space where you will not be disturbed. Choose a spot on the floor to represent the present, and imagine sorting your life's experience along a continuum within the space available, with

the past on one side and the future on the other.

2. Consider your past, from various perspectives in the room, both close to the line (point A in the figure on p.59), and some distance off it, where you can perceive the whole (B). What patterns do you recognize in your past? How has the past shaped your present? What is likely to happen in your future if your past continues to influence your present in the same way? What won't happen in your life if the same patterns and trends continue?

3. Physically place yourself in the future towards the completion of your life (C). How does you life appear, given present trends, from a perspective towards the end of your life? If you were to see your own tombstone, what would be your epitaph? How does you future appear as a whole (D)? Are you satisfied or would you have it different? If you would have it different, notice what might need to change in your present life. Check inside that any changes are in alignment with who you are as a person and with your life as a whole.

4. Returning to the present, imagine you are at a fork in your life's path. What happens if you continue in the old way (curved line F)? What happens if you make some of the changes you have been considering (curved line G)? Walk along both options sensing the difference.

5. From point B, notice what aspects of your past experience support the changes you want to make. Take some time to enliven within you a sense of those past experiences and your learnings from them.

6. Return to the present, what are some concrete next steps in your life?

Imagine your learnings from the past and intentions for the future crystallizing into an icon or symbol with a particular note or sound. Allow this image-sound to draw you into the future, and let it go.

7. Finally, in the present moment, simply be with a sense of the present, linked backwards in time to your past and forward to the future within the simple continuum of now.[2]

TIMELESS MOMENTS

Accounts of experiences of heightened awareness commonly emphasize the timeless quality of such moments. Time seems to stand still and the experiencer no longer identifies with that part of themselves which is measuring time and is subject to change. Instead awareness is dominated by a sense of simply being, existing in a pure state which always and only is. 'Now' becomes far more real than any 'then', including the present, as it is ordinarily experienced. As Tennyson put it, death seems "an almost laughable impossibility".

What experiences of timeless presence can you identify in your own life? What triggered them? What are the experiences like? What do you experience in your mind and body at such times of timelessness?

In timeless moments, people commonly report a diminishing of internal dialogue, the eyes in 'soft focus', noticing the whole field of vision, rather than being sharply focused on detail, the body calm, breathing somewhat lower in the chest, awareness not just in the head, but including the chest. How about you? Does this match your experience? How is it to remember such experiences now?

What happens, if, for a moment, you allow inner chatter to subside, your eyes to be softly open, taking in receptively the field of vision as a whole, rather than staring, your breathing to be calm and in the chest, your awareness in the chest as well as head? What happens as you contemplate your environment. Do you sense the timelessness in time, a little?

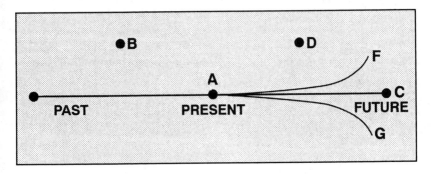

LEARNING FROM EXPERIENCE WITH A PHYSICAL TIME LINE

TAPPING THE TIMELESS

That which is non-changing is the creative ground of transformation. Yet too often we seek our solutions to life's challenges in the same realm as that in which they occur — the field of change. We seek answers from anywhere in time, rather than withdrawing, even briefly, to the timeless source from which the universe springs in its incalculable creative abundance. Yet any brief moment we do so, offers an opportunity for the surprising unseen or unheard solution to manifest in our minds.

Take a moment to identify a memory. Imagine that you enter into it, fully associated into your then body, as if you are seeing what you saw through your eyes, hearing what you heard and feeling those feelings. Allow yourself to oscillate between being in that memory and being fully present here and now. Allow yourself to notice that level of awareness which is background to both.

Let yourself enter and prolong that in-between state of now. This is the creative source of solutions, the well-spring of the new in our lives. Notice how your body and breathing are, as you touch this state.

Identify a challenge you are facing in your life. In that quiet in-between state of now introduce a keyword or image representing the challenge you are facing. Let it go, and wait. Notice what comes up for you from the void in relation to your challenge. If necessary, gently resettle into the timeless and reintroduce your keyword or image, notice what else comes up. Repeat this process two or three times, until you are satisfied with what this source of wisdom has given you in relation to the issue you face. Acknowledge this aspect of awareness with quiet appreciation and return to activity.

Notice that wherever we travel in time, when we squarely invoke 'now', we are instantly reconnected with the common strand to all these possible experiences, the present moment — our irreducible only reality, the one we are experiencing right now, whether masked with the images of time or in its full, timeless, awareness-presence. This the best present we can give yourselves. From wherever we are in time, whenever we look to the heart of now, living awareness is always here — changeless continuum-void, yet mirror to the potential myriad selves and subjects of our time-travelling, position-shifting, level changing life. There really is no time like the present.

NOTES

1.   This process owes much to psychotherapist Roger Lindon.
2.   This process adapts formats developed by Robert Dilts *et al.*

CHAPTER FIVE

Unity in Diversity: Living in Wholeness

Summary
Pure awareness surpasses our sense of individuality, providing a unified ground to experience. Closer inspection reveals it to be a kind of knower, what is known by the knower, and a knowingness that connects these two. Through its three-in-one nature, pure awareness remains a unified simplicity, yet engages in the many forms of 'awareness of' — taking different points of view or 'perceptual positions', shifting through discrete layers or levels of experience, and appearing to move through time. Human experience involves permutations of these elements — the key components of a unified field theory of experience. Knowing oneness in the many helps us be effective and at home in the all.

> *From the one, two; from the two, three, from the three, four,*
> *and from four, the ten thousand things . . .*Lao Tse

The Drive for Unity

Like homing pigeons heading straight for their place of origin, we instinctively gravitate towards the unified. Whether in art, literature, science, or social relations, we prefer symmetry, balance, closure, and completeness. We may expect complex and subtle shifts and differences of tone or colour in a symphony or a painting, but we find these satisfying only in the context of a sense of something that welds the differences into one.

This thirst for unity drives the underlying patterns of growth and development described in Chapter Three; it is our ultimate intent, as if pre-programmed into every cell from the moment of our arrival into this world. Our taste for integrity of design in art and architecture, in our institutions and our analyses of the natural world, are reflections of an underlying urge to be at one with the intrinsic unity of life itself. Our personal evolution is in many respects an undoing of attempts to unify our life around parts of experience that eventually prove insufficiently inclusive. We identify by turns with our emotions, our egos, our minds, our bodymind, and our inner being. But nothing less than all-embracing oneness provides ultimate satisfaction. That unity abides in our own consciousness, the ground of all we encounter.

Our common-sense attitude to consciousness is that it is an emergent property of an increasingly sophisticated nervous system. We assume we have more consciousness than a snail or a stone. Yet, in his pioneering study of expanded awareness, or 'cosmic consciousness', R. Bucke showed a hundred years ago that people from around the world entering such experiences receive a common insight. In states of great openness and wakefulness, consciousness is recognized with utter certainty to be not only in us but in all things.[1] The flame of life burning in us also ignites the dust and debris of our world, and fans through every particle of air and the space that interpenetrates each atom of our universe.

Such experiences, known deeply, intensely, and magically in the only laboratory that we ultimately possess — our own psychophysical system — are self-confirming. They are overtures of a concert of truth that sings, "Know this to be so: this universe is alive, a dance of one in peacock colours. Ordinary experience reduces a richness of colour to tired greyscale. We are not a beacon of consciousness in a desert of night, but an eddy of awareness in an ocean of life. Our nervous system does not generate consciousness, as a light bulb does light. Rather it modulates the energy and intelligence of existence itself, allowing this universe to rediscover and enjoy itself. Individuality is a riddle we have set ourselves in order to surprise ourselves with the discovery of what we have always been."

And yet this resolution of differences requires difference. Without the distinction of one place from another, everywhere would be the same. Activity or motion depend on our ability to tell one thing from another. Differences keep us awake, lively, and moving, stimulating learning and creativity, as our worlds constantly evolve and change. To paraphrase Heraclitus, we can never shop in the same supermarket twice. Our world is always changing as we do. The challenges we face are always shifting as our skills and understanding evolve and mature with experience.

In that sense, the balance and coherence of our lives is a constant dance between the drive for oneness and the need for difference. Of these two sides of the coin of life, difference is the most obvious, because it characterizes the contents of consciousness in our usual 'awareness of'. Oneness is more hidden. Yet both are necessary. The challenge is to find the difference in oneness, and the unity in difference, so that we recover the ultimate satisfaction: the ecstasy of unbounded oneness within the multiple calls and colours of our bodily being in this world.

PURE AWARENESS: THREE-IN-ONE STRUCTURE; HOW THE ONE CONTAINS THE MANY

The dance between simplicity and complexity arises deep in the structure of existence itself. The complexity we witness around us, physicists suggest, exists within deeper and deeper layers of simplicity, and ultimately within the one unified field of existence itself. Similarly, our own pure consciousness, which many identify as the subjective experience of the same unifying field, already contains within its own simplicity the dynamic seeds of difference, the rudiments of the levels of life, the perceptual positions, and punctuation of time that make possible our management of the world of 'awareness of'.

To sense this experientially, take a few moments. Stop, and imagine yourself bereft of images and sounds, not talking to yourself, not wrapped in feelings. Notice what remains.

Perhaps you recognize that, still, you *are*, and you know it. This gives some sense of pure awareness, the elusive bed of the stream of consciousness. It may not seem much, but notice the rich internal structure of this experience.

If you had a sense of underlying awareness, you may recognize that in such moments you are not only aware, but aware that you are aware. So awareness is not only one, but two, containing nuances of a *knower* and a *known*. And it can only be aware of itself, because this singular awareness-existence is a knowing knower. Pure awareness is thus also a *knowingness*. The content-free, untastable, odourless, invisible, noiseless continuing potentiality for experience, then, is not only a seamless unity, but a duality — as subject (knower) and object (what the knower knows). It is also a trinity, as we include the act of knowing or knowingness in which it recognizes its own nature. It is also four. For it is the undivided wholeness which contains these three.[2]

So our simple primary awareness already contains plurality, dynamism, and relationship. Like an ocean, pure consciousness moves invisibly within itself, while resting in its own unity. It provides a simple unitary core whose subtle and intrinsic dynamics permeate and permit all the active phases of our inner life. From the internal creative tension of pure consciousness emerge the more active phases of awareness, played out again and again in the vast drama of life. All existence including our own reflects the unfolding and self-authored theatrics of knower, knowing, and known losing and discovering themselves — as knower becomes knowing or known; and the known in turn becomes new knower, knowing, and known. Possibilities appear, multiplying themselves, like the labyrinthine reflections of an enormous, endless living hall of mirrors.

The facets of knower, knowing, and known and the relationships between them are reflected again and again in the diverse patterns of our mind, body, and emotions. For instance, they reappear structurally in the levels of life. Our sense of individuality involves the knower knowing itself as one. Discrimination is implicit in such knowing, and that implies some mode of knowing mind to register this recognition, which in turn is carried by the known of sensory-specific representations. The contents of consciousness are what we know through the various active modes of knowing. The active levels of experience serve as both means of knowing and, when we become aware of them, what is known from deeper levels of experience. A little fable evokes this process in slightly different terms:

In the be-ginning, if there ever was one, the great Being was lying in bed. Unformed, yet existing, the unexpressed infinite bodymind was at least potentially there. Being, it existed. Existing it was aware. Contemplating its supine status, it recognized that its unity was cleft. It was both subject and object, reflecting itself in the mirror of its own being. It beheld this curious intimacy, the one knowing the other instantly and eternally and intensely, binding and separating itself. Being infinitely intelligent, it was not even a matter of time before it said, "I am". And so it became an in-dividual, with sense of self supreme and, in an instant of eternity, repeating this unexpected discovery, selving selves were everywhere. But to have recognized that was to have made an important decision. And so there was intellection. And intellection articulates itself, so there was mind. Mind you, it didn't stop there, for articulation requires sound, colour, shape, touch, movement, and so creator, creation, and creatures came to be . . . and sometimes in bed, one recoils or recalls that process, and re-creation occurs. For we are in that image and likeness.

Similarly, through the three faces of pure awareness, our experiencing Self enters into different kinds of relationship with itself and its world. Besides the 'vertical' vector of the different levels, it moves 'horizontally' through the various perceptual positions.

The latter are extensions of the ability of our awareness to attend now to the knower, now to the known, now to the process of knowing, and now to the whole of these. For instance, our awareness can become absorbed in self, identified with another, conscious of the patterns of relationship between these, or identified with the whole. Thus in first position, as a self-assured and self-centred 'I', we identify closely with the facet of knower. In second position, as we identify with others and the world out there as if from the inside, we enter deeply into the known, to know it from the inside, and to become knowers of the world from this new place. In third position, as we detach and become aware of both ourselves and others and the relation between them and ourselves, we attend more to the process of knowing. Finally, in the place of 'we', we enter into and sense the patterns of knower, knowing, and known in the system as a whole.

In being the knower and the knowingness that knows itself — knower, knowing, and known — core awareness relates to itself in ways that are at once simultaneous, cyclical, and sequential. Thus it is outside of time in its simple undifferentiated beingness (hence the timeless quality of experiences of transcendental ecstasy and rapture), yet relating to itself in ways that follow a chain from knower to known (and back) that imply transformation through time. As such, pure awareness permits and sustains mental processes that are oriented to the present, recursively past-oriented, or insistently future- and goal-oriented.

We can experience knower and known at one, as when we are simply enjoying our own being, or when we become one with what we know — as in moments of intense love. Or we can become aware of ourselves knowing some object of experience, as when we reach out to see-hear-feel the world.

In such key processes as alertness, intention, and attention, as our awareness becomes more active, we become increasingly committed to the known. For instance, alertness is awareness all dressed up and ready to go out. Intention is awareness with a direction, heading for a restaurant it has not yet reached. Attention is even more honed. It is awareness sitting down to dinner, poised for a great repast.

This linear extension, through the act of knowing, takes us further and further from the knower and into the known, until we forget the ultimate knower, our own knowing awareness, altogether. We even skate over the surrogate knower referred to by the tag-word 'I', and our consciousness gets caught in 'awareness of', dominated by the objects of experience.

This happens, for instance, when streaming thoughts capture our attention, and we do not even realize that we are lost and distracted in them. We have lost the knower in the known. This is not inevitable, however. Thoughts can take place in a quieter train. Then we are aware of their coming or going. We know that we are thinking and sense the gaps between them and the gentle space in which they occur. We breathe softly and awareness extends to include chest as well as head. We recognize river as well as fish. Here knower and knowing accompany the known.

Such connecting back restores and renews. It releases creativity. A phase of silence, simplicity, not doing, in which mental activity settles back into the knower allows new knowing and known to manifest. The creative process is so fulfilling precisely because it involves reconnecting to and enlivening wholeness, launching a new spiralling out from the coiled and collected centre where knower, knowing, and known are still unified facets of each other.

The subtle internal dynamics of pure awareness thus permeate the way we think. Our mental processes have their roots in the paradoxical coexistence within pure awareness of singularity and difference, the dynamic copresence of subject and object, of knower, knowing, and known. Their internal relationship are reflected again and again in the structural patterns of our minds as we engage in the more active phases of 'awareness of', as the following chart illustrates, summarizing some of our typical patterns of thinking:

KNOWER	KNOWING	KNOWN
Beginning	Middle	End
Source	Course	Goal
Producer	Process	Product
Inside	Connection	Outside
Subjective	Link	Objective
Subject	Verb	Object

THREE-IN-ONE STRUCTURE OF AWARENESS REFLECTED IN COMMON
PATTERNS OF THINKING

The intrinsic unity of pure awareness drives our deep desire for the simple, the unified, the undivided, and the one. At the same time, its binary nature fuels our tendency to think in terms of dichotomies and dialectics, subjects and objects, forms and contents, male and female, up and down, inside and outside, right and wrong, similarities and differences. For pure awareness offers the primary state in which sameness, difference, and the relationship between these, occur.

Along with its unity and implicit dualism, its three-in-one nature is also reflected in our personal patterns. It underlies our quest for that which connects and balances, while giving relationship, direction, and progress. Finally, its quaternity of knower, knowing, and known, existing as one whole, makes us want to square things up, integrate, complete, and make whole.

The same internal dynamics that we find in our own consciousness are reflected in the burgeoning multiplicity we witness around us within the endless envelope of our universe. The simple unmanifest complexity of our own awareness is both metaphor and model for the universal processes which we identify, not only in our habits of language and mind, but in the world around us. The being of our awareness is being-at-large experienced within. It is both the unchanging, ever-present now, and the ground of change. Its unmanifest internal dynamics give rise to the critical patterns of nature, as well as mind.

For instance, just as in our internal world, the knower knows itself instantly or proceeds linearly to the known or returns through the known to know itself, so in nature, against the backdrop of featureless and timeless existence, some things happen at once. Others have a beginning, a middle, and an end, like a firework first lit, then exploding, then fizzling out. Others have a beginning, middle, and end and then return to their beginning, like the cycle of the seasons.

We are as the world is and the world is as we are — permutations within the immutable — apparent events within the one as it explores and knows itself. The drive to organize and evolve that is inherent in matter eventually brings to it the capacity to knowingly rediscover an awareness of its own nature. It rediscovers that all along it is knower. Our own awareness is the subjective side of an existence that all things share, and which is as alive as we are. Our own management of diversity in simplicity is repeated on a cosmic scale in nature at large.

Activities

PATTERNS IN OUR LIVES & IN THE WORLD AROUND US

However you respond to this notion of a universal being-awareness manifesting the diversity of creation within its own unique consciousness — and lived experience is more important than theoretical concept here — recognizing that the patterns in our awareness and in our lives are part and parcel of the patterns present in the larger whole can transform our lives. A sense of connectedness with the larger whole releases greater comfort and ease; separateness can engender a defensive fortress mentality. For that which is small and separate is inevitably vulnerable.

Take some time with a piece of paper to identify some of the patterns and processes that you notice occurring in nature which also occur in your life. Take any process that you can identify in nature, and ask, "How might this be reflected in my life?"

Conversely, what are some of the patterns in your inner life. How are they also reflected in nature and in the universe at large?

Recognizing awareness as knower, knowing, and known

1. Allow yourself to settle inwardly somewhat, breathing for a few moments a little more slowly and deeply than usual. Take your time with this exercise. Don't rush. Take a few moments with each step.

2. Allow the ordinary contents of experience, whatever you usually perceive inwardly or outwardly, to fade away for a moment. Notice simply how thoughts and images may come and go. If there is any inner busy-ness, let it settle. Notice what is there between each thought or image. Become aware of the silent gap-continuum.

Become aware of that underlying awareness which is the experiencer at any moment. Experience yourself for a moment as the still and unchanging pure **knower**, that awareness which is experiencing whatever falls within it. What is this like? How does it influence what you perceive . . . inwardly . . . and . . . outwardly, when you are this knower?

3. Experience this awareness for a moment as that which you **know**. Recognize that your awareness can be both **knower** and **known**.

4. While you are aware of this quiet ground of awareness, recognize that it is also a knowingness, a continuing process or act of **knowing** or perceiving. This knowing connects knower and known. It enables the knower to know and be known.

5. Recognize simple innocent inner awareness as at once a knowing

knower and a known. Recognize that you are this wholeness containing and uniting them. How is this? How does identifying momentarily with this wholeness affect what you experience . . . inwardly . . . and . . . outwardly?

How are you now? What happens if you consider some current preoccupation in your life?

PUTTING THE UNIFIED THEORY OF HUMAN AWARENESS TO WORK

Perhaps you are facing a challenge. Take a moment to think how you represent this challenge to yourself. What do you see, hear, or feel within as you bring this challenge to your attention?

How do you respond to these perceptions? How do you think about this challenge? How do you think about your thinking? Who has this challenge? What is the nature of this 'who'? What perceptual positions do you use in thinking about the challenge? Where does your attention move in time in relation to it — dwelling on related past experiences or projecting into the future or even resting in now?

Where lies the nub of your difficulty: in the knower? In the process of knowing? In the known? Or in the relationship among these elements?

Allow yourself to let go of all your thinking about this challenge; release the perceptual positions you take; let go of the various levels of experience; let go of past or future. Simply settle into the undifferentiated now, void of content, position, or level.

Then return to the challenge. Notice how else you might conceive it now. What different level of experience or perceptual position attracts you? What pops to your attention, spontaneously from the null space?

Unified Field Theory of Human Awareness

To sum up, then, pure awareness provides the core element of a unified field theory of human experience. Our simplest, unified state of awareness manifests within itself the triple modalities of knower, knowingness, and what is known. The interaction of these modalities gives rise to the more active aspects of our inner life, and notably to the three primary vectors of our experience: perceptual position, level of life, and time. These in turn are the building blocks of all more complex states and operations in our consciousness. And from them, the complex patterns of personality unfold.[3]

Within the one field of our awareness, the permutations are endless and of wondrous complexity. We shift in an instant from one point of view to another on any level of life, attending to the world around us, our perceptions, our perceiving, our capabilities, our feelings, beliefs, even our sense of who we are, and the centrality of our own awareness. What our awareness attends to changes constantly as we shift perspective, level, or time frame.

The different perceptual positions, levels of experience, and movement through time are like the fingers of a hand, connected to and extending from the palm. Pure awareness like the palm of a hand provides nourishment, support and relationship to the fingers, which are actually part of it. Without a palm our fingers would be hopeless isolated digits. Without fingers, the palm would lack the dexterity and power to hold things, whether large or small. Together these elements form a hand with which to firmly grasp life itself.

To realize our possibilities and become who we are requires familiarity with, and ease across, the range of the different levels of life and the different points of view. It also requires being in the present with a comfortable relationship to our past and our future, learning from our past and creating a satisfying future, allowing our present to create an irresistibly attractive direction for the future. And the doorway to that lies in a large measure in uncovering and freeing the core awareness which animates and contains them all.

In these opening chapters we have laid out the broad lines of a unified field theory of awareness that helps us understand and appreciate how each aspect of experience can bring us closer to our inner home, rather than taking us further away. Subsequent chapters help put this understanding to good effect in relation to key areas of experience in our lives — through meditation, movement, body, mind, senses, and so on.

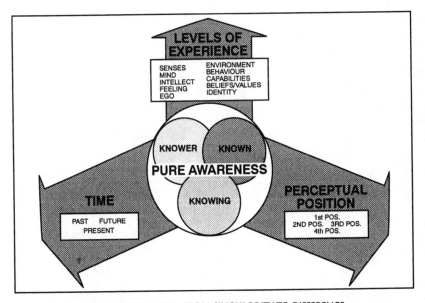

LIVING AWARENESS - FROM SINGULARITY TO DIFFERENCE

NOTES

1.   "So when a person . . . enters into cosmic consciousness — a) He knows without learning (from the mere fact of illumination) certain things, as, for instance: (1) that the universe is not a dead machine but a living presence." *Cosmic Consciousness*, p.76.

2.   I am indebted to Maharishi Mahesh Yogi for this key insight into the paradoxical nature of pure awareness as one and yet many.

3.   In the mid-1980s, Robert Dilts developed a "Unified Field Theory of NLP", using the elements of perceptual position, logical levels, and time. It takes something like consciousness, however, to unify these three. More recently, Charles Faulkner's 'perceptual cybernetics' treat perceptual position, time, and levels of experience as vectors of attention within a consciousness field-space, but the emphasis remains somewhat (and usefully) on the structure and relationship of contents, rather than on the nature and possibilities of the container itself.

CHAPTER SIX

Pathways to Awareness: From Movement to Stillness

Summary
Pure awareness is both static and dynamic. Unmoving and unchanging, it contains the possibilities of multiple points of view and the complete range of our experience. We can know it through both stillness and through movement. In this chapter, we consider the pathway of stillness, through meditation.

A mind that has understood the whole movement of thought becomes extraordinarily quiet, absolutely silent. That silence is the beginning of the new.

Krishnamurti

From my window I see dragonflies dart across the pond. Sky and clouds are mirrored in this inverted eye. Waterweed is scattered over the surface, between the lillypads on either side. The surface stirs with breeze-blown ripples that don't disrupt the clouds. Beneath the surface, a quieter world, where a few fantailed fish feed, slowly stirring fins. I notice the many levels on which my attention can settle, as it gets drawn, losing definition, to the peace of hidden depths . . . .

Stillness and Movement

There are two prime pathways to pure awareness — through stillness and through movement. This is because our inner being is itself a paradox of motion and stasis. Core awareness is both dynamic and still. At one extreme is the impulse to stillness. The release of rest, settling into the soft folds of inner space. Muscles relaxing, mind disengaging. Awareness luxuriating within itself. At the other extreme is the impulse to energy, eccentric effervescence, catherine wheels spiralling incandescent traces from a whirling centre. Oceanic silence suffusing billowing waves of activity. Irradiations of sheet-lightning, surging life-energy promoting change and transformation.

Each beckons and betrays. Too much movement, and we lose ourselves to the shadows and bustle of the world's restless ride. We engage, mounted on the hot-flanked horse of life. But this horse so easily loses the rider. Suddenly the horse is careering away and the rider hanging on, just. Or the rider forgets the horse, waking only to recognize that it is now in other places. And the time quietly to chew hay is long overdue — the bodymind's rhythms stretched though action beyond its natural need for renewal.

Yet too much stillness can leave us dull and inert, sapped of vitality. A lively silence, cool and renewing, becomes an unwanted absence of aware-ness and attention. Without the cleansing vector of dynamic action, the body becomes weary and weighted, tired limbs dragging in a passionless circuit through the day.

Over the years I have pondered the paradox of stillness and movement, recognizing the importance of both rest and exercise, but also experiencing rest that did not restore and the laboured disappointment of joyless exer-cise. Too often I have noticed torpid states transformed by some unexpected good news or a chance encounter. Suddenly resources of vitality reappear and the body wakes up like slack sails catching a sudden gust of wind. And yet in the body's case the wind is not from outside. It is some inner barrier that has shifted. The energy was there potentially all along. I have learnt somewhen unwittingly to shut myself down. In monitoring this curious trait I notice that it is often when I have not been attending to what my inner self really needs. The tragedy is that the more I shut down, the less re-sources I have to extricate myself from my personal slough of despond.

These days, rather than relying on external events to reconnect with core awareness, I find that sometimes, by settling a little into inner silence or by moving the body, I can shift inertia and reconnect to my core energy and awareness, and then direct that energy where it is most needed. It is a question of responding to the right need at the right time in the right way.

That can be quite an art. Our physiology, too, has countermanding ten-dencies towards excitation and inhibition. Our neurones have inhibitory and excitatory biases. Whole systems are geared to wake us up, ready for any event, others to dampen us down for rest and renewal, so that we don't burn up. Childhood and social conditioning to be quiet when we would be wild mean that these two basic physiological tendencies, which should com-plement each other, instead often conflict. Sometimes we drive our highly tuned body-car with our foot on the brake and the accelerator at the same time. Or we go forward in reverse. Or we drive on neglecting to stop for fuel or servicing. The trick is to stop when we should stop and go when we should go.

Attendance to pure awareness helps to bring balance, because it is the source and integration of these opposites. It is so still and silent compared to the restless chatter of the mind's more active phases. And yet it is so utterly alive that those who glimpse it fully consider it the most subtly elec-tric experience possible. From the still-moving core, we are more likely to perceive and follow our real needs. The key is to find helpful pathways to pure awareness.

Reflecting the dual nature of pure awareness, the practical ways to ac-

cess and enliven it tend themselves to emphasize either stillness or movement. I begin here with the still way, in part because that is where I began
my journey. At the same time, culturally, we emphasize what is outside rather
than what is within us. We favour excitement and movement, finding it
easier to do than to be. Stillness is missing — so much so that there is more
to be gained for us from learning simply to be than from finding one more
way of doing.

REFLECTION: BALANCING STILLNESS AND MOVEMENT

Before proceeding, take a moment to consider how you balance the need
for rest and stillness with the need for dynamic activity. Do you have the
proportions and timing of these right? How could it be better in your life?
What might you gain in body and mind if the balance were better?

The Still Way

*It's April, 1970. We take the bus from Ipswich to Woodbridge in Suffolk. Robert
and I each have apples and oranges, a new white handkerchief, and some daffodils. The sun is shining, with that thin spring warmth; enough to let you know
winter is over, but not enough to let you cast off jackets and jumpers. She picks us
up again in the VW camping bus. Her eyes are bright and alive, sparkling with
warmth and welcome. Her house, a Georgian farmhouse deep in the country is
besieged by armies of daffodils and pansies giving colour to the smooth, green
lawn. The willows reach down to the river. It's peaceful inside, the sun shining
through the windows. She likes rich warm colours; they are everywhere in the rugs
and fabrics of the house.*

*I wait while she teaches Robert, sipping tea, and wondering, stroking the cat.
Then it's my turn. I take my little tray of things. Incense turns lazily in the air. It
feels peaceful, though I'm wondering what's going to happen. She takes the flowers and motions me to wait while she performs a short ceremony. She says some
words in some other tongue. Time seems slowed, letting things — walls, tables,
chairs, curtains, vases — hang in the stillness as if transfigured and articulating
that presence we usually have no time for. (As in those afternoons when I was
sent to rest in bed as a child and couldn't sleep but watched the patterns on the
curtains and the shapes and shadows of their folds). I'm feeling peaceful and just
a little nervous. She turns and has me say a word that I'm to take within. I'm
sitting, eyes closed, the word almost has a life of its own, pulsing in the mind and
passing quickly into quieter echoes of itself. My mind seems to expand and open
into soft and gentle spaces of beauty. I feel enormous yet subtle and understated
peace and joy. It's as if the hard paving-slabs of too-much-lived life crack to reveal
soft and rich earth underneath, ready to sprout with green shoots, yellow-flowers
and new life. I recognize that 'there lives the dearest freshness deep down things',
but especially in me. I am not lived-out as I thought, I am these cool waters, these*

bubbling springs of awareness-feeling, deep beneath the dross of habits of mind and feeling, of workaday routine.

She comes to collect me. The afternoon is still rich with silence. We leave with our bits and pieces, a piece of fruit and a daffodil apiece, trumpeting emblem of renewal. Everywhere I turn my eyes, things seem to greet me in their generous ordinariness, as if for once I appreciate how good it is just to be alive and enjoy this extraordinary display of the too often unnoticed — the cracked fences and fields, dustbins and tarmac, buses and trees.

Meditation is the classic pathway to stillness. There are many forms of meditation, each with its own emphasis. I have chosen to emphasize Transcendental Meditation (TM) here for a number of reasons. First, I am most familiar with it, having practised it daily for over 25 years. Second, decades on, the criterion which convinced me to select this approach over any other form of meditation still seems paramount. It is natural. There is no effort or concentration in TM. TM uses the inherent tendency of the mind to go towards greater happiness. This it finds naturally as it settles into deeper levels of itself. Third, there is a global network of trained teachers, teaching the practice in the same way, so that there is a large measure of consistency in its teaching. Fourthly, TM is perhaps the most researched form of meditation, with several hundred studies pointing to a wide range of physiological, psychological, and even social benefits.[1] Finally, TM illustrates principles that are useful for understanding and evaluating other meditation techniques.

Strictly speaking TM, like most forms of silent and sitting meditation, is a mental technique. But although the practice is mental the body is closely involved. We park the body quietly and comfortably in a sitting position and begin the practice with eyes closed. From then on, once the mental practice begins, the body settles into a state of deep rest, deeper than sleep, with profound changes in almost all aspects of bodily functioning. And in that sense this mental technique is also a very physical one with profound effects on our physiological well-being.

Rest can expand awareness. When we stop doing and simply take it easy, it is as if the crumpled wings of our bodymind unfold and dry in the sun, ready to carry us on to new things. It's a common experience: when we are focused on a problem, either alone or in a group, stopping to take a break allows the answer to emerge almost unbidden. It's as if when we stop funnelling the bodymind down to the point of the problem, we release the boundaries we were imposing and open up to the possibility of solutions from that wider part of ourselves in which all our creativity manifests.

TM takes this principle of rest a stage further. It offers rest to the mind by allowing it to settle from applied content-driven thought to floating on gentler content-free thought-impulses within the expanded spaces of our consciousness. This is restful subjectively. Thoughts arising in this state are typically no more than passing traffic in a larger quietness. And because this state brings lively restfulness to the bodymind, it translates subsequently into improved performance on a vast range of mental and physical tasks.

It offers rest to the body. Physiological functioning slows to a distinctive fourth state of consciousness, different from waking, dreaming, or deep sleep. Breathing and heart rate slow, the biochemical effects of stress are neutralized, while the brain functions in a more coherent, unified, and orderly way. This state of restful alertness offers mental and physiological renewal that is in a similar direction, but — so the research shows — goes far beyond simply sitting and relaxing.

The actual practice of the technique involves effortless internal repetition of a content-free word or mantra. Absence of content allows the mind to disengage from everyday reflection and to settle into states of reduced internal activity, as it perceives the mantra at quieter and quieter levels of manifestation — the inner equivalent of attending to a recurrent noise receding into the distance.

The emphasis is on increasing stillness, but like the lapping water which soothed Rousseau into a state of restfully awake expanded awareness on a Swiss lake, the mantra gives the mind an element of focus and liveliness as it settles down. There is some gentle internal movement that becomes less and less, until, in principle, even this fine activity ceases and the mind for an instant or longer becomes aware of what is there when there is nothing specifically holding its attention — just simple awareness.

Creases and crinkles in the bodymind soften and melt. My mind listens to receding ripples of its own activity. I cast away from the shore of firm-boundaried attention. I settle into myself, easing into the warm bath of my own being, where images and impulses from daily life come and go as I flow with the slowing internal rhythm — settling, emerging, settling deeper, and emerging again — according to the bodymind's natural internal rhythm on that day. And at moments, I just am. Unbelievably and indescribably, empty-full-something-nothing-anywhere-somewhere-wordless-knowing.

And afterwards I am as if bathed and cleansed. My eyes don't burn to hold with hard focus, they embrace the world more widely and softly. The eternal chatterer inside is quieter, and I feel smoothed and connected in some quiet and underlying inner space. Some of that inner awareness stays with me as I re-engage into activity. At least for a while.

So the experience of pure awareness, at first fleeting and elusive, becomes increasingly recognizable with practice and familiarity. Furthermore, repetition on a twice-daily basis of this experience of our inner ground makes it begin to be part of our active lives. We sense a core of being and silence inhabiting all our conscious experience. As Paul Valéry puts it:

But every life, however unique, possesses, at the depth of a treasure, the funda-
mental permanence of a consciousness that nothing supports; as the ear finds and
loses again, through all the changes in a symphony, a deep and continuous sound
that never ceases to reside there, but which ceases at each instant to be picked up,
so the pure self, that unique and monotonous element of being, lost by itself again,
eternally inhabits our senses; this deep note of existence dominates, once one hears
it, all the complexity of the conditions and variety in life.[2]

And this is another reason for opening this section on pathways to awareness with an account of meditation. Daily experience of inner stillness
cultures the bodymind to greater flexibility. For it finds itself accommodating extremes of action and silence, the full range of our experience. Whatever
else we learn, we learn more easily. We have learned how to learn, because
we know both this empty inwardness and all the prismatic possibilities of
action that can fill it. The deep rest to the body and the dissolving of rigid
boundaries of separateness in our active experience of different things, pre-
pares the bodymind to accept more newness and difference. In this way, the
daily dive into our own awareness and the lively stillness enjoyed by the
body enables all our other activities to be more profitable. Whatever else
we do, we get more out of it. Through deep stillness in body and mind,
other pathways to potential are cleared. We are more receptive and flexible.

Movement in Stillness, Stillness in Movement

Paradoxically, the stillness in meditation is a lively one, and even here movement has its place. Traditional Sanskritic accounts of meditative practice,
such as Patanjali's *Yoga Sutras*, describe the process of meditation as one
involving a combination of stillness and movement. Patanjali talks of a
settled but lively internal state *samadhi* — collected (*sama*) intellect (*-dhi*)
— which is reached through two basic mental processes *dharana* and *dhyana*.
Dharana is mental fixity or focus. *Dhyana* is mental flow. Often these are
understood as consecutive processes. In fact, any mental activity is likely to
involve both direction and flow at once. For instance, in TM the attention
gently directed (*dharana*) to the mantra, flows (*dhyana*) into quieter and
quieter emergent impulses until movement ceases, like waves settling into
stillness. This is *samadhi*, the blissful balance of these opposing mental dynamics.

So even in a meditative practice which appears totally dedicated to silence and stillness, movement has a quiet but necessary role. Conversely,
at the other extreme of vigorous physical movement, silence is also present.
Stillness is both the foundation and ultimate goal of movement, as we shall
see in the next chapter, where we look at ways of enlivening and exploring
awareness through movement.

Awareness Activities

TAKING A BREATHER — THE 'BREATH OF PEACE'

Our breathing is intimately connected to our awareness. Through breathing, as Rilke put it in the *Sonnets to Orpheus*, we are engaged in 'rhythmic exchange' between our inner and outer worlds. Our breathing is like a pulse or wave within the great 'world-inner-space'.

Take a moment to notice your breathing. What happens to your awareness as you breathe in? As you breathe out? What happens at the junction point between the two? Allow yourself to breathe just a little more slowly and deeply than usual, noticing as you do how your awareness shifts. Inhaling tends to give a sense of contained expansion; exhaling, a sense of relaxation and release. But notice what happens to your awareness in the moment between the in and out breaths? What happens to inner chatter? Is this a place, where you 'see into the life of things'?

Notice which parts of your body you are using as you breathe — nose, mouth, throat, ribcage, muscles in the back . . . Notice the rhythm of your breath, rapid or slow, shallow or deep.

Allow yourself to be aware of the differences in breathing: shallow, high in the chest; at the level of the heart; and deep in the belly. How do you habitually breathe? What is most comfortable for your?

Allow the rhythm of your breath to slow a little, so that you have a sense of 'resting' on the breath, your attention floating gently on the inner and out breaths and opening into the gap between the two. It is as if your awareness and breath are one, as if you are expanding, contracting, being still with your breath. As you continue to breathe in this way for a few minutes, be quietly present to the world around you. Notice how relaxing and refreshing this can be. You can do this at any time or in any place where you are not actively engaged in activity. It is an especially valuable way of relaxing and refreshing awareness at hectic times, during breaks, and before and after challenging events, and in those dead times, waiting in line for bus or train.

AWARENESS MINI-BREAKS

Those moments of in-between time in our routine are particularly valuable for briefly reconnecting with our deeper awareness, and thus experiencing renewal and fresh energy.

During a break, take some time to notice how you are when you are relaxed or relaxing. How many times in the day are you very relaxed and at a standstill in body and mind? When are you relaxed? How is your body? How are you perceiving? How are you thinking? What are you feeling? Do you often relax and just be? Is it easy? Is it difficult? Take a moment to check how things are now in the bodymind. What's still? What's moving? Do you give yourself enough such breaks?

Take some time each day, particularly in those in-between moments — in the bath or shower, in the toilet, in the train, at the traffic-lights, or during tea or coffee breaks — to simply rest. Give yourself a stretch, maybe a yawn, let your body relax, rest your eyes by closing them, or allow them to open to wider vistas or settle on something charming, like a flower or plant. Don't stare, simply notice what is perceiving inside your body. Allow yourself to be with whatever is happening in the moment. Just notice that quiet part of yourself that doesn't move, even if the grasses are dancing in the breeze or the tops of trees rippling in the wind. Take some time to notice that part of yourself which is outside of time, for which there is no time . . .

And then gently return to whatever you need to do next.

DEEPER REST

At least once, and preferably twice a day, I would strongly suggest disengaging fully from activity and settling more deeply into inner awareness for 15-30 minutes.

One simple practice, which I call 'Pulse Meditation', involves sitting poised quietly with eyes closed, and noticing the underlying rhythms present within the bodymind — whether those of breathing or of the heart rate, or of some deeper underlying life-pulse. Simply allow yourself, without strain or effort, to attend to any rhythm or pulse you perceive within you and allow it to slow, like a wave that becomes slower and broader. As the rhythm or pulse becomes slower, and you become increasingly settled, simply rest in your own being. If your attention wanders away, when you notice you have wandered, simply resume noticing any pulse that is present and allow it to settle some more. After 15 minutes or so gently and slowly return to an awareness of your surroundings and to your active life.

You may already have your own form of quiet meditation. If this is working for you, by all means continue with it. You may find the criterion of naturalness a useful one for evaluating meditation practices. According to the founder of TM, any technique that systematically leads to the transcending of its own activity, allowing the practitioner to go effortlessly beyond mental activity into the state of pure being-awareness, can accurately be termed transcendental meditation.

If your practice isn't self-transcending and involves mental, emotional or physical effort and activity holding you to the more manifest levels of thinking or feeling, you may consider exploring a simple technique, such as TM, that will take you effortlessly towards your essence. Meditation is a delicate process, better learned from a teacher than from a book.[3]

NOTES

1.   Scientific Research on the Transcendental Meditation Programme, Collected Papers, MERU Press, Livingston Manor, N. York, 1977, Vol.1.

2.   Paul Valéry, *Oeuvres*, Gallimard, Paris, 1957, I, 1228. My translation.

3.   However, see also *Moksha: A New Way of Life*, Peter Wrycza and Dr. Luh Ketut Suryani.

CHAPTER SEVEN

Moving Being

Summary
Awareness has a bodily base. The body is a community of living cells that together modulate pure awareness in a variety of ways. At times our awareness may be more centred in the head, at other times more grounded in the heart or in the body as a whole. Such grounding is important for integration of neglected parts of ourselves, for living in greater harmony with our unconscious, and for benefiting from our inherent 'body-wisdom'. Such grounding can be enhanced by allowing time to be in and to explore the body. Dance and movement are particularly powerful and pleasant ways of culturing a totally fulfilling awareness-in-the-body — especially free and spontaneous dance and movement, but also some more structured forms.

> . . . *dancing is also speaking the language of animals, communicating with stones, understanding the song of the sea, the whisper of the wind, discoursing with stars, approaching the very throne of existence.* Maurice Béjart

Body Awareness

Awareness is both in the body and of the body. But it is not the same as the body. Each of our cells is a living being. We have trillions of cells in the body. Our awareness is the fruit of their collective functioning. The body is alive. It has its own awareness and intelligence and it contributes to the collective awareness we each call 'me'. The sensuality of touches and tickles remind us of that aliveness which can hum with pleasure or pain. The body is the known to the 'I', the knower, but this known is also its own knower as it experiences its own sensations, which 'I' savours or shivers away from.

Some parts of me are centres of knowingness. 'I' may inhabit my cranial cave, but when I feel tender, the gentle stirrings in my chest send glowing fronds of connection to the big bulb on my shoulders. If my emotions are stronger, I may feel fire in the belly and the energy flush of passion or anger may dissolve the heady glow into a larger body-bonfire in which awareness is alive and electric. Boundaries melt and it is hard to know where I begin or end. Aliveness whirls beads of hot wax in a galaxy of happening.

Sometimes I feel like a light-bulb, as if my awareness is glowing in my head, shining within my body and spreading out in the spaces around me.

But the rest of the body is in shadow, like the base of the bulb. It is both me and not me. It sustains the light, but is somehow separate. Yet it also has its own life and awareness.

At such times I may experience my awareness as a still clear pool and be virtually oblivious of its banks and basin, enjoying awareness but forgetful of the body that sustains it. When I am still, I may allow my migratory thoughts to settle like wind-whipped eddies and ripples back into a more unified state of being. This is not necessarily disincarnate. For when I am still, my body is still and *vice versa*. But some states of stillness give a cerebral awareness, centred in the head. My inner voice quiets, and I listen in the emptiness to the faint threads of being-textured multi-stranded unified thought. I am as close to knowingness as to knowing anything in particular. If my eyes are open, I see without judgement in simple recognition the silent shapes and colours that are around me.

It feels good, up there in the head, soft, still, open and receptive, and down there, I can feel, should I so choose, my breath an almost absent undulation in the stillness. My heart is beating so gently it is imperceptible. The feeling is quiet and peaceful. But the whole pulse of life is centred on that awareness up there, and the awareness up there is both resting and restful. Like liquid in a full cup.

This is an important kind of awareness, but awareness-in-the-body can be other and more than this. When my awareness is an awareness-in-the-body, something in which my parts participate, I feel best of all. Conductor, orchestra, and music are at one. Awareness becomes so much more rich, vibrant, and heart-warm.

Our body is a complex self-regulatory system of infinite possibilities. Consider the enormous variety of ways in which it is used in the different pathways and pastimes in the various cultures of the world — everything from cooking to computing, welding to wine tasting, sumo wrestling to bird watching, soldiering to synchronized swimming. And yet of all the possibilities most of us use only a few. Most of our working and playing just uses selected muscles and methods out of all the permutations.

Usually our body obediently obliges. But take its point of view for a moment, and compare it to a large organization, where the individual cells are like workers organized into specialized units or departments. Perhaps the work force are overextended in some parts, underused in others, but generally loyal and committed to the daily routine.

But as anyone who has worked in large organizations knows, there is almost invariably a huge amount of wastage and frustration. Wastage, because talents go unnoticed and unused, because hierarchies almost invariably disempower, restricting the freedom of movement and choice necessary for growth and life. Those at the top of hierarchies cannot possibly know and meet all the needs of those in their charge. Moreover, the need for order in the whole organization means that systems and rules are established that benefit the coordination of the whole, but not necessarily the needs of the individual.

Consequently, it can be like a breath of fresh air, when with a change of management or attitudes, the leaders of an organization try to find room for individual creativity to flourish, for possibilities of learning and feedback that stimulate the individuals and help the whole to become more alive and responsive.

It's a bit like that with the body. We are like old-style autocratic bosses. We give our bodies a restricted range of experiences — lying in bed, eating, walking, sitting at desks or in cars, trains, and planes — and even these repeated in ritualized, somnambulistic ways. How many people walk with the grace and awareness that is so pleasing to experience whether from within or as observer?

In the factory, there are breaks and holidays, but for our bodies these are often of limited relief. We take our habits with us, and above all our habits of mind. These are of control, suppression, or deformation of almost all our natural urges — right down to the need to yawn or fart. We are taught to eat by a timepiece and don't really know what either hunger or satisfaction is. We oscillate between repressing our natural needs and compulsion and excess. If we managed an enterprise the way we manage our bodies, most of us would have had numerous strikes, industrial relations disputes and probably be sacked by the shareholders. With our bodies, the stoppages and disputes we have — they're called illnesses and internal conflicts. But generally the body and its parts is patient indeed before striking.

So it would seem only fair to give the body its head. Or rather relieve it of the control of the head. Give it a chance to do exactly what it needs and wants to do. Allow the parts of the body to be and move in ways that they need.

Our bodies have innate wisdom. After all, the heart pumps, the lungs breathe, the kidneys eliminate, the stomach and intestines digest, without any conscious management by us. We really couldn't consciously control the myriad microscopic transactions that finely adjust our corporeal pharmacological equilibrium at every instant. We can at best support our body's wisdom.

Yes, our body's wisdom. This body that has had such a bad press down the ages as saints and seekers after a finer level of equilibrium have struggled with the ins and outs of the mind-body divide. Seeing the body from the mind's standpoint, they have made the spirit willing and the flesh weak. Weak or wanton, the body is branded as Satan's whore, the seat of temptation, fallen from all that is good and true.

Yet body-wisdom is present here too. The bodymind is a system of one-yet-two. And when we split body and mind, we invite disequilibrium that the body wisely finds ways to countermand. Temptation is the body's version of parliamentary democracy. Her majesty's opposition maintaining balance by pulling in the opposite direction. Sadly, it so often takes a crisis to establish a government of national unity.

Body is wordless; it links more directly to our unconscious than our conscious mind. The impulses and images, signals and symptoms of the unconscious are the very language of the body. Our unconscious is the wordless life-stuff, the essence and effect of melded mind and matter. Our unconscious is really our body-consciousness. We acknowledge it as the protective peripheral servant of our focused foveal vision, yet fear it as the harbourer of imprisoned passions and inadmissible drives. Our unconscious is in reality our wider self. It is an awareness behind our awareness. As a beam of light can be pencil thin or broad-beamed, so can our awareness be tunnel-tight or broad and all-encompassing. Our conscious mind can settle more deeply into and include more of our unconscious. Heightened awareness is also deepened awareness.

Awareness-in-the-head already simplifies and opens. Awareness-in-the-body expands and enlivens that awareness to include the almost indescribable delight of ecstasy. This delight is our birthright — cellular celebration, the creative energy encoded in our genetic promise and dampened and endungeoned by our almost inevitable (and perhaps necessary) childish acquiescence to adult conditioning.

Awareness-in-the-body helps us retrieve the simplicity of core awareness. When we bring our awareness into the body, we connect, as it were, the grossest and subtlest aspects of the bodymind — the physical body and our inner awareness. This links the full range of our lives and relieves our attention from its often excessive involvement in the intervening levels of experience — dizzy thoughts, whirling emotions, restless beliefs, or insistent identity. We simplify our experience to simply be in our multicellular being. Without preoccupations and distractions, our awareness can expand to a state as deeply sensual as a hot-chocolate fudge sundae, as effervescent as a cool fizzy drink on a hot summer's day, and as gentle as love and morning sunlight.

A key way back to this awareness-in-the-body is simply regularly to take some body-time — time dedicated to the body, the body's own time. The body is a self-regulatory system. It normally needs no injunction to be well. If sick, no doctor heals it; it heals itself. With sleep and rest it sustains itself through countless labours. In body-time, we reverse the usual hierarchy of things and place our conscious selves at the service of the body. Christ washes and anoints the feet of Mary Magdalen. Body-time allows the body to use its natural self-regulatory powers to restore the balance and flow of energy. This may be in stillness, as in sleep or meditation, but it can equally and desirably be in movement.

Moving Ways to Awareness for Body-time

STRUCTURED MOVEMENT

There are many pathways to awareness through movement. They vary in the degree of their formal structuring. My own preference is for the relatively unstructured, though both formless and structured approaches can be valuable. Structured movement may be more appropriate when there is a great deal of fear about letting go or if one has a history of powerful psychological disturbance that makes letting go without a framework of guidance and support risky.

Almost all forms of structured movement can be valuable, provided they do not strain the body. Formats vary in the balance they strike between stillness and movement. Some lean towards stillness, like *Hatha Yoga*, in which a succession of gently-held positions and the quietly body-centred moving into them take the bodymind into complementary and contrasting arrangements. This process flushes out the residue of stress and leaves the cells singing in synchrony and the awareness, calm, creative, and present. Structured movement is particularly valuable when it takes us into unusual ways of moving the body. *Hatha Yoga* involves taking uncustomary postures that stimulate and stretch different muscles and organs of the body. To those who have practised this discipline even a little, it is no surprise that research shows *Hatha Yoga* more beneficial in neutralizing stress and creating well-being than bodybuilding and other forms of supposedly superior aerobic exercise.

The Chinese and Japanese also developed simple stretching and breathing exercises to align and balance the bodymind. Some, like *Ba Dwa Jing*, are very ancient. *Tai Chi* leans further in the direction of movement than *Hatha Yoga* or *Ba Dwa Jing*. With its ritualized balletic sequence of movements, it reeducates the bodymind to balance and wholeness. It can be practised as a solitary meditation in which consciousness sculpts space through its body-presence. It can also be a way of furthering awareness in our relationships with others through paired exercise and practice. Some of its variants, such as Al Huang's 'Tai Chi Dance' can also be practised in a more formless way, once its essence has been grasped.

Other martial arts lean further towards movement, *Ki Aikido*, for instance, energetically emphasizes and develops presence of mind and body. This discipline brings our attention to patterns of energy in our own bodies and how that energy collides, flows, and combines with the energy of others, in vigorous contact and tumbling. In this way, it activates a lively feet-on-the-ground power-in-the-belly awareness-in-the-body, and, with that, a readiness for whatever happens.

In the West, more recent explorers have developed new approaches.

With the Alexander Technique and the Feldenkreis Method, gentle aware-ness-guided movements and positions help realign mind and musculature misused in our goal-getting tarmacked lives. Bringing the attention to sim-ple ways of bending, turning, standing, sitting, and lying allows the body to rediscover the poised patterns and freed grace of early childhood. With this comes some of the soft focus and settled fluidity of balanced and aware movement.

Unfortunately, some of these forms of movement can become habits done in a bored or hurried way. Some people are more easily distracted, losing interest in routine or repeated activities than others. If you are moving in a bored or absentminded way, you will find your movement far less effective and enjoyable. If this happens, identify the state you need to be in to do your movement or exercise in a way that fulfils and renews. Take a minute or two beforehand to breathe a little more slowly and deeply, placing your attention in the body. If necessary, vary your pattern of exercise slightly, perhaps giving more emphasis on different days to a particular posture or set of movements, in order to recover a sense of freshness.

This freshness of approach to structured movement is important, be-cause even when the postures and movements of systems such as *yoga* or *tai chi* become familiar, they remain beneficial if practised with awareness, at-tention, and enjoyment. They allow the body to move in ways that contrast with, and complement, the rest of the day's patterns. When we do them with awareness, for their own sake, we place our attention back in the body, which allows us to enjoy and feel the process of moving and stopping. This enlivens awareness-in-the-body, which remains with us afterwards, with-out our trying to hold onto it, when the demands of work and other people press upon us.

Some people argue that formal training in forms of highly structured movement, such as classical dance, can inhibit free movement. The body appears unable to escape from the patterns that have shaped it and been imposed upon it, often since childhood. From observing people moving, particularly those who have been grounded in the balletic, I agree that this can be a problem. But I don't think it is inevitable; sometimes it's simply a matter of lightly inhibiting the familiar and letting the new and unfamiliar move the body.

And usually, some background in forms of structured movement can be a resource. Experience of forms of structured movement can help our intui-tion to function more freely during more spontaneous forms of movement. If we have already moved and allowed the body to move in many different ways, it is as if the body already has a rich potential kinesthetic vocabulary and syntax — even different kinesthetic languages — that allow us to ex-press ourselves easily and freely. We have also developed our relationship with our body and a measure of trust. We are not so shocked or surprised by what our body does. We recognize and accept what is happening as rhythms and postures shift spontaneously — from, say, the yogic to the gymnastic, from complete stillness to a hesitant slow-moving sculpting of space or the active and chaotic with everything-happening-at-once. And we still find those places and permutations that are never before encountered, which take us to the edge of where our bodies hold trapped energies and residues of past experience — limiting body memories of anger, pain, panic, or even joy.

MORE VIGOROUS EXERCISE

Most of the approaches alluded to above contrast with the vigorous aerobic type of exercise which has been popular in the West since the rise of the British public school. Here the emphasis reflects our cultural mind-body split, with the aim often being to overcome the limits of the body. And sometimes when the body is pushed towards its limits, stillness does emerge as the ecstatically enjoyed rich ground of movement. Some runners report passing through a barrier of discomfort, until the running runs by itself, and inner awareness is superfluid and expanded. I too have experienced that vigorous exercise of this type can shift states, shatter inertia, and move mind and body to an electric rhythm.

Unfortunately, running is not always so fruitful. It can become a dull and mindless pounding in which the doorway to ecstasy or even feeling good jams tight, leaving only sweaty fatigue. Sometimes the mind flags as the body struggles, with little delight, as we push towards some external target in time or distance. And even after, the bodymind can feel altered, but not always improved, sometimes even brutalized, its fineness blunted.

If walking is goal-oriented locomotion from A to B, running can be even more so. This end-gaining, to borrow Alexander's term, means our mind is ahead of our body — already in the cookie-jar before our fingers get there. Goal-driven running rushes the knower (runner) towards the known (time-distance target), diluting, even deleting, the vital connecting process of running. It is so easy to do such exercise without full attention. Muscles may move fast, but without the lubricating energy of awareness-in-the-body, they may move jerkily.

Yet the most satisfying running, both to experience and to watch, is 'in the body' running, where the curving back of the attention onto the process of running, allows mind and body to unite in a lithe and loving sensual process. Then we savour the bliss of roller-coasting on the unctuous sensuality of our own cellular and muscular articulation. Our greatest athletes have been goal-oriented, hungry for records and medals, but they are consummately in the body as they compete, giving a graceful sensuality and simplicity to their movements that is a delight to watch. The Peles and Coes have something more than ambition, something that touches the spectator with its ease and magic.

Exercise restores and revitalizes above all when it is pleasurable. Recent research suggests that harsh end-oriented exercise is stressful and hence unhealthy. Pleasure comes from our being centred in the body and exploring through and in it what and how it needs to move. This integrates the three facets of core awareness: knower, knowing, and known. Awareness-in-the-body moving, flowing, shifting, shaking, slowing, brings together the extremes of our physical beings, our most manifest level of life and our inner attention, and allows them to interact so that what needs to happen for muscles and cells to feel alive and free happens. Any inner knots and blocks can undo themselves in what I call 'Self Unfolding'. Self Unfolding allows the Self to unfold itself to itself through movement in its own way. It integrates being and being-in-the-body and allows us to enter fully into that state of wholeness, which is, quite simply, total aliveness, ecstasy, bliss.

For me two of the most satisfying forms of Self Unfolding through movement are self-unfolding movement and free dance. The two are closely related, the key difference being in the much greater use of music in free dance.

The Dancing Path

Dance is an ideal way of enlivening of awareness. Dancers and dervishes delight in the 'still point in the turning world'. Music provides an internal focus to which the body can align itself. Sound saturates the senses, dissolving and rippling through the bodymind, as limbs and trunk, organs and cells move to the music of life.

Many people gain great enjoyment from mastering dances with specific steps. Once the steps are automatic, the rhythmical and repeated movement, regular but adequately varied, entrains the body and entrances the mind, releasing deep feeling.

I find learning steps difficult, though after painful practice in which anxiety interrupted early enjoyment, I now understand the power and pleasure in it. (I was long hampered by discouraging memories — such as one of the convent girls brought in to help us sixth formers learn the art of dance saying loudly: "If you step on my foot one more time, I'll kick you in the shin.")

Free movement comes more naturally to me: I love allowing my body to express itself spontaneously, following and exploring its wishes, shifting as the mood or the music or the limbs suggest.

In dancing I allow movement and music to merge. From sometimes laboured beginnings, dancer, dancing, and dance become one. I am danced. As the dance gains its own momentum, my awareness expands and explodes with waves of energy and enjoyment. Droplets of pure pleasure ripple like hot honey through the bodymind, showering my head with light and sweetness and my heart with almost painful golden-treacle tinges.

I have long known that sometimes the body needs energy raising and sometimes energy settling. And at the right time and in the right mix. But quite how energy raising and settling fitted together, I wasn't sure. Understanding and experience took a large step forward when I had the opportunity to work with a wonderful dancer and most present person, Gabrielle Roth, whose self-confessed specialization is ecstasy.

She stalks in, black haired and black leathered, like a large raven in human shape. Immediately her humour flashes, with some throwaway line. She shimmers, her mood shifts mercurially, her voice sliding across scales expressing lyrical lights as silvery shafts of energy dart from alive-eyes glowing beneath a black fringe. Sixty people enter a magical space she throws around them. She is present, humorous and strong, irreverent and tender, thoughtful and provocative, and also fragile and vulnerable. She offers an example of what it means to be simply human and to let it show from every angle. She leads you into that same open place of trust and spontaneity, seeding needed transformations to sprout and spread in other times and places, when she is elsewhere.

And then she dances. In deep gentian blue, smoking African violet, she weaves and moves. Poetic, humorous, robotic, angular, sweeping, moving in and out of the present, self-contained, sharing, tickling group awareness to self-expression with electric intensity.

Over many years Gabrielle monitored her own pathway to ecstasy, eventually distilling her discoveries into a simple map of five basic movements:

Flowing — Staccato — Chaotic — Light/lyrical — Stillness

These five types of movement — for it is a question more of a mode of movement within which the form is free, rather than tightly structured steps or positions — blend into an organic sequence.[1] This sequence takes the bodymind quite naturally through gentle undulating 'feminine' warming (flowing), to 'masculine' and energetic cutting and thrusting (staccato), thence surrendering to the bursting of boundaries in energetic and control-free intensity (chaos), then lightening and lifting in the clear calm after the wild winds (lyrical), to end with the most self-contained of subtle shifts of movement or short shifts from one paused posture to another (stillness).

The sequence is satisfying and complete. It moves through the bodymind's major modalities, gently shaking off inertia, flushing resistant channels, and then calming, balming, sweetly soothing back to a lively stillness and loving life-readiness. It draws core awareness out of quiet recesses in the bodymind and leaves it glowing in the eyes and on the cheeks, anticipating the enjoyment of whatever one is to do next.

Self-unfolding Movement

Self-unfolding movement is a natural process. Our bodies are made for movement and are constantly in movement, internally and externally. We have
hundreds of muscles, billions of cells, countless neural pathways, channels
of energy and communication linking foot to head, enabling and sustaining
the flow of information, nourishment, and energy. We are a moving matrix
of movements.

Unfortunately, our static and selective repertoire of movements — it is
said we use as few as 50 of our 600 muscles each day — makes us like a city
where certain routes are so overused that they never get properly repaired,
while others are so underused that they fall into disrepair and neglect. Drains
get blocked with leaves and debris; waste water cannot escape properly.
The system as a whole functions poorly.

Self-unfolding movement allows the body to bend and flex itself, in whatever way it needs to clear blocked energy from one part or to open a needed
channel elsewhere. Muscles move as and when they need to restore themselves to optimal functioning. As a result, the body comes into balance,
with energy flowing wherever it is needed. Frustrated cells and cell-groups
feel vital and alive; we move on to ordinary action enlivened and aware;
we sense grace, presence, and poise in the body; we enjoy ecstasy and bliss
— awareness-in-the-body.

Allowing ourselves to move spontaneously in this way is a bit like letting
the dog take us for a walk. Usually, we take the dog for a walk. It's leashed
and at our heel. We maybe give it a bit of lead to sniff here and there, to
stop for its needs, but basically we are in control. When the dog takes us for
a walk, we must be ready to stop and sniff where it wants to, to ferret here
and there, to charge through the undergrowth, to run and jump or simply
stop and pant, pausing for whatever scent on the wind captures the interest. We must be willing to accept a measure of adventure and discovery. It
may be slightly unnerving at times, but it is tremendous fun and highly
refreshing for both dog and owner.

SOME GUIDELINES FOR SELF-UNFOLDING MOVEMENT

1. If possible, wear loose-fitting clothes. Or if you fancy, none at all. But
don't let lack of the right clothes at the moment stop you giving the body
what it needs!

2. Be still. Turn the attention inside. For most people it's easier to close
their eyes. Notice how you are feeling in mind and body.

3. Allow movement to start wherever it wants to. I find that often movement may begin with small micro twitches in the fingers or the toes. Or
perhaps there is a slight swaying or flexing in the arms or the legs at the
knees or at the shoulders or pelvis.

4. Allow this movement to amplify as much as it wants, so that, for example, twitching fingers lead to the arms moving, and thence to the whole torso and body moving.

5. Allow whatever movement that happens to happen, whatever it is. Movements may include:
* stillness in almost any conceivable posture
* very slow almost imperceptible movements
* shaking or trembling of the limbs or trunk
* flowing sinuous movements
* harsh abrupt movements
* tender, primitive, or sensual movements
* single movements
* repetitive movements
* movements that seem completely new or unexpected
* familiar movements that one might experience in *yoga, tai chi*, dance, etc.
* and any combination of the above.

Whatever happens, take it as it comes and let it go as it goes. Trust your body; work with it; it won't betray you.

6. Allow yourself to experience any feelings or emotions that come up with the movement — including laughter, tears, joy, sadness, rage, etc.

7. Allow yourself to breathe and for your breath to take any pattern it needs. If you feel sounds or noise want to come out, let them, freely (neighbours permitting!).

8. If you feel you've 'lost it', that you are no longer moving spontaneously, but have fallen into boring old unconscious habits, or have got into too much conscious control, or simply have got sidetracked into thought, don't mind. Come back to the point of stillness, and allow whatever movement that comes up to begin a new cycle.

If all your movements seem unspontaneous and hackneyed, settle more deeply into what is happening in the body. Is you mind making you mismatch it by moving too slow or too fast? What state is it in, where is the energy held or blocked? Once you recognize what is really happening in the body, and your awareness aligns itself and enters into the real state of your bodymind, the body knows exactly what to do. Just allow it to happen.

9. When you have finished, sit or lie quietly for a few minutes to allow your energy to settle and align itself ready for your customary activity.

10. Initially, if you are unused to self-unfolding movement, you may wish to do only a few minutes. As is comfortable, build up to 20-30 minutes.

11. You may sometimes prefer to enjoy self-unfolding movement in the context of dance. Choose music you like with a varied range of rhythms, preferably with nice long tracks. Gabrielle Roth has produced some excellent tapes.[2]

For myself, I like to vary what I do, sometimes using music, sometimes not, depending upon how I feel. Sometimes, I feel I need music to provide a framework, a structure, and lead. Sometimes it intrudes and allows movement to be less than spontaneous and authentic. Feeling can be a helpful guide. This time is for you and not a chore; be sensitive to what supports deepest renewal and enjoyment.

BEGINNING SELF-UNFOLDING MOVEMENT

If you are new to self-unfolding movement and if the whole idea of the body moving freely in its own way is hard to imagine, here is a simple way to begin:

1. Begin with one hand, right or left, and allow the finger tips to begin to move in their own way, as if they are telling their own story. Be curious, now, and throughout this exercise. What will these fingertips do left to their own devices? If nothing at all seems to happen, just begin something and be very curious as to how it might evolve. It may take a little while to recover the sense of freedom and play that children have so easily. But be sure, it is there, built into the bodymind. Allow the movement to extend into the fingers, and from thence into the hands. Let the movement develop in its own way, gradually allowing it to include the wrist, forearm, and upper arm.

2. Repeat this process with the other hand and arm. You may allow the first arm to continue moving in its own way, if it seems to want to. If there are moments of very slow movement or stillness, that is fine. Let the attention be in the body, innocently enjoying whatever happens. Then allow the different parts of the face to express themselves in their own way, moving as they feel inclined to move — mouth, tongue, eyes, ears, and nose.

3. Allowing the ears and nose to move will probably get the whole head moving with the neck. Allow the head and neck together to move freely, and then, progressively, the shoulders, the upper torso and the lower torso. Allow each part to express itself in its own way, to tell its own story in movement.

4. And so on to the pelvis, and from there let movement originate in turn from the thigh, knee, ankle, foot, and toes of one leg, and then the thigh, knee, ankle, foot, and toes of the other leg.

5. Then allow both legs to move in their own way together, letting the movement spread progressively up the legs to include the pelvis, and thence the torso. Eventually the arms can move, too, and again allow the neck and head to become involved.

6. Till now you have been directing the attention in turn to different parts of the body which for that time become the centre of free movement (although at no stage do we try and interrupt movement in any other part of the body). Gradually you have allowed more and more of the different

parts to move freely together. By now you should be ready to make a small leap of faith and allow the whole body to move freely and spontaneously, with the whole or any part expressing itself in its own way for the next several minutes. It's a bit like jumping into the water after dabbling and splashing about. Don't be concerned, the water is warm and not deep. You won't drown! After some minutes, take a few moments to rest. Lie still with your attention gently present in your body, in the legs, arms, trunk and head.

SELF-UNFOLDING MOVEMENT — BACKGROUND

Recognition of the power and importance of self-unfolding movement as I have come to enjoy it didn't come overnight. Many experiences contributed to it, including experiences with *yoga asanas* and meditation, spontaneous movement experienced along with powerful feelings in a therapeutic context, dancework with Gabrielle Roth; authentic movement as used with other artforms at Natalie Roger's Person Centred Expressive Therapy Institute, and chance meetings with people such as Tony Crisp who had begun to work with themselves and others in this way.

Self-unfolding movement is not a new phenomenon, and it is quite natural. Stretching and yawning when we wake up or are tired involve natural spontaneous movement. Anyone with some in-depth experience of *yoga* and meditation, may well have encountered self-unfolding movement, either as a direct experience or among people sharing this path. At certain times, during meditation or even in bed at night, the meditator can be in such a deep state that energy starts to move in the body. Going with this energy (which happens very naturally when in a deep and inward state), the meditator can find his or her body moving through a series of postures, even for an hour or so that seem to result from, and to allow, the opening of new channels and pathways of energy in the body.

Such powerful experiences have led individuals to allow such experiences to occur and to systematize their insights into an approach that they share with others. Examples are Janet Adler's Authentic Movement and Tony Crisp's Coex.[3] Gabrielle Roth's dancing path includes a powerful element of spontaneous movement in what she sometimes calls 'the wave' through the five rhythms.

Aspects of self-unfolding movement are present in various therapeutic techniques such as Bioenergetics, the popular breathing technique of Rebirthing, and Arnie Mindell's 'process-oriented psychotherapy'. The names of religious groups, such as the Quakers and the Shakers, bear testimony to their roots in aspects of spontaneous movement.

To be moved by the spirit is to be moved by the great force of life that is within us, and we witness aspects of self-unfolding movement every time we encounter an inspired artist who has passed beyond conscious control to allow whatever is happening to happen. When this occurs, as at peak moments of improvisation, we sense something powerful and transcendent raising the work to a higher level of life that takes us as audience with it, to bathe and renew us.

SELF-UNFOLDING MOVEMENT AND INTUITION

Self-unfolding movement is an enjoyable and intriguing experience in its own right. It has direct benefits in daily life by increasing our sense of creative vitality and well-being. It leaves us feeling more aware and opens our intuition.

Much of our social and educational conditioning is directed towards forcing us to exercise conscious control — whether by trying to get us to weigh immediate gratification of present urges against longer term consequences (e.g. educational success and career prospects tomorrow versus having fun with friends now) or to inhibit our natural urges to meet the expectations of others ('people won't like or accept you if you do that in their houses'). As a result of this emphasis on conscious control, we have suppressed our natural urges, and with them much of the spontaneous and creative response to life we call intuition. Not only do we not follow our intuition, we have suppressed much of our ability to even notice those faint impulses of thought and feeling.

In the pathway of stillness, sitting in meditation with our eyes closed, we effectively raise the threshold that inhibits thought from becoming action. This allows the self to settle into itself, and the active phases of the awareness to subside back into the simplest state of consciousness. We learn to allow unhelpful mental 'noise' to dissipate, creating more room for us to experience the true creative impulses of being in our life. This sharpens our intuition from one direction.

Conversely, with self-unfolding movement, we lower the threshold so that the censor obstructing fresh and immediate responsiveness to life no longer stifles spontaneity. We find ourselves following impulses and urges that seem odd but prove to be incredibly appropriate during self-unfolding movement. This spills over into the rest of our lives with a greater tendency to respond elegantly and intuitively in the dance of life, with sharper hunches about people and situations that are easier to follow and usually beneficial to us.

This recovery of intuition is an important side-benefit of self-unfolding movement, because it makes us much more likely to live in harmony with ourselves, and hence to do what is necessary to maintain well-being for us in our present context. Living with awareness involves spontaneously knowing and following what is right for us in the life-constellation in which we find ourselves at any moment.

An important part of this development of intuition, as Tony Crisp suggests, involves recognizing and responding to any visual images that arise during self-unfolding movement. These are often powerful communications from the unconscious and much can be gained from exploring them from different perceptual positions by dialoguing with them directly, by reflecting upon them with the conscious mind later, and by associating into them and allowing them to move you in self-unfolding movement.

If you are not particularly visual, key words and phrases that arise may also be important handles to understanding what is happening and hence in allowing it to unfold fully. Allow them to resonate in your body during movement or use them later as a starting point for freewriting. Self Unfolding can continue through a variety of expressive media, including writing and sound.

Other Activities

SELF-UNFOLDING SOUND
Giving voice to sound is an important vehicle for Self Unfolding. Sounds may be a spontaneous expression of shifts in the body during free movement. Allowing vocal sound to unfold is also very liberating in its own right. It often helps one enter more quickly and deeply into self-unfolding movement. Like inner-directed movement, self-unfolding sound brings our attention fully into the present moment and thus develops awareness and spontaneity. Sounding can be very healing. It releases tension and, through its vibrations, it massages and tones up parts of our head and body from the inside.

Before sounding, take a comfortable stance, where you are not likely to be disturbed nor to disturb others, and allow your mouth to open. Let a long deep 'ah' sound come out. Notice where you feel the sound in your body. Allow the sound to go up and down the length of your body, noticing how it becomes deeper as it drops from your head down to the depths of your belly. Let the sound move up and down as it seems to please. Allow your mouth to change shape and let the sounds change freely and spontaneously however they seem to wish to. If your body seems to want to move, allow it to move in any way it wants.

Alternatively, notice how you feel inside and allow any sounds that seem to match those feelings to come out fully. As your feelings change, let the sounds change freely. Use self-unfolding sound from time to time, either on its own for fun or release or as a prelude to, or part of, self-unfolding movement.

AWARE WALKING
Walking offers a wonderful opportunity to enjoy some moments of simple

awareness-in-movement. Take some time to walk for its own sake. If you can do this in a park or in nature, so much the better, but, if not, wherever you will be relatively undisturbed.

Notice how you are walking — speed, rhythm, etc. Where is your attention habitually as you walk, on internal matters or external? If the latter, on what — sounds or sights? How do you use your body? You may need to slow down a little as you allow your attention to be more in your body, while continuing to be present to the world around you. Be in the process of walking. Notice any places where you feel tension in your body as you walk. Have the gentle desire and intention to let go of tension. Let your body adjust itself, as in self-unfolding movement, as it lets go of tension. Play with your walk a little, exaggerating the sway of your hips, the swing of your arms, etc. Allow your body to find a rhythm and way of walking that is just a little more elegant and effortless than usual, walking with economy, ease, and pleasurable sensuality, grace-full.

Be aware of a sense of poise and balance, as your body manages the relationship between the ground pulling you to it through gravity, yet providing the solid support for the upward counterthrust that helps keeps your body up and your head skyward.

As you become comfortable and aware in your walk, allow yourself to rest a little on your breath, breathing a little more slowly and deeply for a while. While continuing to walk, notice where your attention falls. Notice how your attention shifts from one thing to another. Notice the transition point as your attention passes from one object of attention to another. If you find you have become distracted, return to aware walking, being in the body, enjoying the process for its own sake, resting on the breath, and enjoying and delighting in what you see, hear, feel, and smell.

POSTSCRIPT: WATCHING DANCE

Watching dance can sometimes be as refreshing to the body as actually dancing, as the watcher's body can make micro-muscle movements as if subtly dancing in sympathy. Watching dance brings subtle movement into stillness. When watching, allow yourself to go to second position for an extended period with a dancer of grace and beauty. This process can work well with any form of classical dance and with contemporary dance. Notice what changes in your sense of your body afterwards. Be moved and you will move differently, and still be you, too.

NOTES

1. See *Maps To Ecstasy*.
2. The Moving Center, P.O. Box 2885, Petaluma, CA 94953, USA.
3. See *Mind and Movement*.

CHAPTER EIGHT

From Sensing to Transcending

Summary
In the two previous chapters, we considered approaches to awareness at opposite ends of the experiential spectrum — allowing awareness to express and reveal itself through moving the body, and settling into the inner experience of that consciousness which underlies all the more active levels — ego, feeling, intellect, beliefs, values, mind, and senses. In this and subsequent chapters, we explore ways in which awareness is essential to the full functioning of all these levels, and how each level can contribute to the unfolding of awareness. Here we consider how the senses, the intellect, and values levels can all be both impediments and vehicles towards unfolding awareness.

It is likely that a good education of the olfactory sense will develop flair; of the tactile sense, tact; of taste, taste . . . but not only in the true sense of the words, but in the symbolic sense for the intelligence, which would have strength (hence penetration), flair (hence intuition), tact (hence sensitivity), taste (hence discernment). One can, in this sense again, speak of the sensibility of intelligence, which, thanks to the education of the different senses, will harvest its fruits.

Antoine de La Garanderie [1]

Marshmallow puffs melting into sweet gooey gelatinous lumps. Sausages sizzling in hot spitting fat. Logs creaking and crackling, flame-giving, spark-throwing, glowing, red-white-red-white. Acrid smoke curling in darkness, pungent, crinkling nostrils, making eyes water. Hot to the front, cold to the back. Voices floating in and out amid strands of music from another time. Dancers holding hands, circling by the fire, stepping in time to the tune, shadow-cast faces, now inward to the dance-flow, now smiling across the darkness. Eyes gazing into the incandescent core, pulsing, edgeless, drawing you in and down into the shapes and shadows of dream-time. Fire-world, friend to a thousand thousand forebears, gazing in quiet thoughts, as stories shape themselves again, anew. Once upon a time . . . .

Senses and Sensing

Attitudes to the senses have oscillated wildly down the centuries. Considered now Epicurean ends, now obstacles to apprehending the ineffable, and now gateways to all there is — the world of phenomena. The different religions, too, have gone from puritan iconoclasm, stripping distracting images and colours seen to mask and belittle the One, to catholic sensory celebration, marshalling sounds, sights, and smells to celebrate the sacred and make it palpable in swirling incense, icons, gold brocade, bells, and chanting. From God transcendent, wholly other, beyond all our sensing, to God immanent, essence of all things, the very breath and tissue of our sensory selves.

From St John of the Cross:

Estaba tan embebido,
Tan absorto y ajenado,
Que se queds mi sentido
De todo sentir privado,
Y el espmritu dotado
De un entendir no entendiendo,
Toda ciencia trascendiendo.

I was so whelmed,
So absorbed and withdrawn,
That my senses were left
Deprived of all their sensing,
And my spirit was given
An understanding while not understanding,
Transcending all knowledge.[2]

to Thomas Traherne:

How like an Angel came I down!
How bright are all Things here!
When first among his Works I did appear
O how their GLORY did me Crown!
The World resembled his Eternitie,
In which my Soul did Walk;
And evry Thing that I did see,
Did with me talk.[3]

Again and again, in East and West, the senses are held as both gateways and impediments to a deeper or higher awareness. And in one way this perception is just. Jesus' parable of the prodigal son warns of the dangers of over-identifying with sensory experience to the loss of our inheritance. In another story from a different tradition, Indra, ruler of the heavens, tests life on earth as a boar. He is so comfortable in the mud, with his sow and litter, that he forgets his true nature. His divine colleagues are unable to remind him of his real status — until they slay his porcine wife and children. Sexual and chemical excess, addictions to alcohol, drugs, and even food can all represent a kind of triumph of sensory awareness that both intoxicates and disappoints. The siren senses can both exalt and enchain.

We can understand this paradox a little by recalling the map of the different levels of awareness from Chapter Two.

Environment	
Senses	Behaviour
Mind	Capabilities
Intellect	Beliefs/Values
Feeling	Identity
Pure Awareness	

LEVELS OF EXPERIENCE

The senses mediate between the outer and the inner. Information and experience pass via the senses to the inner screen of consciousness which enables us to perceive. But the act of perception can inundate that inner awareness. Our senses flood our awareness with coloured contents, Christmas-tree baubles, Nature's bonfire, in exchange for the immortal diamond of consciousness.

And yet perception is a paradox; through our senses we construct a universe with every appearance of reality. We call it reality, act as if it and all the things in it really existed, forgetting that whether or not they do depends upon the magic lantern of the mind. Our senses don't simply register what's out there; perception is creation. The 'out there' exists for us only through our internal construction or reconstruction of it, projecting it into an as-if-out-there, whose as-if-ness we overlook. From one point of view, there is no 'out there', there is only consciousness. Our perceptions are fluctuations of our own consciousness. Fleeting shadows on the screen.

That is why sensory perception is not only reviled for shortchanging us, but revered for revealing something that surpasses our ordinary mudwalled world. If what we sense is not only content, but also the container of all our experience, any moment of perception can explode its present boundaries and take cosmic proportions. When our internal functioning is even subtly changed, we can create very different realities.

Consciousness as tri-faceted knower, knowing, and known is in its very nature, self-interacting, self-exploring, self-discovering, and self-knowing. Any act of perception worth its salt is flavoursome oceanic being. The fullest perception is inevitably self-referential.

Whenever something is exquisitely beautiful, delicious, or even extraordinarily ugly, our attention is drawn both to appearances and to deeper levels of the act of experience itself. Heightened perception is inseparable from some simultaneous heightening of the knower.

That is why poetic descriptions of sensory beauty rarely linger in the gleaming of dew-bedecked vein-threaded leaf and flower without reaching into the larger meaning of the moment in the poet's psyche. Moments of heightened perception at the very least speak of us, at best "yield drops and flow, ring and tell of him".[4]

The mistake we sometimes make is to locate the magic in the trigger rather than in what is triggered. That is the root of addiction and what in the East is called 'the binding influence of experience'. This landscape, this artefact, this melody, this lover, or this armchair are identified as the source of comfort and consciousness. Sometimes they are faithful ways of allowing us to live more of what we are. But they also easily become substitutes whose worst effects we observe and experience in addiction and dependency. The free Self is chained to a substance, promising release and freedom, but wrecking the body and creating chaos in the lives of loved ones and even strangers.

There are four key ways of responding to the senses in the interests of greater consciousness: withdrawing, witnessing, enjoying fully, and becoming one with.

The first follows St John of the Cross and other saints and seers withdrawing from active experience into that state of unknowing-knowing, beyond senses and mind. It is the pathway of meditation, where with eyes closed we experience quieter levels of the mind, until transcending even these we rest in the state of being-awareness. Sensory contents yield to awareness in its pure state.

The second way of responding to sensory experience in a manner that safeguards the knower is to rest in that state of inner awareness, while continuing to accept the contents of consciousness. Douglas Harding talks of 'leaning back', 'staying at home', and simply allowing whatever sensory experience there is to be there, in that silence. In such a state, it is as if I am the indescribable, unbounded awareness that witnesses all that falls within it, but remains unflurried. Like those tranquil surfaces of water, which are both surface and depth and can reflect and contain trees, plants, people, sky, but which not even the breeze disturbs.

Whereas the first two ways suggest a kind of detachment from sensory experience — as experience rather than attitude — the third way involves entering more deeply into sensory experience, often from that place of stillness. When our awareness is fully awake, there awakens with it a greater capacity for appreciation for what falls within it. With greater appreciation comes also greater recognition and enjoyment.

Many artists and writers take this route. "With an eye made quiet, we see into the life of things".[5] Visual and auditory contemplation from a state of stillness reveals more of the subtle inscapes of things around us. We sense 'the dearest freshness deep down things'; things 'catch fire, ring, and speak of him'. This opening to the wonder of the world in the simplest flower or thing leads to a profound appreciation of the cosmic artistry present in nature, and beyond to a celebration of the unseen artificer of all things. "He fathers-forth, whose beauty is past change, Praise him."[6]

Opening to receive the reflections of reality in awareness or delving deep into the beauty of all things often lead to a further recognition: that the knower and the known are one; that perceiver and percept are not different.

Higher States of Consciousness

These four ways of relating to the senses correspond to the higher levels of development described in Chapter 3, and (according to Maharishi Mahesh Yogi) to four higher states of consciousness beyond the three ordinary states of waking, dreaming, and deep sleep.

The fourth state, the introvertive quiet of pure transcendental consciousness is reached by withdrawing in meditation from outer sensory experience to lessening inner sensory experience.

Eventually fifth state of witnessing sensory experience results from alternating inwardness in meditation with everyday activity. Eventually, inwardness is sustained naturally along with outer activity.

The sixth state grows out of deeper appreciation of what we experience through the senses; the somewhat cerebral witnessing of outer activity from the stillness of awareness-in-the-head is 'warmed up' more and more by the heart, revealing deeper layers of charm in sensory experience.

The seventh state sinks deeper still. Sense of a separate self lessens. There may be an 'I' and a 'that', but now I recognize that 'I am that', as is everything and everyone else. Unity prevails; all this is that, too.

This map of higher states of consciousness suggests why attitudes to the senses have varied so much. With different experiences of consciousness, the relationship to the senses shifts — from the senses overshadowing awareness (ordinary waking) to them pointing to something else (fourth and fifth states), to them being a source of delight in their own right (sixth state), to them being transparent vehicles to the one universal awareness (seventh state).

Depending on which part of this map one is relating to (and often people have often only had fragments to guide them), the senses can be interpreted as either friends or threats.

What may be appropriate at one stage of our personal journey in unfolding inner awareness may be totally inappropriate at another. There is a time for sensory reserve and a time for sensory abandon. After all it is a rhythm that nature parallels in its annual cycle through the seasons, from the buds and shoots of spring to the ripening of summer, the falling away of autumn and the long rest of leafless winter.

Not everyone develops in the same way in relation to these states. We may pass amongst them all, emphasizing now one, now the other. We may have many glimpses of them coming and going before they begin to predominate and become permanent modes of our awareness.

Like Paul Valéry, Douglas Harding (citing the south Indian sage, Ramana Maharsi) compares the indwelling awareness to a note in music that once properly heard is present through all the different strains of the music, sometimes predominant in our attention, sometimes peripheral. For this to happen, we may need to return many times to that simple single note, before we are so familiar with it that no matter what parts of the orchestra are playing, no matter what we are attending to, it is always at least in the background of our experience.

This map of different states of consciousness resolves some of the controversy surrounding the senses. Knowing that they have their place in higher states of consciousness, it becomes unnecessary to deny them. So long as we remain aware of our central concern — living awareness — appropriate use of the senses can be an important part of doing just that.

All the senses are important, but in this chapter we will pay particular attention to the three primary senses of seeing, hearing, and kinesthetics (sense of internal body-feeling and sensations; touch; and also proprioception).

Developing Awareness in and through Sensory Experience

MEDITATION

At first one might expect meditation to be an unusual way of heightening sensory awareness. It appears to emphasize an eyes-closed inwardness that discounts the senses. However, as we have seen, meditation is a central pathway to that heightened consciousness which includes greater sensory awareness. This starts almost immediately. It is a common experience of meditators that two daily 20-minute periods of withdrawal from the senses actually heightens them. After meditating, what we look at seems brighter and more beautiful. Sounds are richer and fuller. Food tastes better and our touch is more sensitive.

These subjective experiences are borne out by research: greater visual acuity and reduced auditory thresholds, greater hand-eye coordination and so on. Research on meditation even suggests that it reverses some of the sensory decline that accompanies the ageing process.

APPRECIATING WHAT'S THERE

One of the biggest impediments to sensory awareness is our failure to attend to and appreciate what's there. This may be due to tension in the bodymind, closing down the receptive senses and making it difficult to let the world in fully, while sending us scuttling anywhere but the present moment, away on thoughts and anxieties to do with the future or past.

One of the simplest ways to enhance sensory awareness is to first relax the bodymind fully, to breathe a little more slowly and deeply than normally, until the bodymind is more settled. Allow your attention to acknowledge and be with any tense or tight feelings in the body until these melt enough to feel more comfortable.

Then take a moment for the following exercise. Simply notice what you are seeing at this moment in time. Notice the brightness or lack thereof, the quality of colour, the sense of depth. Notice what you hear. What tone, timbre, and volume is there to the sounds? Notice any sensations where your body is making contact with something else — perhaps the pages of this book or something you are sitting or lying on. What textures do these sensations have — sharp, dull, continuous, intermittent? What sensations are there inside your body right now? Are they spread all over, localized, light, heavy, pleasant, unpleasant, etc.?

Take your time to explore and recognize your sensory experience at this moment in time, firstly sense by sense. Then easily, without straining, allow yourself to be aware of all sensory channels at once.

Now allow yourself to be aware of who or what is perceiving.

Who or what is the perceiver?

Who or what is seeing right now?

Who or what is hearing right now?

Who is feeling right now?

Who or what is seeing, hearing, fling right now?

What is the perceiver's relationship to what is being perceived?

When you have 'downtime' (waiting for a meeting, a train, in a bus, in the bath, or shaving), take a moment briefly and instantly to inventory what is happening in the bodymind. Breathe more slowly and deeply allowing the in-breath to fill the whole body, and the out-breath to release any tightness or tension. Be aware of the moment between the in and out breaths. Rest for a moment on your breathing, as suggested in the 'Breath of Peace' pattern. Then simply allow yourself to be in the present moment, seeing what you see, hearing what you hear, feeling what you feel. There is no need to reach out strongly or forcefully to the world. Allow a feeling of opening in the heart and senses, and allow the world of sights, sounds, and sensations, flowers, sky, clouds, brick walls, to come to you. It is surprising how fascinating even a little piece of wall can be in its tones and textures when you allow it to come to you. This is an inexpensive way to enjoy great riches at any moment.

Writers such as Proust, Hopkins, and Rilke were reported to spend hours like this contemplating a flower or stone. Wherever you are right now, try it. Allow yourself to become open and receptive and welcome whatever your attention falls on. If your attention wanders, gently come back to what you are perceiving here and now in the moment.

SENSORY BIAS

Generally, we tend to favour one sensory system over another, both for inner and outer experience. What is your sensory bias? Take about ten minutes with eyes closed to notice where your attention goes. Is it to visual images and your eyes-closed visual field? Is it to external sounds? Or to internal dialogue? Or to the feelings and sensations you have in the body? Maybe you notice switching from one channel to another. Which channel do you come back to repeatedly?

Continue sitting for a while with eyes open. Which sensory channel predominates? Is it the same as when you have your eyes closed?

ENJOYING OUR SENSORY BIAS FULLY

Often one mode of experience becomes a habit. We may use it in an automatic and unconscious way, without really appreciating how we are using that channel or what we are experiencing within it.

Give yourself 10-15 minutes with eyes closed to pay particular attention to the sensory channel you tend to favour. If it is visual, notice the size, shape, location, colour, and other characteristics of the images that come to you. Are they big or small? Do they fill part of the visual field or are they panoramic? Are they bright or dim? Are they 'abstract' or 'representational'? Still or moving? Are they single or multiple? Do they follow each other in quick succession? Are you in the images or are they things seen as if through your eyes?

What happens to your experience if you begin to modify some of these sensory 'sub-modalities', for instance making pictures of a pleasant memory larger or smaller, closer or further away, brighter or dimmer, and so on?

If the auditory channel predominates, does your attention go more to external noise or more to internal dialogue? If to external noise, what are the characteristics of what you hear? What can you notice about the tone, timbre, pitch, and volume of the sounds that you have never noticed before? How do your ears cope with location (the sense of where the sound is coming from)?

If your mind is filled with a lot of self-talk, where do you hear this, 'inside' or 'outside' your head? Centrally or off to one side? Whose voice do you hear? What is its tone, pitch, tempo, volume? How is it talking, as a helpful friend or as a critic? How do you respond to this voice? Is there more than one voice? If so, what is the relationship among them?

What happens if you modify the pitch, tone, volume, or location of your inner voices? What happens if you talk to yourself differently, using for instance the voice of one who really loves and cares for you?

What happens if you allow the inner voice to become silent for a while and simply rest in the silence?

If you are more aware of your internal feelings and sensations, become fully aware of these. Where are your feelings and sensations located in the body? Are they static or moving from one part of the body to another? Are they of constant intensity or do they fluctuate? What are their characteristics ('lightness' or 'heaviness', sharpness or smoothness, pleasantness or unpleasantness)? What parts of the body are you not feeling? What happens when you allow yourself to be aware of feelings in those areas?

Notice what happens to your experience as you pay particular attention to the features and characteristics of your preferred sensory channel.

Repeat the exercise with eyes open.

BECOMING AWARE OF NEGLECTED SENSORY SYSTEMS

Typically, our preference for one sensory system over the others can lead to one or more channels being underdeveloped. Our sensory preference has wide implications, affecting even our personality. Whether we prefer visual or auditory modes of thinking, for instance, can affect how we relate both to self and to others. (A visual bias can make it easier to speak frankly and see things clearly for instance; an auditory preference may involve a greater need for 'harmony' in relationships.)

Repeat the previous exercise, but this time switching from your favoured sensory channel to the one that you seem to use least. What happens if you deliberately switch to a relatively unused mode and stay with it for a while? Is it easy? What do you discover in using this unfamiliar mode? Notice how your attention in that channel may influence what is happening in the other channels.

What are the implications of your experience in this exercise? How can you bring more balance to your experience? What might you do to make better use of a neglected sensory system?

Practise giving more attention to a neglected channel in your life for a week or two. What else do you notice happening as you do this?

TWO-WAY SEEING

Two-way seeing is a way of at least getting a sense of what the fifth state of consciousness is like. It is one of a number of experiments in awareness developed by Douglas Harding and his friends. In ordinary seeing, we look out at the world. In two-way seeing, we look in at the perceiving awareness at the same time.

One simple way in which Douglas helps people to do this is to have them point at the world with the index finger held about a foot or two from the face. Try it. Then slowly lower the finger, till it is pointing at the ground. Continue pointing the finger further and further down, until you are pointing at your own feet. Point to legs, torso, and gradually point it towards your own face. Point directly with your index finger held about a foot away right towards the centre of your field of vision, towards where an outside observer would expect your eyes to be. Try it. What is your finger pointing at? What are you aware of when you look out towards the pointing finger? The edges of a coloured world around it, and then a kind of empty space, which is at once nothing and not nothing, a kind of lively void? Do you get a sense of the witnessing-seer?

Now, with your other index finger held at the same level, but pointing outwards, allow yourself to be aware of what you are pointing at in both directions.

MASSAGE

Massage can be a very powerful way of heightening the sense of touch, whether you are massaging yourself or someone else. This exercise involves massaging yourself.

Take some time in a private place to stroke yourself. Perhaps one hand stroking the other arm. Allow yourself to have your awareness first of all in the stroking hand. Then have your awareness in the area that is being stroked. Notice how the experience shifts as you shift the locus of your attention. What happens when you have your attention at the same time in both the area you are stroking with and the area being stroked?

Notice the feeling that you have as you touch yourself. Imagine that you are someone you really care about. Touch yourself with a feeling of deep love and appreciation. Now begin to massage yourself, starting with you head, taking as much time as you need, with that feeling of love and care, and then working your shoulders, each arm in turn, then your trunk, including the stomach area, then your pelvis and each leg and foot in turn. Enjoy.

You may chose to repeat this exercise with a partner. Notice again what it is like to place your attention in your hand, in the place you are touching, and simultaneously in both. Notice how your touching changes when you bring a deeply loving and caring feeling to it.

FROM UNDERSTANDING TO APPRECIATION, TO OWNERSHIP

The senses are not innocent. I can contemplate this oak with mind-seeing. Noticing the shape of leaves, their colour, now green, recently spring-yellow. I can notice this crinkle on that leaf. That curl on this one.

Or I can look at it with heart-seeing, allowing its glorious profusion of sameness and difference — repeated patterns of serrated leaves, all held in organic harmony, overlapping, dancing singly and in clusters in the wind — to resonate in feeling. Do I see and feel its beauty? Or does my beauty welcome it home, acknowledging it as long lost kin to my inner essence?

When I see with the belly, there is no doubt. This tree is my tree. I embrace it as emblem and icon of my inner nature. I am the tree. The tree is me. I own what I see. And so with the other senses.

Try it. Look at something with your attention a little more in the head, the heart, and then the belly, as you perceive. Repeat with the other senses. Notice what you find.

Lying on my back on the grass. The sky is blue. Fleecy clouds litter the sky, like discarded cottonballs on a cobalt dresser. I'm tired. I close my eyes. The early June sun warms eyes and sockets. The space is golden. My body melts, resting on the ground. The wind picks up, sieving itself forcefully through the beech trees. I feel warm, but not hot. Fatigue slips away, a knot in my forehead eases. Mental space expands, golden and edgeless. Thoughts stir, ideas surface from nowhere. Half-posed questions answer themselves and I am ready to write.

Mind/Intellect

The notion that the mind and intellect can serve as pathways to awareness may seem strange. A common complaint is "I can't stop my mind thinking". Racing thoughts can seem like midges on a summer's evening, irritants that remove any inner peace. One of the commonest observations about states of heightened awareness is that there is less self-talk; internal dialogue quietens.

In unfolding awareness, it is not necessary to have a giant intellect. Like the senses, the intellect can misdirect and mislead, as when it becomes an end in itself or when dedicated to lesser ends — say, towards the acquisition of trivial knowledge, even of an academic kind, or the accumulation of wealth, as the only aim and purpose of life.

In fact, the intellect is arguably unnecessary for unfolding awareness. With the development of fine feeling also develops the kind of subtle intellect that helps us understand and appreciate who and what we are.

Yet the mind and intellect can help unfold inner awareness in a number of different ways. Firstly, part of the function of the mind and intellect is to set intention, thereby directing attention. In a real sense, what we turn our mind to becomes more prominent. Whatever our routine preoccupations, they increase in our life. If it's making money, we will be alert for opportunities to increase personal fortune. If it's scientific knowledge, that will increase. If it's our performance at golf or growing prize pumpkins, we'll get better at those things.

Once we realize that our awareness is the means whereby we enjoy anything at all, and start to give it its due importance, our mind and intellect can help direct our attention to opportunities to understand, enjoy, and expand our awareness. This can take many forms. It may involve choosing moments to just enjoy what the senses are perceiving. It may mean taking time to reflect not just on what we are experiencing in our life, but how we are experiencing — is it what we desire? Is it nourishing? It may also mean following up potential sources of greater understanding of who and what we are, whether it involves reading, or talking and listening to others with knowledge and insight.

The intellect can be helpful in another way. Its function is to analyse and to synthesize — to break things into their constituent parts and to recognize the patterns and relationships among things. Ordinarily, we apply these skills to the phenomena we encounter in our daily life. We analyse issues in our relationships, in our working environment, in the political and economic spheres, as well as in the more traditional fields of analytic enquiry that are taught in schools and universities. We generalize about people, places, things, information, and ideas.

While it is a mistake to live only in the world of the head, these activities of analysing and synthesizing — universal mental processes, even in the untrained mind — lead us in the direction of unified awareness. It doesn't take much to extend them both towards enhancing our experience of wholeness. For instance, if I take the process of analysis to its ultimate, whether in the world of objects or in my own internal experience, I arrive at that which is smaller than the smallest, that unmanifest awareness that is the field within which all things occur. If I attempt to synthesize the disparate elements of my experience, from inner thoughts and feelings to my outer perception of this world and beyond to the vast intergalactic spaces of the enormous universe, I arrive at that which is larger than the largest, larger than me, but still within my unbounded containing consciousness. If I try to understand how things fit together, seeking with Bateson 'the pattern that connects', and I group ideas, experiences, or things, my intellect leads me again to that which connects all things, my existence, my intelligence, my awareness.[7]

So a trained mind can be a trap, but turned in the direction of understanding who and what we and all of this are, it can point us towards that pure awareness, which is always there. Besides, as we shall see in later chapters, much of the way we stop ourselves from living awareness results from the intellect's mistaken evaluations of experience. These create distorting and limiting filters to our personal reality. One way to undo these mistakes is to involve the intellect in the unravelling of those same mistakes and misperceptions.

This function of the intellect in deconstructing the imprisoning scaffolding of limitation and in unfolding truth explains why in the East there is an intellectual path to enlightenment, called *sankhya*. We may end up finding with one of the West's greatest intellects, Aquinas, that all our rumination is so much chaff, but that very realization is in part a fruit of the intellect's continuing exercise.

Ultimately the intellect's gift is priceless. The intellect recognizes, acknowledges, and names that indefinable being-awareness, which is so subtly but permanently there, whatever the fluctuating contents to consciousness. The intellect lets us know actively who and what we are. Without the intellect, we might not recognize that subtle nothingness, apparently so inert and useless in some moments of perception, which is the silent Self, source and centre of ourselves and every other thing.

Exploring Awareness — Exercising the Intellect

WHAT AM I?

Take a moment and close your eyes. Imagine without straining or trying hard to do so that you have no thoughts, no images, no sensations. What remains? What is that silent and colourless continuum which is there between and beneath all mental activity? Allow your intellect to recognize and name that unnameable being-awareness which is the container of all your thoughts, which is there as any inwardly whispered 'I' fades away. What qualities does it have that makes it an unmistakable experience?

CHUNKING — MENTAL GROUPING

The intellect typically works by splitting things up or grouping them together. Two ways it does this are by going from parts to a whole (or vice versa) or from members of a class to a class of things (or vice versa). We go from parts to a whole when we take the different bits of a car — engine, upholstery, exhaust, etc. — and assemble them as a car. Conversely, we go from the whole to parts when we strip the car down to its nuts and bolts).

We go between classes and members of a class when we recognize that cows, cougars, and camels are all mammals or that roses, violets, and irises are all flowers. Both ways of organizing information are important for intellectual activity and can be developed.[8]

Here are some activities to cultivate the intellect's ability to group experience, relevant to our concern here with awareness:

1. Make a list of ten things that are as different from each other as possible. Now ask yourself 'what do they have in common?' If you haven't already done so, add yourself to the list. What do all these have in common?

2. Take three things. Imagine that you were to break them into smaller and smaller pieces. Imagine going deep into the molecular structure of each item and beyond. What happens when you get to the finest level of each item and imagine going beyond? What happens if you imagine exploring your own body in this way?

3. Take a piece of paper and note your answers to these questions: What

are some of the possible ways of grouping things? (e.g., animals, businesses, planets, etc.) When you have a goodly collection of classes of things, ask yourself: what would group all the classes of things I can possibly think of? Take your answer and imagine for a moment that you are that item or class which groups all other classes of things in the universe.

4. Allow you mind to range freely through some of the disparate aspects of your existence: home, family, friends, work, play, country, habits, hobbies, etc. Ask yourself: What is the pattern that connects all this? Allow the answer to come and explore how it feels and the implications of it for a few moments.[9]

WHAT'S THERE?   WHAT'S MISSING?
In grouping experience, the intellect directs the attention — either towards detail and specificity or towards pattern and generality. Another way it does so is by influencing whether we pay attention to what is present or what is missing in our experience. Take a few moments now to pay attention to what is missing in your experience right now, what is not there. Notice what happens inside yourself. How do you feel?

Now take a few minutes to pay attention to what is present in your experience. Allow your senses to open and breathe more deeply. Notice fully what is there in your physical environment. Notice what happens inside yourself. Which experience is more satisfying? Which is more typical of your way of relating to the world?

Paying attention to what is missing can be useful in refining our creativity and problem solving, as it motivates us to improve on what we have. But it can also be a recipe for dissatisfaction, with our seeking for what is not present in our life and failing to appreciate what is there.

Consider taking a few moments each day to enjoy fully what is present in your environment. This enhances peace of mind and living with awareness in the present moment.

When you need to solve a problem or want a creative change, ask internally: 'What have I not considered? What's missing? What else is needed?'

Values

Our values are what we hold to be important in our experience. Applied to the contents of consciousness, they determine the criteria by which we judge whether something is worthwhile or not. Thus, if we value money, we may reject people or activities that do not support this value. 'Money' becomes a criterion we use to judge experience — whether we should associate with certain people, or whether to spend or save, for instance.

Values thus set the filters directing attention to some things rather than others. Values also motivate. They influence what we move towards or away from.

Conflicts may occur between values. For instance, some values may be mutually exclusive — like those influencing the desire to be slender and those leading us towards cream cakes. We may then oscillate from one value to another — and shift in our behaviour from overeating to crash dieting. On the other hand, some values may consistently override others — for a workaholic, work may win out over play. All values are valuable, but some are more valuable than others.

Values operate on different levels of life. For instance, we may value material things like money or good clothes, relationships with friends or family, or more abstract things like beauty, peace, or truth. Generally, we move towards things that make us feel more happiness, satisfaction, and self-worth, while avoiding the unpleasant and painful. As these are also values, we see that deeper values ultimately give value to surface values and actions.

At deeper levels, the values behind our values turn out to be important qualities of our own beingness, such as 'fulfilment', 'well-beingness', 'peace', or 'lovingness'.[10] These 'core states' or 'core values' are states of great and expanded self-awareness, close to pure consciousness itself. An in-built — and generally poorly recognized — drive to reconnect with what we truly are thus underlies all our thoughts and actions. Our values structure a recursive urge to be ever more closely aligned with our own essence. As we gradually discover that the value of what we thought was valuable lies in something deeper, we return closer and closer to our deepest Self, our own living awareness. We may love a particular sport, a line of work, or our family, but we do so through what they awaken within us. Discovering this doesn't make them less valuable; it merely subtly recentres us, making us less dependent on externals, which are always subject to upheavals. Loss of job or loved ones may remain painful, but much less so when the very qualities that we appear to lose are recognized as part of what we inevitably are.

Usually, we know some of our values at the conscious level, recognizing, perhaps, that 'love' or 'kindness' are important to us. Other values may be unknown to us, but yet influence us. Both the values we are aware of and those we don't know can influence us unconsciously. When we find ourselves feeling uncomfortable or rejecting something because it 'feels wrong', it is generally because some value is active. The value may not necessarily be in our conscious awareness, but nonetheless influences its quality and direction. If we value 'excitement', whether we realize that we do or not, this guides our choice of activities and affects our awareness.

Becoming more aware of our values and how they relate to each other helps us become more aware of what is motivating us, allowing greater choice. Recognizing deeper values helps resolve internal conflicts, as our deepest values form a common ground uniting and reconciling all our diverse drives. As we discover what's truly important to us, our life's direction naturally comes into alignment with that. Realization of deep values is thus both an outcome of a life of quality and a means to it.

Increasing Awareness of our Values

IDENTIFYING AND GROUPING VALUES

What are the values that motivate you? Take a piece of paper and note the question: 'What's important to me in my life?' What do you consistently give your time and attention to? What's also important to you that you neglect.

Look at the list. What patterns do you discern? Revise the list, clustering values that seem to belong together. Are there any values that seem to underpin groups of your values? What are those values?

VALUES AND LIVING AWARENESS

Identify three or four things that you do which support a satisfying quality of awareness in everyday life. What values are implicit in these activities that are supportive of living with awareness?

Identify three or four things that you do which have the effect of impairing the quality of your awareness. What values are implicit in these activities that lessen your awareness?

How are these two sets of values related? What might you lose if you succeeded in giving more weight to one set of values? What is the value that makes what you might lose important to you?

What value or values reconcile and contain both what you gain and what you fear to lose?

If you imagine having that value or those values as your starting point, how does that appear to influence your behaviour? How might your life be different if you are close to that value?

HIERARCHY APPROACH

Some values have an apparently equal weight for us. Other values have far more importance for us. Asking the question "What's important about that?" or "What does having that get you?" reveals the value behind any given value. Take one of the values that seems to have key importance for you in your list. And ask, "What's important about that? What does having that do for me?" With each answer that comes up, ask the same question again, until your answer remains constant or you find yourself looping round in a circle.

How has this value affected what you have paid attention to in your life? How has it directed and impacted your awareness? Is this a value that you wish to continue to guide you? How is it likely to impact you in the future?

VALUES MANDALA

The values mandala offers a structured way to explore how values relate to each other.[11] It helps identify the values behind our values, and ultimately a value that may have overriding importance in our lives. If you are not used to thinking in this way, this exercise may stretch you; be patient and take your time.

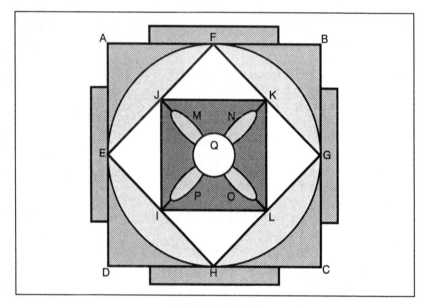

VALUES MANDALA

1. At each of the corners of the largest square (points A, B, C, and D) write down four things that are important to you.

2. Take the words you have written at points A and B and ask yourself: 'What is there that is common to both A and B that makes them both important to me?' Write your answer at point F. Don't rush this process, at the same time don't ponder overlong. Just allow yourself to identify a value that makes both A and B important to you. Rather than analyse mentally, identify experiences of both A and B and feel what quality is common to both of them that is important to you. You will repeat this process a number of times with different combinations to unfold a core or deeply held value that is of pervasive influence in your life.

3. Repeat step 2 three more times for B-C, C-D, D-A in turn, writing your answers at G, H, and E respectively.

4. Now ask yourself: 'What is there that is common to both E and F that makes them both important to me?' Write your answer at point J. Repeat for the other three sides of the diamond (F-G, G-H, and H-E) in turn. Write your answers at points K, L, and I respectively.

5. Repeat this process with the words now at the three corners of the triangle, J-I-K. Ask yourself: 'What is there that is important to me that is common to J, K, and I?' Write your answer in the petal M. Repeat this process for the triangles J-K-L, K-L , and J-L-I in turn. Write your responses in petals N, O, and P respectively.

6. If you have different words at M, N, O, and P, ask what is it that is important to you that is common to them all. Write your answer in the middle of the central circle Q. If your words at M, N, O, and P are the same, write that at Q. Is there anything even more important than this for you? If yes, add this to the centre.

7. Notice how this value makes you feel. Allow yourself to experience it fully in your awareness. How has this value influenced you in your past, as a child, adolescent, and adult? How is it influencing your life at present? How does it guide you towards the future? How is it related to your sense of your own essence?

Our values may be evaluations or decisions about what we want to have more or less of in our life, and thus appear to be functions of the intellect. And some of our values do reflect intellectual judgements about what is important or worthwhile in our personal worlds. But ultimately all such judgements are guided by what leads to greater or less well-being in some form in our life. The feeling level ultimately determines the types of value we have and our ability to fulfil them. In the next chapter, we consider this feeling level in a little more detail and how living awareness involves freeing feeling.

NOTES

1. *Pédagogie des moyens d'apprendre*, Centurion, Paris, 1982, pp.45-46. [My translation.]

2. *The Collected Works of St John of the Cross*, trans. Kiaren Kavanaugh, OCD and Otilio Rodriguez, OCD, PCS Publications, Inst.of Carmelite Studies, Washington DC 1973, pp.718-719.

3. Thomas Traherne, 'Wonder', *Centuries, Poems, and Thanksgivings*, ed. H M Margoliouth, OUP, London, 1958, II, 6.

4. *Sermons and Devotional Writings of Gerard Manley Hopkins*, edited by C Devlin, S.J., OUP, London, 1959, p.195.

5. "Lines Composed A Few Miles Above Tintern Abbey", *The Poetical Works of William Wordsworth*, ed. E de Selincourt, Clarendon Press, Oxford, 1952, p.250.

6. The three quotations in this paragraph are from Hopkins.

7. It may be that this holistic function of the intellect is responsible for the tendencies of 'intuitors' (in the Jungian model) to live longer than 'sensors'. The former experience the parts of experience as part of a larger whole. The latter fragment the world into atoms of detail. This may be more wearying for our bodies to sustain.

8.   Reuven Feuerstein's 'Instrumental Enrichment' helps learners acquire basic grouping skills. Buzan's 'Mind Maps', Gowan and Nowak's 'Concept Maps', and the Maharishi's 'Unified Field Charts' used at MIU, Fairfield, Iowa provide visual ways of showing the relationships among ideas and help develop hierarchical thinking.

9.   Other exercises in Chapter Eleven and Twelve on patterns and on values and purpose are also relevant to the exercise of the intellect in the service of awareness.

10.   See Connirae and Tamara Andreas' *Core Transformation* for an account of core states.

11.   The values mandala was inspired by Douglas Pride's Criteria Awareness Triangle, described by him in an article in the British NLP newsletter, *Rapport*.

CHAPTER NINE

Awareness-with-Feeling: Freeing the Emotions

Summary
Feeling, particularly the subtle backdrop of 'finest feeling', gives texture to pure awareness, and supports and guides the more active levels of experience. The delight of feeling is ultimately what makes life worth living. Here, we consider ways to free feeling, notably, through the 'creative connection', the sequenced and free use of the expressive arts.

So feeling comes in aid/Of feeling . . .   Wordsworth

Finest Feeling

Feeling is the inner essence of a satisfying quality of human life. How we feel influences how we evaluate our experience, positively or negatively. Feeling takes many shades and qualities of intensity. The foundation of all feelings, though often overshadowed by our more dramatic emotional states, is 'finest feeling', the simplest quality of feeling, in which our awareness is simply open with a quiet and satisfying sense of warmed-up fullness and well-being.

When we experience the finest feeling level, it is as if we are attuned to the junction of abstract consciousness and the physical body. We experience a deeply fulfilling state. It is like basking in a bath at just the right temperature with all cares dissolving, or relaxing in spring sunlight with thoughts absent or so quiet they barely ruffle the smooth surface of being. Finest feeling is a simple state of presence and grace. It is the core of what some commentators call 'essence', a state beyond the emotions, which can yet be coloured by such qualities as pure love, joy, or beauty, etc. These transpersonal 'qualities of essence' delightfully tinge pure awareness, delicately personalizing the impersonal.[1]

Finest feeling is the deepest part of the intellect (as the centre of discrimination rather than rationality). It connects all parts of the bodymind, head, heart, and visceral instincts. It is the basis of our intuition, our being able to 'know' instantly what is true, right, and appropriate. It is the touchstone of centred certainty. Whereas the more analytic phases of our minds take time to compute logically, finest feeling processes all the implications of a situation from within that state which is 'the home of all knowledge' and delivers the answer with doubtless clarity.

Finest feeling is the platform of our stronger emotions, but is somehow beyond them. As the ocean supports the pulse of the planet's rhythms, swelling under the influence of moon and wind into rising waves that break in different showers on the shore, so fine feeling gets pulled into our various emotions. The active emotions — such as passionate love, fear, anger, or sadness — involve strong physical sensations. As they arise they become like waves that not only enliven, but swamp.

Our active emotions are nature's way of mobilizing responses to practical challenges. Fear in the appropriate context galvanizes defensive action. Anger sets the bodymind to safeguard its integrity. Passionate commitment engages us 'whole-heartedly' in a course of action. However, most of us do not experience emotional lives of such simplicity. Too often, when we would feel, we are numb, and when we would respond, we inappropriately under- or over-react.

Emotions are triggered by inner or outer sensory stimulation. The latter may have an almost intrinsic pleasing or displeasing quality, or an acquired meaning that determines a personal response. Sunsets over oceans are almost universally delightful. Old black dogs may trigger affection or fear, depending on prior experience and associations with such animals.

Children express their feelings naturally and immediately. If something they wants is taken away, they cry. If they see, hear, or touch something or somebody they like, they respond immediately. They don't ask themselves whether they should have such a feeling, or how they should respond. Unfortunately, growing up and becoming socialized is an education in deceit and denial. Innocent and spontaneous responses don't necessarily meet with adult approval; in fact, they may have painful consequences. As a result, we learn to dissimulate our true feelings from others and come to distrust and deny our own impulses. We end up deceiving both others and ourselves.

By habitually blunting our immediate responses, we not only suppress the subtle impulses arising within finest feeling, we often fail even to register them. As a result our feelings must grow in intensity to gain our attention. What may have been easily dealt with if we had responded to it in the moment, such as a mild annoyance, may finally be the target of full-blown anger.

Sometimes we have so cauterized our ability to feel that the latter becomes an alien modality. We become numb from the neck down, living in a cerebral world of words and images, alienated both from our active emotions and from their ground in fine feeling. We can become cold and 'unfeeling', dulled against our own and others' pain and joy. Not only is such a state unpleasant to be in, once we begin to feel it (just as we can feel a local anaesthetic), but it saps our energy and vitality for daily life, draining creativity in a wasteful holding operation.

Freeing feeling allows energy and awareness to flow more fluidly in the moment. It allows us to ride life's surf, to live with creativity, intuition, humanity, and wisdom.

FREEING FINE FEELING — REST AND EXERCISE

Rest, particularly the deep restful wakefulness of meditation, is an effective way of restore the fulsome charm of fine feeling. Too many members of our alarm-clock society have sleep-debts and underlying fatigue that blunt the senses and coarsen feeling. As a result, we need depressants to relax and stimulants to pick up, and our feelings have to be over-activated to gain our attention.

Meditation on a daily basis, with occasional deeper retreats, allows the self-healing mechanisms of the body to throw off tension and tightness and relax into a suppler and softer sense of Self. In offering an experience of the settled Self, meditation provides a platform of tranquillity that enables us to enjoy the wilder swings of life from a place of peace. We need less stimulation to feel good. Small joys have a greater meaning — the sight of flowers, or a walk in nature — go deeper as a result. Big experiences are better coped with. They are contained within the larger space of the experiencing Self.

Exercise, from simple stretching to vigorous aerobic exercise, also frees feeling. Exercise flushes out the toxins left by overactive or unpleasant emotions. It centres us in immediate activity and the enjoyable feelings resulting from using the body. Participating in sports can channel and release aggressive feelings in a fun way, while, as we have seen, self-unfolding movement and dance also activate and shift stuck states.

FREEING FINE FEELING — INTROSPECTION AND ART

To recover fine feeling, we may need first to acknowledge and experience the more active emotions that overlay it. Our surface emotions, because unpleasant or unwanted, may themselves lurk beneath our conscious awareness. If we first recognize what we are actually experiencing in the moment — which may be some 'negative' emotion, such as anger, sadness, or frustration — we can discover that these states in turn conceal more subtle facets of our own being or essence. As we accept fully the emotional states that are present in our awareness, they naturally transform and evolve. In doing so, they reveal more subtle states of feeling; we discover pure states of inner peace or joy, facets of finest feeling.

One effective way of returning to what we are experiencing emotionally, and thence to unfolding our inner essence underlying it, is by the free use of the expressive arts. The expressive arts free feeling in a particularly powerful way. The arts tap into the right hemisphere of the brain, which has less language, but is sensitive to colour, shape, sound, melody, rhythm, space, and movement. If the left hemisphere labels experience, the right hemisphere appears to store the non-verbal gestalt of images, sounds, and associated feelings. It is thus closely involved in our emotional life. Artistic activities, especially where they are undertaken for purely expressive purposes, rather than to create aesthetic effect, access the right side of the brain. External expression using the arts — verbally, through sound and writing, visually through art, and kinesthetically through sculpting and movement — activates and releases feeling states otherwise locked in the bodymind.

Using the arts for emotional expression requires a very innocent approach, without expectation or design, and no emphasis on creating aesthetic product. As people become 'experts' in artistic fields, they begin to use more of the analytic capabilities of the left hemisphere. This is an appropriate part of growing mastery and the controlled use of the arts to communicate a message to a wider audience. But it is not necessary when using the arts for self-unfolding or healing. As such, there is no advantage in being artistically gifted or trained to use art to free feeling. All that is required is to be willing to relinquish tight conscious control and allow things to develop and unfold. If you are artistically trained, you may find this quite challenging, but it is not really difficult. Using unfamiliar media — clay instead of paints, writing instead of the visual arts, for instance — can help restore innocence, as can working with the 'non-dominant' hand, the one that we do not usually use. This immediately takes us out of familiar neural pathways and allows something fresh and unexpected to happen. Our dominant hand is also usually closely connected with the accomplishment of our conscious intentions. Using the other hand allows other parts of ourselves in the shadow to come to awareness.

FREEING FEELING WITH THE 'CREATIVE CONNECTION'
Using several of the arts in a single session can be a particularly powerful way to explore and shift stuck states and open feeling. Natalie Rogers, founder of 'Person Centred Expressive Therapy' calls this approach 'the creative connection'.

Natalie developed the creative connection from a personal need for balance. In attending her father Carl's conferences, she found herself going 'stir-crazy' after days spent sitting and talking. She began to introduce creative activities, such as movement and art, to achieve balance. She found that others enjoyed and benefited from these breaks. Eventually she realized that powerful as the arts were in uncovering and articulating the inner workings of our feeling-life, their sequenced connection was even more powerful.

As people shift from one artistic medium to another, the feelings and threads tapped through one medium often unfold more thoroughly and intensely. For instance, as feelings are channelled into painting, they may become stronger or transform themselves. A state of dull stuckness may shift to anger, anger to sadness, and sadness to peace. Taking the painting into movement or writing often amplifies the feelings or brings out new facets, revealing further chapters of the story in a different way. Along with this activation and release comes understanding of how we might have been limiting ourselves and what we might be. Through the use of the expressive media, issues and experience that might have been beyond the fringe of our primary focus, finally get full attention. More of the whole Self unfolds.

We may have suppressed parts of our experience in the past in order to cope with difficult situations. The creative media help us express what we are experiencing — whether as feelings or as images — in the present moment. In the process, portions of buried experience which may need resolution for us to move forward in our life may surface. The expressive arts enable us to bring our attention to 'the edge of the beam'. We may choose an art form in the same sensory channel we are already using — painting images we see, singing or making sounds we hear inside, or moving from our feelings, for instance. Or we may choose an art form that invites us to transpose our experience into another sensory channel — drawing from feelings, moving from images, or writing from clay pieces, for instance. Both approaches can be valuable.

When aspects of repressed experience come up more strongly through one sensory channel, using this already activated channel for outward expression in the corresponding art medium has two important effects. First, it orients the attention towards that part of deleted, distorted, or generalized portions of our experience which are already beginning to manifest-whether in words, images, or feelings. It makes use of what is already almost there. Second, as the experience is explored through the channel where we have greatest awareness of it, other dimensions of the experience emerge. For instance, as we move, visual images or lost memories may come up; through painting more feeling or words may come up.

Conversely, switching sensory channels to one which we usually use less can also work powerfully. As we shift to another art medium, we also shift to the sensory channel associated with that medium. This can help us focus more deeply on parts of the experience that are less conscious and trigger yet more freeing up, with still more discoveries coming into awareness. If we begin to use a relatively underused sensory channel, we may discover much, as we are likely to have less conscious dexterity and hence less control and organization in that channel. More can happen spontaneously. It often happens that an underused channel is one that we had blocked off, because there were things in that channel which we didn't want to hear, or to see, or to feel in the past.

Along with the emergence of portions of experience previously out of conscious awareness, our present self gains insight and understanding as to how its current life is influenced by past choices and experiences. For instance, one person using the creative connection saw clouds of poisonous gas when talking about her relationship with her mother. Drawing these clouds and then letting the drawing inspire spontaneous movement allowed her to experience enormous rage and anger and recognize that "my mother wouldn't let me breathe". Her mother's oppressive behaviour had stifled her ability to express herself and influenced her whole life. After recognizing and to some extent releasing this, she was finally able to access — again through drawing — an image of orange, which was accompanied by great peace.

The expressive media not only help one to reach into and resolve negative or restrictive states, they also help unfold positive states. These are after all the essence of normal healthy life. And they become more prevalent as the obstacles to their experience — the negative beliefs and states — dissolve.

The creative connection provides a self-unfolding process. It neither privileges the positive, nor does it deny the negative. We don't set the agenda. We start with wherever we are, with whatever is happening in the moment. We follow our own unfolding drama at our own pace. This pace is considerably accelerated by the use of the creative media, but it still proceeds in relation to our own desire and comfort.

The expressive media allow fuller understanding of the meaning of the images and feelings that come up to emerge. This understanding is helped by writing, personal reflection, and by verbal sharing, whether with someone in a counselling role or with another sensitive explorer. There is no attempt to force feelings or images through an analytic grille. Putting the images out in expressive works allows us to take a fresh perceptual position. If we have been in first position — expressing what is arising from an associated state in which we are inside our own experience — seeing or hearing our work allows us to take a little distance and process what has arisen. We may discover new meaning and connections, which may in turn inspire a new round of expression and discovery.

Written words or painted images provide a visible and tangible reminder of sometimes fleeting states. They help us digest what has come up. Previous images may suggest new ones or contain a depth of meaning that emerges over time as we continue exploring our response to the image. If the image had not found its way into some form of art, it might have been forgotten or simply returned to the unconscious from where it emerged.

As feelings unfold, they may be accompanied by symbolic or archetypal images of numinous intensity. These images may evolve as they recur in a series of works or sessions. Intense images of the natural world or of the gods or traditional symbols, such as swords or crosses, represent deep transformation within the bodymind and may punctuate transition points in a mythic or archetypal journey. The creative connection allows people to enter deeply into this journey and to reflect upon it. Such images do not require expert interpretation. Usually the same innate wisdom that produced them will provide the understanding needed, though some people enjoy exploring how such images — swans, trees, suns, flowers, etc. — may have come up in the literature and art of the traditions of the world.

Writing a story, with very little conscious thinking, from a series of drawings or pieces of work produced over several days, also crystallizes a deeper level of understanding of the states one has been experiencing. A deeper pattern implicit in the various pieces of art, and their relationship with each other, emerges when all the works are passed through the creative process again. This process is much easier when there are physical pieces of art tracing the various states one has been experiencing.

SOME BENEFITS OF THE CREATIVE CONNECTION

The creative connection, not only frees feelings in the moment, it leads to powerful changes in our values, and in how we live life.

The expressive media offer physical release through the somatic discharge accompanying the creative process. People may access painful states in the bodymind as they open up in the creative process. Using art and movement releases these states and allows access to states of healing and integration. By releasing deep blocks in the bodymind, the creative connection allows new pathways to achievement to open.

Opening blocked sensory channels and releasing constrictions in them frees whole ways of being in the world — really seeing or hearing or feeling, almost for the first time, and with that gaining in strength and confidence in life as we become a plane that flies using all engines, rather than having one or more shut down. Our trapped vitality is freed and becomes available for fresh creative endeavours in our life.

Creativity is like breathing. It is part of the rhythm of life, going within and coming out, as we alternate between inspiration and expression. It turns outer awareness back into itself, reconnecting knower and known in a moment of inward knowing. This creates a space to acknowledge and recognize what is there and for what is within to flow out. To create is to express who and what we are. It is to take what is inside and put it outside. The creative connection builds familiarity with this rhythm of going within and coming out. It opens the channel between core awareness and physical expression in the world. The connection between inner conception and outer realization is opened up. We achieve more and achieve it more easily in our lives.

The practice of picking up feelings and expressing them also develops an ability to be sensitive to what is happening in the moment and to respond to it. By culturing attentiveness to what's happening in the now, we grow in the desire and ability to be present to our experience, both in our inner and our outer worlds. We become more aware. We begin to attend more fully to our sensory experience. We respond more quickly to unfulfilled inner needs.

As a result, we become more congruent — all parts of ourselves unite to give one single and convincing message. We find ourselves more sensitive to what is phoney in ourselves or others. It is harder to accept situations in which there is some fundamental denial of truth. Because incongruence in our environment stifles the atmosphere in which we live and move, we are readier to act authentically and draw attention to what is being negated.

This makes the creative process both a spiritual and a revolutionary act. It opens the channels of our inner life like a floodgate and this is intrinsically liberating and fulfilling. We recognize that our birthright is to be free and creative beings, co-participants in the incredible creative act that the universe is. We feel more complete, vital, and true. Such experience affirms that I can only be fulfilled in being true to who and what I am. If I let others make final decisions for me, I give away my integrity. That is why the creative process is anathema to totalitarian systems. People become centred and grounded in their own awareness. They begin to think more for themselves and expect freedom and dignity for themselves and others.

Using the Creative Connection to Unfold Awareness

To use the creative connection you will need some free time and some materials: a selection of oil pastels and chalk pastels; coloured pencils; paper of various sizes — at least A3 or (11 x 17ins in the USA), and some bigger; writing paper and pen or pencil. It can be helpful to have a supply of modelling clay. If you want to use paints, you will need paints of your choice — a selection of water colours, acrylic, poster paints, and brushes. You may need space to move and some music if you like to have music in the background or while you move.

You can do the creative connection on your own, but it can be enjoyable and helpful to have a sympathetic friend or two to share the process with you.

Generally, it is a good idea to start the creative connection with some movement to connect with what one is actually feeling and to ground the awareness in the body. Start any movement with gentle stretching and warm up comfortably. Allow yourself to follow how your body wants to move, letting it make any movements or take any posture that it seems to call for.

From movement, you might consider working with one of the visual media — drawing, painting, or clay-modelling. Start with how you are feeling now in the moment or pick up any powerful images or sensations that come up in the movement. Or if appropriate, take your attention to some major issue in your life.

Take a moment to settle inside and sense what seems to be going on within you. Using your non-dominant hand, allow yourself to work quickly and freely, just following inner images or letting feelings move your hand. Let the drawing or painting unfold before you — whether as identifiable images or simply as abstract expression. Don't worry about getting it right. Let the process unfold by itself. When the drawing seems complete, sit back a little and let it communicate to you. What is it showing or telling you? How does it make you feel? Allow a few keywords to come up and write them on the painting.

You may feel moved to take what you have done into another painting or drawing or into another medium altogether — freewriting or movement or clay, for instance. If you do use clay, try working it with your eyes closed, and allow the clay to form itself in its own way in your hands. Be sensitive to your intuition, it will guide you to what you need if you are open to it. Be willing to experiment and try things out. This is your own journey with yourself.

If you do have a journeying companion, take time to share, either as you complete one phase of the process or as you complete a cycle. Each talk about your own work first and what has come up for you, before sharing what the other's work triggers in you.[2]

COLLAGE

Collage can be a quick and friendly medium for those intimidated by creative materials. Collect a stack of magazines from friends and neighbours. Have scissors, glue, and a large piece of paper handy, A3 or larger.
Take a moment to get a sense of how you feel in your life overall.

Working quickly, flick through the magazines identifying images that seem to catch your attention. Pull or cut them out. When you feel you have enough, lay them out on the paper and stick them down. Again, don't analyse or think, just let it happen quickly.

When the collage seems to be complete enough, step back from it. What messages does it seem to have for you? What feeling comes across overall? What images have attracted you? How have you arranged them? How have you juxtaposed them? How do they relate to your life-themes and issues?

Take the experience into five or ten minutes of freewriting, starting with any feelings or images triggered by the collage. Just begin writing, letting the writing take you where it will. If you have a friend with you. Take some time to share your experiences, without judging each other's work. What does the other person's work communicate to you?

ART JOURNAL

Keeping a journal of our explorations also helps unfold inner awareness, as we give time and attention to what we are aware of. The journal is even more powerful if we use the creative media in it. Expressing creatively what is happening through freewriting and through drawing with coloured pencils and pastels can be a very powerful way of both tracking and accelerating our journey of self-discovery in living awareness.[3]

I remember one day driving from a mountain retreat to Lucerne. The streets were thronging with people in bizarre masks and costumes, sounding horns, marching to rhythmic dirges. People were playing pranks on each other, children sousing grownups with water, confetti, streamers, and shaving foam. Bewildered, I asked one child what was happening. "It's Dirty Thursday!" he exclaimed. "What does that mean?" I asked, hardly the wiser. "You can do anything that you want!" he shouted, showering me with confetti. And all was clear.

Here were the orderly spotless clockwork-thorough Swiss with their own creative escape mechanism, balancing the 360 days of precision with some days of creative mayhem. Firstly in designing and making outfits expressing unexpressed aspects of the psyche — alternative identities from the macabre and hideous to the dotty and twee. Then in wearing them and marching to dislocated mardi-gras music in the dark of night, going on to dance and revel, discharging collectively the accumulated debris of their shadow selves.

Bridge

The creative connection helps unfold the emotional activity obscuring fine feeling, the warmed up edge of pure awareness. But our emotions are not only the cover of subtler levels of experience, they are reactions and responses to inner and outer triggers that determine how we give meaning to experience. Interpretation of what events in our life mean precipitates emotion, and emotion in turn influences interpretation, which in turn shapes emotion. Much of meaning is coded in language, which, with emotion, sets our underlying beliefs about ourselves and our world. These in turn direct our attention and awareness profoundly and pervasively. The next two chapters thus explore the influence of language and beliefs on our experience of both pure awareness and 'awareness of'.

NOTES

1.   Notably, A. H. Almaas in his various writings; e.g. *Diamond Heart*, Vol.1, p.26; *The Pearl Beyond Price*, pp.72-74.

2.   For more information on the creative connection, see Natalie Rogers' book on the subject or contact the Person Centred Expressive Therapy Institute, 1515 Riebli Road,

Santa Rosa, CA 95404, USA. In Europe, contact Dinah Wrycza, 18 Rowan Lane, Skelmersdale, Lancs, U.K.

3.   Jung kept an important art journal. See also Joanna Field, *A Life of One's Own*, Virago Books, London, 1986; and Lucia Cappachione, *The Creative Journal: The Art of Finding Yourself*, Swallow Press, Athens, Ohio, 1979.

CHAPTER TEN

Language and Awareness: The Syntax of the Self

Summary

Language is a mixed blessing. Mirror and mediator, between our inner and outer worlds, it can both open and obscure awareness. Carrier of the core mistakes of the mind that overshadow wholeness, it is also a means to their resolution. It communicates both conscious and unconscious intents. Through syntax and non-verbal signals, it conveys either integration or incongruence. It speaks through our body and of the body, indicating both blocks and well-being. Used appropriately it can assist in identifying and dissolving those blocks, helping the healing balm of awareness restore balance to the bodymind. Greater awareness of its patterns can simplify communication with ourselves and with others.

Language is the mother of the universe.

The Veil of Language

Language is like water. It has both surface and depth, reflecting an inverted world of oaks, ashes, and clouds or fracturing that world in rippled wind-flurried fragments. It can offer a limpid window to deeper dimensions, revealing waving fronds of waterweed in slow currents, half-hiding perch and pike. Dense and opaque, it can be like a brown sediment-soup, holding darkly, years of rotten leaves, broken branches, twigs, and lost coins and rings in silted sludge. It can be stale and stagnant or fresh and vital, still or flowing, calm or flash-flooding, sweeping old stumps, loose stones, and soil before it.

Shortly before her death, Marilyn Monroe absented herself from the set of 20th Century Fox's production of "Something's Gotta Give" to sing 'Happy Birthday' for President Kennedy. Famed for her erratic time-keeping, she was introduced as "the late Marilyn Monroe". These words in her unsettled state, when her work in progress was also affirming that 'something's got to give', may have tipped the balance of an unstable mind. Her introduction, implying that her appearance was already posthumous, that she wasn't just late, but had already ceased to exist, may have nudged her towards suicide. Within weeks she really was 'the late Marilyn Monroe'. Coincidence or injunction? Impossible to say, but language influences us intimately and unpredictably. It affects what happens in our awareness in ways small and large.

Conversely, awareness also shapes our use of language. If we are in align-ment with pure awareness, our speech tends to be softer and pleasanter in its vocal qualities and life-nourishing in its content. Living with awareness we can support a life of quality in others through the impact of our words on them.

Like awareness, language resists easy exploration. As attention turns back on itself, words become both objects of investigation and vehicles for ar-ticulating the results of that investigation — both prosecution and defence. Torchlight turned into its own shadows, awareness catches words slithering as they would reveal what they conceal, and as they conceal what they might reveal.

Language directs the attention. Whether words come from outside or arise within, they colour consciousness with their contents. Awareness sur-renders to the images and sensations conjured up by inner dialogue. The often swarming thoughts of future plans, present possibilities, and past joys and woes saturate our sense of self with content. And we are not even aware of this self-reduction as we forget who and what we are, immersed in what Mallarmé so aptly called "the choir of preoccupations".

What we think sets the direction for what we experience, both inwardly and in relation to the world around us. Hence the importance of positive thoughts. We create within us representations of whatever we conceive mentally, as words, images, or feelings. Naming summons what is named to the inner eye and ear. This is so, even if we negate what we are thinking. As Valéry said, to deny A is to show A behind a grille. If we decide not to think of chocolate, we have to think chocolate in some way, and with it some-thing of the flavours, taste, and other associations of chocolate. If we think illness or ugliness, we create that within our consciousness. This may not matter much for an instant. But if such thoughts are sustained over time or held with intensity, the consequences are potentially enormous. Our inter-nal representations impact us physically. When we think of movement, our muscles respond. Fleeting thoughts may have a temporary impact on our bodies. Deeply and frequently held ones shape us in sickness and in health. And our patterns of thinking are often ingrained. Of the thousands of thoughts we think each day, the vast majority have much in common with those of yesterday.

These recurring patterns of thought also feed and form our sense of self. They shape who and what we take ourselves to be. Our individual self is a matrix of interlocking concepts, constructed from our ideas of what we are. Though much of the premises and parameters of our self-concept are usu-ally hidden to us, our thoughts are constantly confirming, modifying, and denying that concept. Language sets many of the boundaries of our world.

But if what we speak and hear manifests in our minds, language can also heighten awareness. When we talk, write, read, and think of awareness, language evokes and enlivens something of that awareness — at least tempo-rarily. Patterns of sound, imagery, and rhythm — such as those of poetry or heightened prose can evoke still more intensely. Language that dances and delights the ear with fresh turns of phrase and adroit metaphor can entrain the listening attention to respond not only to content, but to how the con-tent is delivered. The patterns of the language heighten our awareness of it, and like the children of Hamlin, we follow the piper, entranced. We become more aware of the vehicle of meaning, the language itself, rather than passing directly to the meaning it carries. This attending fully to the words also yields a deeper and richer awareness of the emergent meaning.

When the content of heightened language has to do with awareness, we are drawn further into a deeper and fuller apprehension of that awareness and the fine structures and responses that can occur within it. We can glimpse how meaning manifests within our consciousness. The veil of language lifts a little to reveal its own subtle and secret ways of working, its enchanting power to create and to awaken, as well as to entrap and deceive.

Language that springs from enlivened awareness — such as some poetry or expressions of personal eloquence — remains fresh even years after. Read-ing such writing awakens in one's own awareness some of the qualities of the writer's own consciousness. We may recognize a personal quality differ-ent from our own, but we do so within a deeper awareness activated by the charm and attraction of the patterns of the writer's words. We enjoy the radiance of the writer's language within our own awareness and connect, in spite of different personal, cultural, and historical experience, not only with some essential quality of the author, but with the animating energy and awareness that we share. Such is the power of language that is shaped deep within awareness.

Language can thus both help and hinder. In coding, summarizing, and explicating experience, it can be a reductive substitute for aware presence. It can mask awareness by directing the attention to the myriad things to which it refers. Or it can be a vehicle of beauty and truth, raising aware-ness, by enlivening experiences within it that reflect greater consciousness. It can both reveal and veil the deeper Self, focusing the attention on sense of Self or on sausages.

This chapter, and the two following ones, attempt to bring some of these subtle processes to awareness, so that they may be understood and redi-rected for greater comfort and well-being. Attending to language and knowing how to respond to it elegantly can deepen our relationship with it and quicken our progress towards living with what transcends it. Our aim is to enjoy language wisely and well for its capacity to awaken, appreciating its power to enchant, while minimizing its potential to cast spells that ensnare and overshadow.

Language: Mirror of Self and World

Much of the two-edged power of language arises from its curious status as mirror of experience, mediating between inner and outer worlds. It parallels the functioning of each in striking ways. The question raised by sages of old as to whether our universe is a manifestation of an infinitely creative Word returns today in a different form as physicists and philosophers ponder 'the language of nature'. Our universe has language-like qualities, and our language features like those of nature.

Through language we become mini-creators within creation as a whole. In remembering or imagining people, places, things, and events we recreate what has been. In our stories and dreams, we manifest what has never been, but might. Like Orpheus, what we conceive, we create, making striking representations within as we think and dream.

Like these creations of language, physical reality appears more substantial than it is. There is more space proportionately in our bodies than in intergalactic space. The hydrogen atom, for instance, has been compared to a grapefruit in the middle of a football stadium, orbited by a speck of dust. Matter's substance is largely an appearance created by its motion. The superficial solidity of our world matches the apparent reality of the worlds our words conjure up as we get entranced in the creations of our thoughts and speech.

Like both inner and outer worlds, language is organized hierarchically. A selection of the primary units of sound available to the human voice — called phonemes by linguists — are used to form the elemental units of meaning or morphemes, which then make up the words of each language. These smaller units combine to create the potentially infinite number of unique phrases and sentences of each language. These in turn form the larger units of discourse, such as poems, plays, and conversations.

Whether a given utterance is part of a formal speech or an everyday conversation affects how we listen and understand. We listen differently to fact and fiction. Turning on the television, we know instantly whether we are listening to drama, documentary, a news bulletin, an interview with a 'real' person, or a commercial. We automatically adjust how we listen and give meaning to each phrase according to the conventions of the relevant mode of discourse.

Beyond that our awareness ultimately provides the most encompassing dimension of language. All elements of sound and meaning are generated and apprehended within it. It is the silent ground and source for all our expressions and understandings. If silence corresponds to pure awareness, which like it is essentially silent, meaning corresponds to 'awareness of'. Sound, is like intent, directing intention to the potentially infinite variety of contents of consciousness that can be reflected in our awareness.

Just as the elements of sound are organized into units of meaning, so our behaviours constitute capabilities which coordinate and give meaning to them. The larger units of meaning — phrases and sentences — are like our beliefs, particular expressions of perceived reality. In fact, our beliefs, when apprehended consciously, are usually expressed in sentence form. Our beliefs as a whole constitute, in turn, like many of the sentences we may utter, a larger whole. Our identity in all its transformations may be compared to the larger units of discourse. And just as awareness offers ultimate coherence by reflecting the meaning of these various macro-linguistic structures, so it underpins and pervades identity.

Language also reflects the structure of nature itself, offering a kind of second universe, a microcosm of creation at large. Elementary particles and waves pulse within the unified field, like sound waves in silence. Just as the limited number of elementary units of sound are the vehicles for meaning in all human languages, so waves and particles form the atoms of the different elements, which in combinations make the building blocks, the structural morphemes of our universe. Connected in the potentially limitless mixes of different molecules, they form the phrases and sentences of our universe.

At the level of greatest complexity, molecules combine to form structures with their own self-renewing identity — living creatures that carry their own blueprint for reproducing themselves. (Not for nothing have the large life molecules of DNA and RNA been compared to language, with RNA reading the information stored in DNA. Language, like DNA, stores information that is potentially retrievable even thousands of years later.)

Living systems correspond to the larger linguistic structures — the different modes of everyday discourse, from news reports to novels — that set the frame in which their individual elements are to be understood.

The self-perpetuating living systems of nature ultimately have nervous systems so rich and complex that they function with a level of sensitivity to their inner and outer environments that we can call awareness. They are aware and able to reflect on their own awareness. And one of the tools they have developed for this is language.

PHYSICAL WORLD	LANGUAGE	INNER WORLD
Unified Field		
Waves and particles	Phonemes	Behaviour
Atoms	Morphemes and words	Capabilities
Molecules	Phrases and sentences	Beliefs
Living systems	Complex linguistic forms	Identity
Pure Awareness		

LANGUAGE: MIRROR AND MEDIATOR BETWEEN WORLDS

Language parallels our inner and outer worlds in other ways, too. We have considered the importance of the primary impulses of stillness and movement in relation to living awareness in Chapters Six and Seven. These impulses are fundamental to both nature and language. Coherent change occurs in nature through a dynamic relation between the forces towards movement and the forces towards stasis. Too much stasis and nothing would happen. Too much movement and nothing could cohere anywhere. Movement and stasis in nature manifest ultimately in process and product-objects and transformations as these objects interact. In nature's deep structure physicists find things appearing as either waves or particles depending on how they are viewed. It is as if at this deepest level things are potentially either objects or processes and only at more manifest levels differentiate themselves. These primary elements of objects and energies infusing, impacting, and altering them correspond to the core elements of our language: nouns and verbs.

Other linguistic elements merely define nature and relationship of these two. Prepositions show relationships between objects in space — on the table, by the sea. Conjunctions connect things and processes with each other. Adjectives qualify the noun to which they are attached and adverbs the verb, allowing greater precision and nuances.

If language is built around the two elements of nouns and verbs, its basic syntax is subject-verb-object. The verb explains the relationship between one noun and another. Each sentence is shorthand for an event in the universe. Something transforms or is transformed by something else. Process does not occur in a vacuum; it is in relation to elements that are affected by it in some way.

This subject-verb-object arrangement matches the structure of awareness, which we described as a singularity with firstly a dual and then a three-in-one nature. Awareness is both subject and object. It is and it knows. It is simple existence and it is pure consciousness. It is a knower; it is aware of itself; it is this being aware, this knowing; and it is itself, the known. Knower, knowing, and known, pure awareness expresses itself through the subject-verb-object structure of our language, where the subject is like the knower, the verb like the process of knowing, and the object, like the known. As awareness knows and moves within itself, this movement within the one is reflected in language. A single sentence reflects the story of creation. The permutations of the relationship of knower, knowing, and known are endless.

Different languages emphasize different facets of this subject-verb-object relationship in their syntax and word order. German, for instance, often uses a structure that at the end of the sentence a verb places. Such features specific to a language result from the tendencies of the speakers of the language and in turn have a subtle impact on them. In the case of German, placing a verb last accentuates its dynamic energy, and reflects a predilection for energetic activity. Germans at the time of writing have no speed limit on their autobahns. In their organizational thinking they tend to be more process-oriented than object-oriented, giving great attention to planning and answering the question 'how' in relation to goals.

Language expresses the various levels of experience, perceptual positions, and time that make up the primary vectors of our unified model of awareness, introduced in the early chapters of this book. For instance, our verb conjugations shift the attention to different perceptual positions and move awareness through time with their different tenses. A sentence also reflects the various levels of awareness, often alluding to several levels at once. A sentence such as, 'I can applaud by clapping my hands at the theatre' covers the primary logical levels — identity (I), belief (can), capability (applaud), behaviour ('clapping my hands'), and environment ('at the theatre'). Tonal emphasis may give more prominence to one or more of these words indicating which level is being emphasized. For instance '*I* can applaud' is very different from 'I *can* applaud' or 'I can *applaud*'.

Language, then, is both a dialect of the language of nature and a metalanguage, able to comment and become conscious of it. It parodies the language of nature, divorcing us from it, but enabling us to parallel, mirror, and 'master' nature through our words and thoughts and all these can do. We interact with ourselves and the world by manipulating, consciously and unconsciously the subject-verb-object relationship inherent in our awareness, in nature, and in language. We become subject and verb to the object of nature itself.

That makes language a mixed blessing. On the one hand, it refers the knower to what it needs to know to survive and flourish. Mediating the relationship between knower and known, it provides a subtle and flexible tool for handling the complexities of our relationship with self, others, and world. It enables us to process, understand, interpret, reflect on, and respond to the outside word or to inner experience. It allows information — news of the universe — to be taken in and to be put out. It informs and guides the knower. It projects out leading to action, informing and impacting other knowers.

On the other hand, it separates the knower both from himself and from nature as a whole. It creates a curtain of fragmented content that hangs between the knower and nature, both our own and that of the world we are in. We no longer recognize who or what we are, nor what anything really is. We are hypnotized by the stories told in the tapestry of words, and forget Self and World in the process.

Language and Correcting the 'Mistake of the Intellect'

Yet language can also help undo that process and deconstruct its own spells to allow the knower to reapprehend that living awareness that he or she is.

The French philosopher, Jacques Derrida, claims that Western philosophy has been beguiled by an illusory quest for an imaginary Logos. He argues that at crucial points our philosophers have made logical leaps in their language to what he considers a comforting crutch, the idea of some primary being that is beyond language and is its source. He suggests that language works through difference, with meaning created out of the relationship between words, their similarity and difference from other words. There is no absolute, he proposes, only a world of relative terms in which one word 'defers' to others for its meaning.

Derrida's difficult writing highlights the flight of attention from language into reductive meaning. In appearing to capture some of that process 'on the wing', and slow it down so that we can notice it, he relentlessly peels away the leaps we make in our use of language, allowing it to seem to mean more than it actually does. He heightens an awareness of the emergence of meaning from and among words.

Paradoxically, for me, in the process he also makes us aware of what he claims is not there — an awareness beyond words. In exposing the slippery edges of language and closing off the bolt holes to easy naming of a privileged source of words, he as it were dismantles all the comforting scaffolding that words usually offer to easy understanding. Words are stripped of their seductive and reductive power. They cannot be trusted to adequately evoke, express, or substantiate the silent being-awareness beyond them. All their attempts to do so fail and often lead us into thinking we know, rather than to being in a state of knowingness. In reading Derrida, I still find some wordless experiencing awareness remains like a void in which language has been occurring. Derrida's writing actually deconstructs our habit-thoughts to yield a sense of a subtle and indescribable nothing — something which they have been obscuring all the time, but which shapes and silhouettes them as negative space (the space between things) defines the shape of leaves and chairs. Yet this space can suddenly become itself the satisfying focus of attention and means to richer appreciation of the very objects it was already defining. Derrida's writing thus offers an example of how language can help free as well as bind the knower, by making us more aware of how it works within us.

Traditional Indian philosophy points in a similar direction in quite a different way. It suggests that all human problems, whatever their superficial differences, share a common deep structure. They all spring from a primary error, *pragyaparad*, the mistake of the intellect. The mistake the intellect makes is to confuse the one and the many. We identify with an 'I' that has separated itself from the unity of existence. In doing so, it also separates itself from its deeper essence. As a result we find ourselves out of balance and alignment both with ourselves and with the larger whole. Unity is fractured and differences predominate in our awareness. All difficulties in life, both personal and collective, may be traced back to some form of this ultimate error. Solutions to problems are piecemeal unless they address this primary mistake and restore our identification with, and experience of, the integrating wholeness which is our true nature, and the wise source and centre of all resolution.

Language is a key carrier of the mistake of the intellect. Language makes distinctions that split and fracture unity. It names, separates, and contrasts. It elaborates a web of constructs that become more real than the real. It makes a map whose shorthand we take for the territory. It drives conceptual wedges between us, and between ourselves and the territory. One of its key functions is to help us manage differences by labelling them, but in so doing it tends to accentuate the experience of difference.

But language can also help identify the mistake of the intellect, tracing lesser mistakes back to their source in simpler, universal errors, thereby allowing wisdom and healing to prevail. Language can help, partly through its very capacity to register differences. Using language, we can identify unhelpful distinctions expressed in words. Conversely, through language we can group, generalize and dissolve differences. Language can acknowledge relationships and include. It can unify.

These twin tendencies reflected in language — to split and to fuse — are at the heart of how language can at once sustain and suspend both the mistake of the intellect and many of our lesser confusions. For NLP trainer Chris Hall, human difficulties arise from two simple miscategorizations that reflect these tendencies of language. We place things in

* the same category that should be in separate categories
* different categories that should be in the same category

As an example of the former, we might say that because we can't do something (sing, walk on water, or learn foreign languages), we are stupid/incompetent/incapable. Here our ability to do something means something about us. What we can do and what we are have been placed unhelpfully in the same category.

Conversely, someone might limit themselves by saying that they can't be both creative and practical. Creativity is perhaps associated with freedom and playfulness; practicality with being systematic and logical. When these two categories are collapsed into one, with practicality accepted as an important part of the creative process, a richer and more productive creativity becomes possible.

These two kinds of miscategorization are key ways in which the primary mistake of the intellect arises and is maintained. We fail to honour unity by placing ourselves in a separate category from the rest of creation. We separate parts of creation from each other, neglecting their relationship and connectedness. We group parts of creation inappropriately, bundling parts of our experience, and disregarding appropriate differences.

By recognizing how we miscategorize our experience with our words, we can undo limitations and open possibilities. Recognizing some of the forms of these two primary miscategorizations can help this process. For Chris Hall they include:

* **confusing internal images with outer reality**

(e.g., I get worried, because I imagine something is going to happen, and forget that my body is responding to the image, rather than reality. It has not yet happened and might never do so.)

* **allowing once or twice to mean always, every, or never again**

(e.g., I try something once, it doesn't work out, so I discount that class of experience for ever; I meet an unpleasant French or German person and take all French or Germans to be unpleasant.)

* **confusing identity with behaviour**

(e.g., I take something I can or can't do and consider it to mean something about me.)

* **forgetting that labels are not the same as what they refer to**

(e.g., Because someone calls me a name it doesn't mean that I am that. Talking about 'love' or 'learning' is not the same as experiencing them. We can call something 'love' or 'learning' but the label may be inappropriately applied.)

By listening carefully to language, we can identify such miscategorizations and sort them out more appropriately. Two key questions can help this process:

Does this necessarily follow?

How do I/you know that?

These questions used internally lead us to listen more carefully, and when used aloud help clarify a person's thinking. The first question helps monitor the logic in what is being said. The second checks that there is valid evidence behind an assertion.

With a friend, if possible, take a few minutes to think of four or five examples of each of these four kinds of miscodings, either in your own personal lives or among people you know.

Recall four or five moments when somebody said something to you about themselves or how they viewed life that didn't quite add up. What did they say? How did you recognize inside yourself that something didn't quite make sense? Was it a feeling or an image that you experienced? Consider what question might have been appropriate to ask and how you might have asked it in a caring way: "Oh, that's interesting, how do you know that is so?" "Oh really, if John leaves his clothes all over the floor, does that really mean he doesn't care about you?"

Imagine four or five situations in the future where somebody says something in the form of one of these miscodings. Imagine noticing your internal cue that you have sensed a miscategorization. Imagine responding appropriately to it.

Language and Aware Communication

Much of what passes for communication involves complacently assuming that information and experience have been accurately exchanged. We assume that the words we speak are understood in the sense we intended them, and that we understand the words of others correctly. In fact, we hallucinate understanding. In order to understand another's utterances, we are obliged to draw on our own representations of the meaning of words. Terms such as 'happiness', 'commitment', 'responsibility', or the 'organization' have a kind of dictionary definition that is to some extent shared. But such words also have intensely personal associations, which easily precipitates misunderstanding. Words are linked to pictures, thoughts, feelings, and sensations — stirrings in the stomach, energy on the inside, murmurings in the mind, expanding and contracting vistas in our inner space.

And not only the major terms by which we define our existence, but the little ones too. Words such as 'I', 'must', 'should', 'later' have a unique set of connotations beyond our usual conscious reach. We have our own images and associations for even simple things like 'cow' and 'milk'. These associations to a large extent define the characteristics of our personal maps. We understand the words we hear by means of our own internal storehouse of experience of both language and world. This is inevitably unique, because no one else has had exactly our experience of either words or life.

Naturally, there are similarities in our experience. We have analogous sensory apparatus. Our bodies have similar structures, with brains and hearts, and so on. Many of our experiences have some universality, such as night and day, sleeping, waking, birth, death, and so on. And increasingly the media offer experiences that are shared in some way around the world. These similarities allow us to share common names for things and thus to assume that what the words evoke are common. But these similarities mask the rough and ready nature of understanding. Even if we are supposedly talking about a shared experience, a party we were at or a book or film we both enjoyed, we are still dealing with unique experiences. If you and I describe a sunset we experienced together, our physical position will be slightly different from each other's. Different sensory and conceptual filters to our awareness at the time will have led us to notice different portions of our experience and give it a slightly different meaning in the context of our personal worlds. If we talk about our experience, my words will invite you to understand me with the elements of your own conceptual and sensory database. You will do this in a different way, recovering images and associations that are not only different in content but in their form. We will emphasize different sensory modalities and be influenced by different 'submodalities' of the same sensory system. If the experience was pleasant for us both, we are each recalling our own pleasure, even if they seem the same.

Because language involves our drawing on our often unconscious personal associations with other words, images, and feelings from our personal history, misunderstandings easily occur. Sometimes differences in our internal understanding don't matter, as we happily imagine our inner experiences to be the same. Sometimes it does, and real disagreements emerge, with added frustration arising from the assumption that we really should be able to understand one another. This we can observe in the futile circular arguments among couples and countries, where we observe the staunch affirmation of one reality (the speaker's) and the failure to understand and accept that the other party's reality is as valid and self-evidently true for them as ours is for you. Without some awareness of how we and others generate meaning, it will be difficult to avoid the continuance of the only real wars, wars between people's maps of reality.

Aware communication thus involves recognizing that

a)   we create our own understanding of what we hear inside ourselves
b)   others understand what we say from their personal experience
c)   what we each understand may be more different than we realize.

Where exact understanding is important, as in communicating information or instructions, or sharing a key personal experience, we can aid understanding by paraphrasing or summarizing what we heard. We can ask questions to clarify what is being said by the other person and to check our understanding. We can make our own language more precise, knowing that more concrete and specific words will invite the listener to draw from their inner database more exact representations of the words we use.

Conversely, where exact understanding is less important, as in some social contexts, we can promote understanding by being artfully vague in our use of language, allowing the other person to understand in their own way.

COMPARING REPRESENTATIONS OF WORDS AND EXPERIENCE

With a partner choose a word that labels a class of experiences that is important to both of you, such as 'happiness', 'satisfaction', 'enjoyment', or 'love'. Ask each other 'What is x for you?' Write down verbatim what is said.

Ask each other 'How do you know when you have x?' Check representations in all three primary sensory systems, by asking 'What do you see (inwardly or outwardly) when you have x? When you imagine or recall an experience of x, what kind of internal image(s) (if any) do you have? One or several; still or moving; near or far away; small or large or panoramic; bright or dim; colour/black and white? What do you hear or say to yourself when you have x? Where are the sounds or voices located? What is their tone, tempo, or volume? What do you feel when you have x? What kind of posture and muscle tonus do you have? Facial expression? What kind of sensations do you have in your body? Where are they located? What intensity and duration?

What sensory systems do you emphasize? How are your representations of the experience similar and how different? What is emphasized or deemphasised? What is similar or different in the language you used to describe x?

SORTING MISCOMMUNICATION DUE TO MISCODINGS

Review some instances of misunderstanding in your personal communication. How might your misunderstanding have been due to categorizing things differently from the other person — perhaps placing things that were probably in the same category for both of you in different verbal categories. (For instance, one person may think they have different expectations in a relationship, one wanting 'love', the other 'friendship', when actually these words may have similar meanings for both of them). Or perhaps things that were really in different categories for each person were described with the same words. (For instance, 'being faithful' in a couple might mean 'emotional fidelity' for one person and 'sexual fidelity' for the other).

Identify four examples of such miscoding in your experience of communicating with others or of observing others communicate. Imagine three or four ways you might have responded differently to sort out the misunderstanding. If these situations are likely to occur in the future, imagine noticing the miscodings and sorting them quickly and elegantly.

Key Language Patterns for Aware Communication

Using language with awareness involves listening to make sure we really understand what is being said. This means paying less attention to content, although this remains important, and more attention to the structure and patterning of how it is said. It involves a kind of dual attention, as if one is asking oneself two key questions:

What does this mean?
What does this presuppose?

The first question draws our attention to what has actually been said. It keeps us aware of what is actually there in the language and how fully we understand it. The second question helps us be aware of other elements of language or experience that have not been expressed, but may need to be made explicit if the communication is to make sense. These inner questions help guide us towards identifying the questions we need to ask in order to understand what is being communicated.

Listening with the filters set up by our two inner questions helps us notice key information that the speaker has deliberately or inadvertently **omitted** or that was implied in what was said, but not clearly specified. In a way, these questions ask us to attend, a) to what's there and, b) what's not there, but could or should be there.

Some linguistic elements may be left out completely, notably:

* the experiencing *subject* of what is being described: e.g. 'Living is easy.' 'There is no solution.' For whom?

* the *object* of the sentence: e.g. 'I am unacceptable.' To whom? 'I am afraid.' Of what?

* some *object of comparison*: e.g. 'I want a better job/house/life.' Better than what?

* the *source of a value judgement*: e.g. 'I am ugly/intelligent/happy, etc.' According to whom?

* the *basis for knowledge of another's internal world* ('mind-reading'): e.g. 'She loves cabbage'. How does the speaker know this?

Listening attentively, we may notice other elements of language, which may be present, but **inadequately specified**, thereby preventing real understanding. For instance, a person may use *pronouns* without it being clear who or what is being referred to. 'It worries me.' 'What's worrying you?'

Any *noun* or *verb* may need some amplification to understand what it means. 'Let's get some results.' 'What kind of results do you want and how should they be achieved?'

Although *adjectives* and *adverbs* are supposed to make the noun or verb they modify more specific, they often reveal very little. They may need further clarification, either in their own right or as part of the noun or verb to which they refer: 'She's a nice person'. 'In what way is she nice?' 'She's treated him kindly.' 'In what way did she treat him kindly?'

One class of nouns may need particular attention. *Abstract nouns*, or 'nominalizations', such as 'love', 'communication', 'relationship', offer enormous possibilities for misunderstanding. Such words summarize so much of a person's experience that it may take a while to unravel the intended meaning. For instance, with the word 'communication', one might need to ascertain who or what is communicating to whom and in what way. One may need to know what kinds of processes are summed up as 'communication'.

Listening with curiosity to what is presupposed by a person's words will also help us notice examples of the **'language of limitation'** — words and phrases that indicate how a person constricts their world. *Modal operators* — verbs such as 'can', 'want', and 'must' — are particularly important. They indicate the relationship between the knower and the action indicated by the main verb. They express what is possible, impossible, or obligatory. Of the three main kinds: Possibility, Necessity, and Volition, the first two are particularly important because they suggest both blocks and compulsions:

'I can't speak in public.'

'I must be good.'

'I mustn't eat between meals.'

If it is appropriate to find out about the nature of the limitation, we might ask, 'What stops you?' and 'What would happen if you did?' These help recover the perceived cause of the rule the person has set themselves and the imagined consequences of breaking it.

Notice also the presence of words that are absolutes, such as 'always', 'never', 'no-one', 'everyone' and 'nothing'. *Universal quantifiers* indicate that the speaker has so generalized their experience that exceptions are discounted. This can be a severe limitation. 'I always say things like that'. 'Always?'

Besides being alert to what is said or unsaid in the words used, it is important to notice patterns that repeat. Some of the language patterns we have described may recur frequently in a person's use of language. For instance, in watching the presentation of an old-style autocratic senior manager to a group of middle managers that a large multi-national wanted to function in a more autonomous and empowered way, I counted in one hour about sixty 'have tos' and 'musts'. In encouraging autonomy, this manager could not forget his old ways nor would his audience fail to notice the fact on some level, even if they were not consciously monitoring his modal operators. Other more flexible senior managers hardly used such modal operators at all.

Identifying recurrent patterns often involves stepping back a little inwardly to notice what happens repeatedly. It is as if we are inwardly asking questions such as: 'What is typical about this person's use of language? What patterns tend to recur again and again?'

SOME OTHER LANGUAGE PATTERNS

We may also notice other patterns in language, for instance, words pointing to a preferred channel of thinking — feeling words, such as 'feel', 'sense', 'grasp', 'moved' or visual words, such as 'see', 'insight', 'look', 'imagine', or hearing words such as 'tell', 'sound', 'say', 'hear'. A person may also tend to use *abstract* or *concrete* words, talking in generalities or specifics. Or the language may be more *active* or *passive*. A person may emphasize *moving towards* what is desired or *away from* what is not wanted. He or she may emphasize what is *present* or what is *missing* and may refer much to self or never talk about *self* and focus exclusively on *others*. Language may also point to preferences in perceptual position, level of experience, and time-frame.

Notice also figurative and *metaphoric* language that a person uses, including 'dead' metaphors. These can indicate important ways in which a person organizes their experience of the world and may need exploration for deeper understanding.

Take some time when you are watching television or listening to the radio (particularly news interviews), when the content is not important to you, to notice language patterns. Listen to the patterns of politicians or other public figures. What questions might you want to ask to engender greater precision or understanding?

With a partner, practise generating many examples of each of these patterns (see the summary chart), one at a time. Practise responding to them. Once you begin to get the hang of each question, make sure you ask it in a tone and tempo that is sympathetic rather than aggressive. Soften your questions a little with phrases such as, 'I'm not sure I've understood you, could I ask something . . .' Or 'That's interesting, what . . .' Or 'I'm curious . . .'

EXPLORING SELF-TALK

And how about communication with ourselves?

1. Take some time to get comfortable and settled. Attend to your inner voice. Is there one or more than one? If there is more than one voice, focus on the one that seems most important. Notice its location. Where do you appear to hear it — centrally or to one side, and if the latter, which side? Is it at the level of the head or lower down at the level of the chest. Does it appear to arise inside or outside the body?

Notice the tone, tempo, and volume of the internal voice your hear. Is it pleasant? Unpleasant? Constant? Does it change of its own accord? What happens if you speed up its tempo or slow it down or increase or decrease its volume? Does it seem like your own or someone else's? If the latter, whose? What type of content is this voice using? Is it giving you information, commenting, questioning, upholding, putting down? What is its relation to you? Friendly, hostile, etc.?

2. Notice what your inner voice is saying. Write it down, verbatim, as much as possible. If there is more than one voice, repeat steps 1 and 2.

3. With a partner, if possible: think of a context where your are successful and at ease, or of a goal that you have achieved. As you imagine being in this context where you are successful, what things are you inclined to say to yourself? Speak out your internal dialogue as it comes up, while your part-

ner writes down what you say verbatim. What kind of voice is it? Does it sound like your own? Where does it seem to be located?

Now, think of a context that troubles you, where you perhaps do less well than you think you could, or think of a goal that eludes you. Again speak out the kind of internal dialogue you might have, with your partner writing down verbatim what you say to yourself.

What kind of voice is it? Does it sound like your own or someone else's? Where is it located? Is there any difference between this voice and the voice associated with the successful context in either its quality (tone, tempo, volume, etc.) or content? Any difference in how you feel in relation to the two voices?

What else might you say in this second context that might be more helpful? How might you speak to yourself more usefully. Try different qualities and content to your internal voice. Have your partner help you by speaking in a way that you can then internalize.

4. Together consider the patterns in the structure of the language. What person does the voice use predominantly, 'I', 'you', or 'we'? What mix of statement, question, and command? What other language patterns do you notice?

5. Repeat steps 3-4, but this time first think about someone you love and get on well with and then someone with whom your relationship is more troubled.

6. Given what you have discovered about your self-talk, how might you talk to yourself differently?

DEEPENING SENSITIVITY TO LANGUAGE
Read the poem (by G.M. Hopkins) below silently to yourself to familiarize yourself with it. Sit comfortably in a poised and upright posture, with your spine vertical and your back unsupported. Then read the poem slowly out loud, as if you are taking your time to enjoy a delicious meal. Take second position with the poem, entering fully into it. Delight in each sound articulating it fully, enunciating it deliberately and with feeling. Exaggerate. Let the sound of the language resonate within your body. Experiment with adjusting the height in your body at which you feel the language — in the head, the throat, the chest, and belly. (Both the pitch of the words and where you seem to be breathing from will change as you do this). What seems to give you most delight in the process of reading? Read the poem a couple of times. How does your experience of the language change?

Now read the poem silently again, allowing yourself to feel the language quietly resonating within you.

PIED BEAUTY
Glory be to God for dappled things —
For skies of couple-colour as a brinded cow;
For rose-moles all in stipple upon trout that swim;
Fresh-firecoal chestnut-falls, finches' wings;
Landscape plotted and pieced — fold, fallow, and plough;
And áll trádes, their gear and tackle and trim.
All things counter, original, spare, strange;
Whatever is fickle, freckled (who knows how?)
With swift, slow; sweet, sour; adazzle, dim;
He fathers-forth whose beauty is past change:
Praise him.

Choose one or two other pieces of writing that you like and repeat this process. Take some language that you don't like or a paragraph or two from the popular press. Notice what happens to your experience.

BECOMING MORE SENSITIVE TO, AND AWARE OF, OTHERS' LANGUAGE

Listen carefully to the voices and tonalities of people you meet and those your hear talking around you or on radio or TV.

Notice people who use language gracefully and are good to listen to (sound and content), and those that appear to make you feel less than good.

When you are not actively engaged in a conversation, practise listening to a portion of speech — from a phrase to a sentence or two. Hear the phrase or sentence and then hear it again in your own head, as if you are replaying what you have just heard. Practise this till you can do it comfortably.

Now, practise listening, replaying a portion of speech internally, and then saying it outloud in your own voice using the intonation patterns of the person you are listening to as closely as possible.

When you have done this for a while, can you improvise speech as if you were this person talking?

What do you intuit about them as a result of modelling their speech patterns?

Language and Balance in the Bodymind

Because language is an instrument of the bodymind as a whole, it expresses more than we may consciously intend — in what we say, what we omit, and how we actually say what we say. Through voice tone and gesture, the bodymind expresses itself more fully than we might wish or notice. Our language inevitably expresses deep and pervasive patterns in our way of relating to ourselves and the world. Attention to language as it is expressed through the body can help deepen our understanding of personal idiosyncrasies. It can highlight both passing and longer-lasting limitations and also indicate pathways to new possibilities.

When we enjoy integral awareness, we enter a state of 'well-being' in which all parts of ourselves are in harmonious relationship with each other. We live a state of balance and alignment in which the wholeness of living awareness gathers the different levels and tendencies of experience into a unified relationship, as the hand effortlessly holds our fingers and thumb in a firm and co-ordinated grip. When we enjoy well-being, our physical self and our ideas about it, our mind and body, and the different levels of experience, are all in accord. We experience a harmony between the different parts and the whole, which is reflected both in our words and in our body language, and in the match of the two. The message in our content is amplified by the message offered by our body. Tonality is appropriate for the content. Gestures tend to be symmetrical and balanced. We are congruent.

Conversely, any conflict or confusion among different parts of our experience with their varying needs is reflected in the language we use to refer to ourselves and our bodies. Voice tonality and gesture may suggest something different than content. Doubts and divisions give double or triple messages. We are incongruent.

For instance, at a job interview we may say: "I want the job" (head thinking the money would be useful). But the voice trails away a little, as a result of the heart musing, "But I'd rather be doing something I really enjoyed", while our arms and legs are crossed and our head leans forward, as if to say "And I don't feel safe with you anyway" (gut). Such mixed communications can obstruct straightforward communication, if we get confused or respond to the wrong part of the message. They can also be a valuable way of moving towards a deeper level of understanding and integration if we are aware of them and respond appropriately.

CONGRUENT AND INCONGRUENT COMMUNICATION — OTHERS'

Review four instances in which you experienced other people being very congruent in their communication. What are the common elements you notice? What lets you know they are congruent? What are the external cues you pick up? How do you respond internally to congruence in others?

Review four instances in which you recognized another person as being incongruent in their communication with you. What was the structure of each instance of incongruence? What were the different messages you were receiving and through which channels?

What were the external cues that let you know they were being incongruent? What was the common cue that let you know inside: 'incongruence'?

Was it a feeling, an image, or something else?

Review the four examples again and notice where you sensed the other person's voice to be located — in the head (nasal), throat, chest, abdomen. How did the voice tonality relate to gestures, posture, and content?

With each of the four instances, review how you responded to the incongruence. Did you respond to the incongruence as a whole or to just one of the messages? If you responded to part of the message, which did you respond to? The verbal or the non-verbal (gesture, posture, tonality)?

Project yourself into four instances in the future where you might encounter incongruence. Imagine how you might respond, a) sooner, b) more appropriately. Identify three possible responses in each of the four situations and imagine yourself making those responses.

CONGRUENT AND INCONGRUENT COMMUNICATION — OUR OWN

Recall four or five instances when you were completely congruent in your communication — your content, voice, and posture supported each other; your whole inner and outer expression was of one clear message, for instance, when very angry or when simply affirming something with complete conviction. Identify the elements to each situation. What are the exact cues that let you know you are congruent?

Take some time to review four or five instances when you noticed you were expressing yourself incongruently, giving mixed messages among content, voice tonality, and posture and gesture.

Notice what are the common cues that let you know that you are being incongruent — feelings in the body, images, or words or voice tone.

Incongruence lets you know that all parts of you are not in alignment. This is a valuable communication, because your unconscious is indicating that you need to take care of something either inside yourself or in the outside world. Explore each instance to identify the structure of the incongruence. What is the mixed message about? What parts of you seem to be pulling in a different direction? Is there a pattern? What positive function is the incongruence serving?

What can you do to respond constructively to your own incongruence? How could you honour the mixed messages you experience, respect their different intentions, and find a way to a unified message? (For instance, checking inside to find what you truly need; identifying what also needs to be taken care of before proceeding; taking time later to sort your own internal division; identifying the purpose and positive intention of the different parts giving different messages; and negotiating a solution that takes care of both needs.)

Take several moments to imagine yourself using three or four new responses in situations where you are likely to be incongruent in the future.

Imagine letting the initial signals of incongruence actually lead you towards three or four new behaviours that will serve your overall needs more completely.

LANGUAGE MATCHING THE PATTERNS AND ORGANISATION OF THE BODYMIND

Just as our two eyes, with their two slightly different images enable us to perceive the world with a sense of depth and distance, so the right and left sides of the body reflect complementary energies that are necessary for coherent functioning in the world — male and female energies, for instance, corresponding to outgoing directness, and flowing receptive energies. These energies need to be in dynamic balance with each other, or we might find ourselves too passive or too active, or lightweight and without stability when we are active, or leaden and inert when we are still.

The two sides of our body express themselves in our language. For instance, we often use the two sides of the body verbally and gesturally to mark out dichotomies of experience, such as past and future, active and passive, mother and father, and so on. Expressions such as, 'on the one hand . . . on the other hand', mark out our dilemmas. Inner conflicts are often described bilaterally, with gestures by each hand in turn, accompanying phrases such as 'On the one hand I want to study and get on, on the other hand part of me just wants to watch TV and eat toasted marshmallows'.

To get a sense of the different energies in the two sides of the body, take a period of free movement without music. Go inside yourself and allow all your movements to come from and express the left side of the body for about five minutes. Only move that side of the body, allowing the other side to follow only as much as is necessary. Take a piece of paper and jot down a few key images and words that seem to express what you experienced with the left side of the body. Then come back to stillness and take about five minutes to allow the right side of the body to express itself. Jot down a few key images and words that seem to express what you experienced on this side.

What is the difference in the type and quality of movements you experienced? Which side of the body do you seem to be most at ease with? Take a few minutes to switch between moving the left and right sides in succession, until an integrated movement emerges that uses the whole body. Enjoy this movement for about four or five minutes, and then come to a place of rest and be still with your attention in the body for a while.

Our body is organized both bilaterally and along the vertical axis. Three main centres — the head, the heart, and the belly or gut — correspond to different energy systems crucial to our well-being[3]. The head is the centre of the subject, conscious awareness, the I, the knower, the seer, the thinker, the organizing centre of our capabilities. In the gut is our visceral identity, the me, the body-self, that is as an object to the knower in the head. The heart is the feeling centre of our life, placed between 'I' and 'me'; it is the locus of our beliefs and values. Traditionally associated with the unifying force of love, its physical manifestation beats steadily, sending life-nourishing blood to all parts of ourselves, from fingetips to toes. Well-being involves equilibrium and cooperation among these major vertical centres of 'head', 'heart', and 'gut', as well as between the two sides of the body.

The key syntactical elements of subject, verb and object correspond to the physiological organization of the three centres, head, heart and belly. Problems manifest in a lack of balance and alignment among these centres. Two of them may be in conflict. Perhaps head and heart are in conflict or head and guts, with heart unable to perform its connecting and unifying role. Perhaps 'I' and 'me', mind and visceral instincts, pull in different directions. Or our energies may be absent from or trapped in some way in one or more of these centres, leaving key parts of the bodymind inert. Perhaps everything happens in the head and we are numb from the neck down, or perhaps we enjoy warm circuits between head and heart, but we are disconnected from our guts and lower organs, disassociated from womb or genitalia. Such imbalances will be reflected in the syntax of our sentences that sum up our woes. They will also be reflected in where we sense the different parts of speech as we reiterate and feel key expressions slowly within.

Perhaps an imbalance will be particularly connected with the subject or object of the sentence, or with the verb expressing the relationship between them. If we have a deep sense of some underlying problem that we express in a short phrase, such as 'I am unlovable', or 'Part of me is false', and notice where we experience each part of the phrase in our bodymind, we may find, for instance, that the 'unlovable' or 'false' are associated with our bodily 'me' in the guts.

Sometimes the statements we make are simply incomplete, with subject, or object or even the verb omitted. For instance, the statement, 'I am not lovable' begs a key question: to whom am I not lovable, myself or others? Who is making the judgment? 'Lovable' is, strictly speaking, not the object of the verb, but the complement to the subject of the sentence, in this case, 'I'. The 'I' is in some sense equated with being 'not lovable'. The 'I', however, is neither 'lovable' nor 'unlovable'. It simply is. It is being beyond attributes. Perhaps the 'I' in the head recognizes that the feelings of not being 'lovable' are located in the heart and really apply to self. Recovering the deleted portion of the sentence, 'to me', activates the belly and opens the way to release.

If we recognize where the energy flows and where it is stuck, it is possible to gently realign the different centres by allowing free-flowing energy to expand to connect with other centres so that the energy of each centre connects with and includes the others. If there is an unpleasant feeling or a block in one of the centres, we can simply allow our awareness to be easily with that feeling until the block shifts and dissolves and that area feels more comfortable.

We might then find a new phrase or sentence that fits the feeling of ease and completion in the bodymind we now have, honours the deeper truth of wholeness, and reflects love and acceptance of self and the inviolate freedom of pure awareness. Listening and feeling, feeling and listening until circuits are completed in the body, we move towards balance.

USING LANGUAGE TO BRING BALANCE TO THE BODYMIND

Think of a personal limitation that you would like to change. Express it in a short sentence (as few words as possible). Consider what is present in the sentence. What does each part mean? Notice what is missing. What is presupposed by the sentence? Do you sense a limitation behind the limitation? If so, form a short sentence and repeat the process you just went through with the first sentence. Recycle as many times as necessary, until you have a short sentence with a subject, verb, and an object that seems to express the essence of the limitation you are exploring.

Silently and slowly whisper each part of the sentence (subject, verb, complement) internally. Where do you sense each part of the sentence? Where in the body do you sense the limitation? Where does the energy seem full and where blocked — head, heart, or viscera? Allow the energy where full to expand and flow to the blocked parts. Allow any tension in the blocked part to dissolve, releasing energy there. Allow the energy to expand to flow to other parts. Continue until you have a greater sense of unified energy field in the bodymind.

What short sentence would express the opposite of the limitation or express its solution in a way that resonates with your sense of inner truth, so that you could say of it, 'Yes, that's it'?

Allow this sentence to resonate gently within you, word by word. Enjoy the sense of the energy of head interfusing heart and belly, of heart spreading to head and belly, of belly spreading to heart and head, and of the whole spreading throughout the body and into the space of which you are part.

Enjoy these feelings as you imagine being in a number of future contexts where you might otherwise have encountered this particular sense of limitation.

An Ancient Ritual for Balancing the Bodymind — The Sign of the Cross

Like many ancient prayers from different traditions, the Catholic Sign of the Cross, unites gesture and language, reminding us succinctly and elegantly to balance and align the bodymind, both within itself and in relation to the larger whole.

It starts with hands joined in the midline at the level of the heart. Then we place the left hand on the heart, and raise the right to the forehead, touching it with the middle three fingers, intoning, "In the name of the Father", (the knower, the transcendent, I, mind-consciousness). As we drop the right hand towards the belly, we say, "and of the Son" (the Christ, the immanent, Hopkins' 'Self of all Selving', me, body-consciousness). Next, we bring the right hand to the left shoulder, saying, "and of the Holy Spirit" (the link between Father and Son, Love), as we cross the midline to the right shoulder. This symbolizes the horizontal balance of the two sides of the body, masculine and feminine, with the heart again the connector ('and of the'). Finally, we join the hands palm to palm, pointing up from the heart, with "Amen".

This short prayer-ritual, done with gentle inner attention, re-enacts the whole process of psycho-physio-spiritual alignment. It honours the essential vertical alignment of the three major centres of head, heart and viscera, and the horizontal balance of the two complementary sides of the bodymind, active and receptive, masculine and feminine.

But its deeper meaning was never highlighted when we were little, and the daily ritual repeated in school before each lesson and meal was etched in memory as a hasty and rather meaningless gesture. Yet it encodes the essence of living awareness.

It summarizes the journey for many — from primary unity at conception to life in the head as language accelerates our expulsion from Eden, to exile in the Land of Concepts. Then we rediscover the unique pulse of our own identity as we begin to connect with our primary life-energies and the process of becoming who we are, in the body, as opposed to just in the head. From there, we complete integration of these by living fully from the great cross-roads of our existence in and from the heart, with the growth of universal love healing our inward psychic divisions and bringing us closer to connectedness with the creatures and creation in which we find ourselves. Finally, we complete our journey in balance and unity, gathered up in the dynamic stillness of being.

The Sign of the Cross is an invocation — 'In the name of' — that identifies gesturally the three persons of the Trinity with the three major centres of the bodymind. (The Father, God transcendant, is linked to the head; the Son, God immanent, to the viscera; and the Holy Spirit, Love, to the heart.) It reminds us of how we are made literally 'in the image and likeness of God'. Our psycho-physiological structure parallels the trinity of divine energies. That is why the invocation is 'In the name of'. We are acknowledging that we are reflections and reflectors of the Divine essence. In making the sign of the Cross with attention, we not only align ourselves with ourselves, but with the larger frame of the cosmic intelligence and energies which interfuse us all.

At the same time, this invocation is a dedication. 'In the name of' is like saying 'on behalf of', with the authority of, as a representative of. We place our major centres of energy and intelligence in the service of the divine energies, as well as inviting those cosmic energies to enthuse us, to animate and make us vehicles of the larger cosmic will, just as the sheriff places himself at the service of the law and makes himself available as a channel for the full authority of the law to uphold and support his actions. When he arrests 'in the name of the law', it is not a personal decision, but an align-ment with a higher authority, which in turn lends its dignity and weight to the actions undertaken in its name. He is able to call on the wider support that would not be possible if acting solely on his own behalf or 'taking the law into his own hands'. It is an act of both surrender and empowerment.

Our language, then, mirrors our own make-up and matches the language of nature as a whole. It remains deeply rooted in our body. Part of the return to wisdom involves recognizing that we not only speak our language, but it both speaks of us and speaks us. We need to be able to speak ourselves and be spoken in a way that allows our body wisdom to be heard by us and to heal us. The next chapter expands upon this theme as we consider the resolution of unhelpful beliefs and patterns in our lives — a process I call 'Open Heart Learning', which presupposes and extends the skills described in this chapter for resolving 'the mistake of the intellect'.

LANGUAGE OMITTING KEY INFORMATION			
MISSING OBJECT OR SUBJECT	*'I'm very curious'* *'Life is but a dream'* *'There's no escape'*	*'About what?'* *'For whom?'*	Recover missing object or subject
MISSING COMPARATORS	*'I want to do better'* *'She's the best cook'*	*'Better than what/whom?'* *'Compared to whom?'*	Identify the ref. point of the evaluation
VALUE JUDGEMENTS	*'He's the best writer'* *'Arabs are patient'*	*'According to whom?'* *'In what way?'*	Identify the nature/ source of the judgement
MIND READING	*'He doesn't like her'*	*'How do you know?'*	Identify the grounds for believing the claim
VAGUE LANGUAGE			
PRONOUNS	*'I like them'*	*'Whom or what do you like?'*	Establish who/what the pronoun refers to
NOUNS	*'I like antiques'*	*'What do you mean by antiques?'*	Identify what exactly the noun refers to
ABSTRACT NOUNS NOMINALIZATIONS	*'We expect success'*	*'Who will be doing what, in what way, to get what, when you have success?'*	Recover the process and subject-verb-object elements
VERBS	*'I am learning French'*	*'How are you learning it?'*	Identify verb's meaning
ADJECTIVES AND ADVERBS	*'That's good'* *'It's big'*	*'What do you mean by good?'* *'Big in what way?'*	Specify the meaning of the adjective or adverb
LANGUAGE OF LIMITATION			
MODAL OPERTORS POSSIBILITY/ NECESSITY	*'I can't do it'* *'I mustn't do it'* *'I have to do it'*	*'What stops you?'* *'What'll happen if you do?'* *'And if you don't?'*	Identify the boundary and consequences of transgressing it
UNIVERSAL QUANTIFIERS	*'I'm always fed up'* *'We never use consultants'*	*'Always?'* *'Never?' 'What would happen if you did?'*	Check for counter-examples and consequences of exceptions

SOME OTHER IMPORTANT PATTERNS

Abstract or Concrete? Active or passive? Moving Towards or Away?

Noticing what's present or missing? Reference to Self or Others?

Point of View: Own (*1st pos.*), Other(s) (*2nd pos.*); Detached (*3rd pos.*)

Level of Experience: *Environment, Behaviour, Capabilities, Beliefs/Values, Identity, Spiritual; Senses, Mind Intellect, Fine Felling, Awareness*

Time Frame: (*Past, Present, Future*) Sensory System: ('see', 'hear', 'feel', 'do' words)

COMMON LANGUAGE PATTERNS IN AWARE COMMUNICATION

NOTES

1.   Deepak Chopra, *Perfect Health: The Complete Mind-Body Guide*, Bantam Books, London, 1990, pp.131-2.

2.   For more on some of these patterns in language, see Bandler and Grinder's pioneering, *The Structure of Magic*, Science and Behaviour Books, Palo Alto, 1975, Vol I.

3.   Some esoteric systems describe a system of seven centres or *chakras*. Here, we emphasize three major centres in the bodymind that easily fit with most people's experience of important differences between the energies of head, heart and belly.

CHAPTER ELEVEN

Open Heart Learning: Updating Personal Patterns and Beliefs

Summary
When pure awareness animates our existence, we feel truly alive, in harmony with ourselves and with the world around us. We know who we are and what we should do. We are balanced and effective in ourselves, and others appreciate our coherence. Although this should be our normal state of life, we mostly settle for less. Here we recognize how limiting and conflicting 'patterns' in our personal maps of reality lead to incoherence in our thoughts and actions. We consider how to realign our maps so that we enjoy integral awareness and its support in our endeavours.

> ....*the world as we know it consists only of an agreement extracted out of every one of us.* Florinda Donner

A True Story

Once upon a time, there was a little girl. It was her first day at school. And she felt very nervous. Such a big place, so many rooms and long corridors. And mummy gone. So many children, some standing quietly, also unsure of themselves, a few quietly crying, some putting on a brave face. Other bigger ones rushing around confidently. A number of strange adults, some with gentle voices and a way of bending down and talking to you that made you feel at home. Others gruffer and more distant.

In the first class, time seemed to drag by. The little child desperately wanted to pee. Too shy to ask the teacher, she waited and waited, till she could wait no more. When it was time to move to the next room for art or games, she left feeling very embarrassed and wet, hoping that none of the other children would see.

They didn't but the teacher found the puddle and fetched the little girl. Towering above, she said sternly, pointing to the puddle: "Did you do that?" The child nodded, head bowed. "Now mop it up, and don't you dare do that ever again." So the child took the heavy-headed mop and pail from the corner and mopped it up.

By the time mother came to collect her, she had learnt a number of things on her first day at school: School is a dangerous place, teachers are not to be trusted, and the only place she was secure and loved was at home.

Many years later, as a mature adult, these learnings were still having a powerful influence on her, although the original incident had receded to a distant part of her memory.

Maps, Personal Patterns, and Coherence

Outer behaviour is an expression of our internal map — our particular configuration of beliefs, values, attitudes, hopes, and fears about self and world. Our map is the sum of these internal evaluations and their dynamic interaction. Through these evaluations we become and express who we are. Conflicts and kinks in our internal map result in incoherence in our actions in the world. And often the world responds accordingly. In contrast, when our internal map is coherent, our outer behaviour is powerful and coherent. We express our being with a force and 'rightness' that harmoniously and potently impacts the world around us. And our personal coherence attracts a positive and coherent response from it.

Our maps are highly structured. Pervasive patterns link the different parts of our individual and collective universes. These patterns are the product of the deep organizing tendency of the mind, which copes with both the singularity and variety of experience by grouping things according to likeness or difference. Grouping determines the internal structure of our maps. We learn new things by associating new elements to old through similarity or contrast. We create by noticing connections we had not noticed before. Through synthesis we unify fragmentation. This applies to learning and to our sense of self. Surface patterns — such as habits, mannerisms, recurring tendencies in speech — are the exposed edge of deeper pervasive patterns. These in turn make us who we are and profoundly influence what we do and how we do it.

Open Heart Learning, as outlined in this chapter, offers a fresh approach to exploring personal patterns in counselling or personal development. It helps us pinpoint and resolve deep and limiting confusions in our internal maps that obstruct our connection with inner being. It thereby helps us live with greater awareness, and express who we are more coherently and completely in everyday life.

Beliefs — at the Heart of Personal Patterns

Our beliefs form the core of our personal patterns. They determine what we give our attention to, what we withhold it from, and how we respond to people and events. They colour our awareness and direct our behaviour. In one direction they shape personal identity, defining what we are. In the other direction, they support and direct all the idiosyncratic manifestations of our personal patterns from where and how we live to the clothes we wear. Our beliefs determine the extent to which we live with awareness. Managing beliefs is an important part of Open Heart Learning.

Beliefs are what we hold to be true. They are generalizations about our experience, especially about *causes, meaning,* and *boundaries.*[1] For instance:
* 'smoking causes cancer'; 'poverty causes crime'; 'love makes me happy'
* 'freedom is our birthright'; 'people are basically good'; 'writing is fun'
* 'murderers should hang'; 'animals can't think like us'; 'I have to be nice'.

Beliefs enable us to live and function in the world. Our beliefs are what we have concluded to be true for ourselves or our world. Through beliefs we give meaning to the variety of our experience. This reduces its potentially bewildering complexity to something more manageable. Beliefs offer orienting signposts to help us navigate the otherwise unpredictable territory of life. Beliefs form the boundaries and contours of our internal map.

Beliefs are at the core of a contradiction. Without them we may be overwhelmed by the 'forest of symbols' unable to make distinctions, identify patterns, and thus to make choices. We may be so intoxicated by the immediacy of each atom of perception that we are unable to piece them together in a way that allows us to care for ourselves in the simplest way. We may miss the whole.

Yet through them we may create unnecessary limitations. Our beliefs may be mistaken, leading us to dead ends and diversions. We may live life at second hand experiencing ourselves and our world through a web of generalizations, deletions, and distortions, losing the beauty possible in our passage through life.

DESCRIPTIVE BELIEFS

Descriptive beliefs affirm what is, or rather what we think is. They ascribe attributes to ourselves or our world. They express opinions about the relationship between elements of our experience, often in the simple form $a = b$. For instance, 'I'm a writer', 'The world is round', or 'Insects have six legs'. Descriptive beliefs often make two longer phrases or sentences equivalent. For instance, 'She's a good person; she gives lots of money to charity'. Here 'giving lots of money to charity' is equivalent to 'being a good person'.[2] Descriptive beliefs may also specify causal relationships in the form $a > b$, or a 'causes' b. For example one may hold that 'a good education leads to success in life' or 'too much money makes you spoilt'.

When limiting descriptive beliefs appear, it is worth checking that the equivalence or causal relationship claimed is, a) intended and, b) supported by valid evidence. You can check that the connection made is intended by feeding back the belief as heard. Check the validity of the connection and the evidence for it by asking: "Does a necessarily $=/>b$?" or "How do you know that $a =/> b$?"

"So you consider that giving money to charity means that somebody is a good person? Does giving money to charity necessarily mean that somebody is a good person?"

"So you say that social security makes people lazy? How do you know that this is so?"

Sometimes reversing the claim may also test the belief: "So if someone didn't give money to charity, they wouldn't be a good person?" "If you didn't have a good education, you wouldn't be successful?"

INJUNCTIVE BELIEFS

Whereas descriptive beliefs sum up what we think we are and how the world is, 'injunctive' beliefs indicate the boundaries we set around self and world. They give permission, inhibit, and compel. Such beliefs indicate what we consider it is possible to be, do, or have. They also indicate constraints that we experience and areas where we have to be or act in a certain way.

The patterns of 'the language of limitation' described in the last chapter often indicate the presence of these beliefs. For instance, modal operators like 'can' and 'is possible' show that the speaker believes the action is possible or permissible, as in 'I can learn languages' or 'It is possible to be poor and contented'. In the negative, these modal operators of possibility and words such as 'mustn't', 'shouldn't', 'oughtn't' indicate restriction or inhibition: 'I can't understand you', 'It's not possible to be liked by everyone', 'I mustn't stay out late', 'I shouldn't think bad thoughts'. In the positive form, this last group of modal operators indicate areas where there is some obligation or compulsion for things to be a certain way: 'I should do my homework', 'I must feed the dog', 'I ought to like my relatives', 'I have to be good in order to be loved'.

Naturally, descriptive and injunctive beliefs overlap. For instance 'Universal quantifiers' such as 'everyone', 'always', or 'never', as in 'Nobody is ever nice to me' or 'People always take care of themselves first' make these descriptive beliefs potentially injunctive, as we find ourselves forced to discount possible exceptions. Expressions such as 'Always smile' or 'Never trust a stranger' are even more injunctive. Their implied modal operators, 'you must' and 'you shouldn't' indicate personal rules that 'must' be obeyed.

PRESUPPOSITIONS

More insidious are beliefs couched in the form: if a, then b. The sentence 'If you loved me, you'd smile more', for instance, contains several descriptive beliefs: You don't love me; you don't smile enough; people who love smile often at those they love; your not smiling means you don't love me. With statements in this 'if then' form, beliefs which are accepted as already true (you don't smile often; people who love smile often) may not be made explicit and hence pass unquestioned. Robert Dilts tells how a doctor who disapproved of the therapeutic work he was doing with his mother when she had cancer, said to her, "If you love your family, you won't leave them unprepared". Dilts aptly calls this statement a "thought virus". It slips into the hearer's mind the doctor's own belief that her cancer would lead to her death, concealed by the more legitimate belief that if we care for someone we don't just disappear.

LEVELS OF BELIEF

Some of our beliefs are close to consciousness and subject to logical scrutiny. For instance, we may believe that the world is flat, and, on being shown pictures of it from space, or on circumnavigating it, or studying the curvature of the earth's surface, change our mind. Such mutable beliefs are relatively superficial. Some would call them 'opinions' to distinguish them from the more personal, patterning beliefs discussed here.[3] Superficial beliefs — such as whether pigs can fly or how full we are likely to be after eating a piece of cake — usually conceal more general and constant beliefs about the nature of reality. Periodically, these may come into question and be readjusted. The resultant changes can be widespread and long-lasting in a person's life. In religious conversion, for instance, a realignment of conscious beliefs profoundly impacts career, relationships, and personal habits, in a revaluation of every aspect of life.

Often the deeper level of beliefs are 'forgotten' and remain unquestioned. These now unconscious beliefs become assumptions that influence us unconsciously. For instance, we may consciously espouse the scientific model at some point in our life. It then forms the basis for a certain way of evaluating our experience of the world and the information that comes to us. We may forget that this whole approach is based on ultimately unverifiable assumptions — such as the notion that there is an objective reality independent of subjectivity.

At a still deeper level, many of our conscious beliefs and the unconscious assumptions behind them may be influenced by beliefs that are so intangible that they are normally outside our conscious awareness, just as we are normally unaware of the windowpane as we look out of the window. For instance, behind our espousal of the scientific method there may be influential feeling-beliefs to do with inner security, such as 'The world isn't safe' or 'I'm not safe' or 'To know more is to be more'. Such beliefs are formed so early on that they are ordinarily consciously inaccessible. These are the 'core' beliefs, the primary beliefs that provide the framework for subsequent evaluations concerning the meaning of our experience. Core beliefs impinge most strongly on our ability to live with full awareness. Open Heart Learning helps us identify and realign such core beliefs and assumptions.

How Beliefs are Formed

Most core beliefs have their roots early on in our life. A belief is an evaluation or decision to enable us to respond to the new with the benefit of past experience. Such learning begins early, at least in the womb. Our infant self is already experiencing pleasurable and painful sensations, sometimes of considerable intensity, with a sensitive, newly formed bodymind that does not have the adult's library of experience and language to explain them. The baby has to make sense of what it experiences, as best it can, particularly as some of what it experiences may be overwhelming. Living awareness may be swamped by intense sensation. The infant 'I' may feel its very existence threatened. The child's mind will attempt to understand and manage such experience as best it can. Typically, it will make generalizations about self, others, the external world, and reality itself. According to what we take our 'I' to be — our behaviour, our body, our feelings, or, too rarely, own being-awareness — we will define our relationship with the larger whole, for instance, 'alone' or 'separate'. By extension, we may decide that we have little power, defining our selves as 'weak', 'vulnerable', 'inadequate', etc. We may decide that we have little worth, that we are 'bad', 'unlovable', 'not good enough', etc. In making the above evaluations, we will also decide whether the outside world is a 'safe' or 'dangerous' place. In effect, we decide to what extent and under what conditions it is good to be alive.

The forming of an evaluation is part cognitive and part affective. The affective part may include the feeling aspect of the experience that the intellect attempts to explain or which motivates the intellect to draw conclusions about associated causes, meaning, or boundaries involved in the experience. The intensity of feeling in some of our experiences — rage, anger, fear, joy, sadness — may subside, but it remains as a memory pattern associated to people, places, things, or situations. Whenever we encounter these again, the original feelings may be triggered in whole or part.

We may also find that the bodymind is locked into an automatic response to stimuli in daily life. We may experience a compelling tendency to move away from things that made us feel bad and were classed as such or move towards things that made us feel good and were classed as such. If being in a group of people made us frightened, we may have decided that being in groups of people is not safe. We may feel frightened subsequently whenever we are in — or even likely to be in! — groups of people. We may simply avoid situations where we might find ourselves in groups, without knowing why. Conversely, if a certain uncle with a white beard was kind to us and made us feel safe and loved, we may conclude that people with snowy beards are good to be with, and find ourselves irresistibly attracted to people with such beards.

Beliefs are thus held in place by compelling physiological and affective forces. Beliefs are connected to the autonomic nervous system; the body responds when deep beliefs are engaged with changes in its internal chemistry whether we like it or not. For instance, when someone believes strongly that 'you've got to be realistic', the origins of the belief may be obscure and the associated reasons for holding it more or less rational, but the feelings held in the body demand compliance. It is as if the body says, this is how it is. The bodymind responds automatically when this belief is challenged, becoming defensive or aggressive refusing compromise or change. This is fortunate for stability and structure in our lives. It would be utterly confusing to alter deep beliefs at whim. But the tenacity of beliefs can make the pursuit of what we truly love and care for extremely difficult.

Beliefs then involve three important elements: a) the belief-forming experience or experiences which provide the initial material to be understood, and b) the evaluation or decision about what the experience might mean for that time *and for the future*. This is cognitive, but closely linked to c) an affective, feeling state in the bodymind, which is triggered in contexts to which the belief is linked. The affective state locks the belief in place and when activated ensures that we respond to it, consciously or unconsciously in ways that may or may not be helpful — for instance, panic arising in the context of public speaking, preventing good performance or even any performance at all.

Two key kinds of experience lead to the formation of beliefs: repetition and catastrophic events. Parts of our experience that are frequently reinforced or are a permanent part of our world influence us by their constancy, just as the dripping of water can eventually wear away the hardest stone. If an experience is repeated often enough, we eventually make generalizations from it. For instance, if we are constantly deprived of attention by our father, we may draw conclusions about ourselves, about men, or about how we have to behave with them — 'I'm not worthy', 'I'm invisible', 'Men are distant', 'I have to whine/get good results/be seductive to get attention'.

We also draw conclusions from major marking experiences or 'imprints'. Any sudden impactful experience prompts our inner intelligence to understand it as best it can, so that we can cope with it in the present and are prepared for any recurrence in the future. A single powerful experience may lead to generalizations that include whole classes of events, to which we respond with an 'avoid at all costs' thereafter. For instance, humiliation in front of a class as a pupil can lead to avoidance of all occasions that might involve speaking in front of a group. One strong experience can result in generalizations that affect how we relate to large areas of our life. Imprints create key filters through which we evaluate reality. They result in many of our core beliefs.

Around our core beliefs, whether formed by a sudden catastrophe or long repetition, other beliefs accrue. These secondary beliefs are contingent upon how our core beliefs lead us to filter reality — safe or shaky, open or fear-based. We may forget the original decision, but it continues to affect us in countless, and not necessarily useful ways. Existing beliefs distort our perception of any new information coming into our world, unless it is so compelling that it can modify or displace the existing structures. Even if it does, the old beliefs may remain in place influencing the new. Religious conversion may result from a compelling spiritual experience. It may turn us upside down changing our conscious belief-set, but we remain who we are, influenced by long-forgotten elements of our personal map. Part of us may treasure a loving God, but at a deeper level, we may still respond to the unconscious influence of a vengeful God we may have created as a child.[4] St Paul's experience on the road to Damascus changes his life, but his new relationship with Christ is mediated through an internal world that colours how that experience ultimately manifests in his life, setting the tone of Pauline Christianity.

Our little schoolchild may well have forgotten the conclusions made on that first day at school, but unless there are compelling contrastive experiences, her attitudes to learning, teachers, the outside world, and home may be influenced for life. She may leave school early, avoiding education and certain relationships. She may not enjoy anything outside the home, even if she really wants to. She and others may just assume that that's the way she is, with no recollection of why she 'naturally' responds to certain people, places, or situations or why part of her seems to sabotage attempts to meet challenges which others take in their stride.

Our unresolved misperceptions may influence us in another powerful way. We may unconsciously seek situations that reactivate aspects of experience linked to limiting beliefs. For example, if we were ignored by our father, being ignored by a man can trigger the original feelings of being rejected together with the related behavioural patterns. We may gravitate towards men who ignore us, until the belief-wound is healed. Our unconscious and in-built desire for wholeness and well-being is tenacious and can persistently lead us to situations for resolving mistaken learning and understanding.

Past experience, then, can lead to unhelpful internal structures in three important ways. First, we may make primary errors about ourselves, others, or the world. These are compounded by subsequent experience, because our starting premises are false. An ordinarily well-nurtured infant's fear and distress on being left cold and wet for some hours may become an inarticulate decision that nothing and nobody can be trusted, because just when he was counting on those basic needs being met, they weren't. Through this filter, all else may be interpreted. Good periods in life are then just fragile 'exceptions' to the rule. Our particular primary errors and their corollaries set the patterns peculiar to our personality.

The second way in which past experience leads to unhelpful internal structures is by our inappropriately adopting others' beliefs. Our core beliefs may have a coherency of their own, matching harmoniously in the bodymind, to create the personal tones and tints of who we are. As a child we may be happy and harmonious and express a personal mix of needs and wants that are very much part of who we are. Every parent recognizes that their new born baby is no blank slate, but already at birth a unique some-body. But through insistence or catastrophe as a child, we may take on the beliefs and values of significant figures around us: parents, teachers, power-ful friends. Important people in our lives may have conveyed through their words or actions a view of reality or of us that we take as our own. To hear repeatedly the message "you'll never amount to anything", or to be treated as if this is the unspoken message, may eventually lead to the belief becom-ing our own. Somewhere inside we may end up saying to ourselves: "It must be true; they believe it so strongly and they are more experienced then I am." And so we have a new belief affecting our experience. Personal pat-terns then may accommodate twisted strands of primary errors, some our own, some ill-matched and borrowed from outside, creating conflict inside us. We may find ourselves pushed and pulled in different directions, even to the point of personal paralysis. On the one hand, we may want to dance and play, on the other, we may have the borrowed message that life is a serious business in which laughter has no place.

We may also be influenced by others' beliefs in a more subtle way as we internalize the unspoken assumptions of our family, society, and culture. Such beliefs are particularly influential as they are often generalizations, not just about one's individual self, but about the world that are taken for granted by many significant others. Examples of such presuppositions are unconsciously held beliefs in the family that 'you've got to take care of yourself' or 'people are self-serving' or 'you've got to put others first'. These may be picked up almost by osmosis, because they influence the behaviour of the social group often without being made explicit or challenged and other beliefs get built around them. In my own childhood, in the early 1950s, there was still rationing in Britain. There was a feeling in the air that 'there is not enough'. That influenced me subtly to believe that you have to make do with limitation. The writer and explorer of authentic movement, Tony Crisp recognized from dreams that although he was brought up in Britain, somehow, through his Italian father, he had picked up an old message from rural Italy that the ordinary person should 'keep his head down'. This un-conscious belief or presupposition had influenced not only his father, but himself.

Whether our limiting beliefs are personal confusions, whether they have been imposed on us by others, or whether they are unspoken assumptions from our family or culture, they ultimately are all of a piece: they fracture wholeness in some way. All these mistaken evaluations, these limiting be-liefs, are subsets of a universal core mistake: *pragyaparad*, the mistake of the intellect. First, we take ourselves as separate individuals divorced from the larger whole. Then we lose our unitary nature in the apparent divisions and differences of all else. All other errors compound this one, generally leading to limiting perceptions about our own power and worth. We may as we mature in self-knowledge and wisdom find that we need to readjust many limiting beliefs and presuppositions. But ultimately they amount to the recovery of an unshakeable realization that our individual self is an expression of the undifferentiated ocean of being-awareness; it is not just within and part of the larger whole, but is one with that whole; the diversity of life is more apparent than real; the larger pattern is unitary.

Before wholeness becomes more than a mere concept, we may need to glimpse it many times. We may need to resolve some of the lesser confusions of our personal patterns and beliefs. And we will probably need to confront the key misperceptions that sustain the primary mistake of the intellect. That is the thrust of Open Heart Learning.

Uncovering Patterns — Open Heart Learning

Uncovering deep patterns — whether our own or another's — is a delightful and liberating experience. For these patterns are the web and woof of who we are, spreading across the various contexts of our life — home, holidays, hobbies, our labours, likes, and loves — and through the different levels of our experience, uniting our often split personal and professional worlds. In uncovering our personal patterns, we recognize how we are who we are.

And it is not difficult. The necessary tools are already inherent in the mind's natural patterning ability, its tendency to differentiate and synthesize experience. The first step is simply to acknowledge our own pattern-making capabilities, to recognize the pervasiveness of patterns in a patterned universe, and allow ourselves to begin noticing them.

Careful attention, not just to the content of a person's speech or behaviour, but to its underlying structure will reveal elements of patterns. Even our possessions, say, a gold ring, a Seiko watch, or a personal organizer, have a relationship, because they are ours. Simple questions inwardly asked, such as 'How does this relate to that?' or 'What are these examples of?' invite us to uncover the thread connecting the apparently unconnected.

Such questions asked of others invite them to discover the unifying pattern, even if they have not been consciously aware of it till then. As elements are connected on one level of experience, they are automatically grouped on a higher or deeper level, just as Herefords, Frisians, and Black-belted Galloways are all cattle, so cattle and cats are both mammals, as are mice and monkeys, and these are part of the larger grouping of vertebrates, and ultimately of all living things. In the same way, our ring, watch, and organizer are connected because of their importance to us. For one person, they may be examples of 'having the right things' or not being different, for another they may be expressions of 'quality'. In both cases, they point to the deeper level of beliefs and values, which colour and create our identity. Simple questioning can also work in the other direction, by allowing us to recover the specific implications of a generalization we may have forgotten. For instance, someone might say that they are easily confused. Confusion is a pattern in their lives. Questions such as 'What are instances of this?' or 'Can you tell me how this actually manifests in your life?' unveil the unique internal representation which accompanies almost every word we speak. They give the specific petals of a pattern.

Normally we are like icebergs to each other and even to ourselves, not in the temperature of our relations, but in the great hidden depths of our private minds which are only hinted at by our outer behaviour. We may guess connections, but it's safer to ask until we are sure that our guesses are accurate. Our guesses from the few hints and suggestions offered by a person's actions, gestures, and words are often shadows of the truth, widely distorted, crudely simplified, and grossly inaccurate. Too easily we create the equivalent of cardboard cut-outs from flesh and blood people. So often we hear statements like 'I can't understand why John does *xyz*.' It is true, we don't understand. And full understanding is unlikely unless we come to inhabit John's internal world. This becomes easier as we come to know the unique contours of our own maps, and the amazing richness and variety of those of others.

A few questions skilfully asked, such as 'what do you mean by *x*?' can be illuminating, particularly once we understand how each of us stores experience in the mind in a unique way, and how language serves as a rudimentary shorthand for the rich resonances of personal experience.

From simple surface patterns, deeper beliefs and patterns easily emerge with careful listening and sensitive questioning. From these it is a small step to the core beliefs and patterns that have a pervasive influence on virtually every part of our lives. Core patterns are often primary mistakes that do some violence to life, either to the wholeness and unity of our own life, or to the outside world and our relation to it. But to uncover a core pattern is to feel that every part of our life, past, present, and even future is connected. This already begins to restore that sense of wholeness so central to personal coherence.

Core patterns surprise us, like long forgotten truths that explain so much. If we already knew what they were, we probably wouldn't be influenced by the surface patterns linked to them that affect our life with compelling irrationality, such as having to wash up, no matter how late it is. In fact if core patterns do not surprise they are probably not core patterns at all. We are not engaged, deeply aware of the fabric of our life, but dabbling on the level of the mind.

To help others recognize incoherent core patterns through Open Heart

Learning takes an awareness that is, ideally, already aligned and imbued with the experience and understanding of that wholeness which supports, sustains, and suffuses all the more manifest levels of experience from identity to action. When we live life from pure awareness, we are no longer the erratic marionette of our own impulses. Nor do we need to try to be who we are, because we are, quite simply, who we are. Pure awareness allows us to perceive ourselves and others within the framework of balanced yet lively wholeness. Our responses are in the moment to the moment, wholly and appropriately. This is wisdom. We recognize this quality when we encounter it in others. But it is very rare, and most of us require a lengthy re-education process in which glimpses and glimmerings lead us towards the quiet core in which we instantly and utterly know what is what.

Until pure awareness becomes the mirror in which we reflect the moment's truth, we benefit from both experiential and intellectual insight into our life's deeper nature. Going to the well, fetching water, learning about the nature of the well and the water, as well as using and losing each draught. For me meditation over long years and the descriptions by my teacher of the qualities of the ground of all things have helped greatly. As awareness and understanding grows, we recognize the intrinsic nature of that awareness more and more easily. What and how it is become self-evident.

Certainty, truth, beauty, life, joy, appreciation, wholeness, peace, unboundedness, reconciliation of opposites, such as balance between inner and outer, poise of dynamic and static energies, combined strength and delicacy — these are some of the qualities that inhere in pure awareness and result from its experience.

Incoherent patterns stand out against this knowing backdrop with grating cognitive dissonance. If there is any doubt check the pattern's impact on the person's life. With incoherent patterns there is always damage and dislocation. When someone says, after a long internal sweep: 'I have never been able to accept myself'; it is clear that this pattern is incoherent. It violates the very nature of life, in which ultimately we are unified and whole. Here part of the self disavows and divides itself. This may have pervasively coloured every fragment of every moment of this person's life, but it is not really who he or she is, for pure awareness is undivided. Nor does it judge. It is.

In contrast, coherent patterns align positively with core awareness and allow the individual to enjoy expressing the pattern harmoniously through every level of the experience. When we are actively expressing a coherent core pattern, the body becomes poised and aligned. There is a glow and joy to the skin, an energy and grace to expression. We are congruent.

In exploring core patterns with people through Open Heart Learning, I have to settle to a deeper level of self and open my heart to accommodate more. To identify a core mistake, I align myself with that state of awareness in which higher truth is self-validating. I have to reduce my own divisions and separations, correct my own mistake. I have to accompany the other person on the journey into deeper levels of self, and open as they open. Coherence communicates; as does incoherence. If the relationship is not one in which there is a sense of engagement, trust, open exchange, in a mutual deepening, it doesn't leave the rutted routes of daily discourse. In moving to a state in which the truth of life is reaffirmed in another, I inevitably reaffirm my own truth. That is very rewarding and enlivening.

Developing Skills for Exploring Beliefs and Patterns

PATTERNING QUESTIONS

Uncovering and exploring patterns, whether alone or with others, requires the ability to sort experience hierarchically. Questions such as those listed below help one to explore the same level of experience, go to a deeper, more encompassing level of experience, or come out to the level of detailed behavioural examples. It is worth practising using these questions with a partner or friend or even by yourself till they become familiar. Eventually, you will learn how to use them flexibly and sensitively in exploring patterns.

QUESTION	PURPOSE
A. What are other examples of this kind of thing [specify it] for you?	To find other instances of a similar type. This question helps us begin finding a pattern. The person asked will group the other examples according to his own organizing principle.
B. What is this [specify] an example of for you?	This question invites the person asked to moves to a more general, grouping level of experience.
C. Could you give me an example of this [specify]? What are some examples of this [specify] for you?	To move from the general to specific examples. This clarifies and builds potential 'leverage', by reminding the person how the pattern actually affects his or her life.
D. How does this [specify] relate to that [specify] for you?	To uncover the connection between one portion of a person's experience and another.
E. What do you mean by this [specify]? What is this [specify] for you?	To identify the specifies referred to by a particular word. To ascertain the personal meaning attached to a word or phrase.
F. What does this presuppose? What has to be true for this to be true?	To find a level of meaning or belief which underlies or is implicit in what is being said.

PATTERNING QUESTIONS

EXAMPLES OF USING THE QUESTIONS

QUESTION A

If somebody has a noticeable behavioural pattern, perhaps he or she complains of never leaving enough time to get to appointments without rushing, or he or she is wearing a splendid collection of rings on all five fingers, you can begin finding more about the pattern by asking some form of question A: 'You seem to like rings a lot, what are other examples of things in your life like these rings?' Or 'You say you have a pattern of not leaving yourself enough time, are there other habits or patterns in your life like this one?'

QUESTION B

Perhaps, besides the rings the person has a collection of necklaces or brass ornaments at home. To find the pattern that groups these together, ask questions such as: 'What are these rings, necklaces, and ornaments all part of for you? What links them all together in your life? What are they examples of for you?' Asking 'What's important about these rings, etc. for you?' will also unfold the grouping pattern, since the grouping element in our personal patterns inevitably involves values and beliefs.

QUESTION C

If someone makes a general statement, such as 'My relationships never seem to work' or 'I'm a failure', it may be that neither the asker nor the person asked are fully aware of the concrete implications in daily life. To open up how the pattern manifests, ask a question, such as: 'Can you give an example (some examples) of this? Can you identify some instances of how this manifests in your life?'

QUESTION D

This question can be useful if we sense that two pieces of information are connected in some way — say a tendency to go to lively parties and to take risks in sport. We might ask how these two facts relate to each other. Sometimes we might be confused by an apparent contradiction and seek to clarify a particlar connection. For instance, if someone says they like fresh air, but stays indoors a lot, we might ask "How does this (the former) relate to that (the latter)? This question can be a valuable one to have at the back of one's mind, because it helps us to be alert for the 'pattern that connects'.

QUESTION E

If a key word or phrase seems to be particularly important, because it groups or summarizes a lot or is marked out by the speaker in some way with tonal emphasis, we might use this question to clarify and open out this part of the pattern. For instance, if after some exploration there is a pause and the phrase comes up, 'I suppose, I've never really understood myself', we might ask: 'What do you mean by 'understood'?' or 'What is 'understanding' for you?'

QUESTION F

This question helps one 'think round corners'. Whatever is being said may imply much more. Together with the question: 'What does this really mean?', this questions helps build intuitions about the deeper structure of our own or other's experience. It is particularly useful when someone crystallizes what they have been saying into a key summarizing phrase that expresses a belief, such as, 'I have to be strong for others'. Asking, 'What does this presuppose?' may draw out more aspects of the pattern, such as 'I can't relax' or 'My own needs don't get met'.

PRACTISING THE KEY QUESTIONS

1. Take any everyday object belonging to the person being questioned (your self or someone else), and ask question A ('What are other examples of things like this for you?', Wait till you have at least two other examples.
2. Ask question B, in the form: 'What are these three all examples of for you?'
3. Take the answer to this last question, and ask question A again: 'What are other examples of things like this for you?'
4. Repeat steps 2 and 3, until you find that you have reached a dead end or are going round in circles.
5. Take what seems to be the most general or 'highest' level of answer and ask: question E, 'What is this [specify] for you? What do you mean by this [specify]? Also ask questions C: 'What are some examples of this for you? Can you give me some examples of how this manifests in your life? How does this relate to other aspects of your life.'
6. Take some time to discuss (or if you are doing this alone to think about) the patterns that came up, both in the answers themselves and how you reached them. What do the patterns that came up presuppose? What has to be true for them to be true? What life-patterns does this exercise bring out?

IDENTIFYING BELIEFS

1. What are some beliefs you aware of? Take a piece of paper and list as many as you can. What do you hold to be true about:
   * yourself
   * others
   * the world
   * the nature and purpose of existence
2. What are some of your unconscious beliefs?
a. Take a piece of paper and jot down some of your interests. Note also some things that you like about yourself, others, or the world around you.

b. Taking what you have written, point by point or in groups of two or three that seem to go together, what are some of the assumptions implicit inyou interests and passions and in the things that you like about yourself, others or the world around you? What is it as if you believed to be true about yourself, people, the world, the nature of life and existence?

c. List some of the things that you do which you dislike. List some of the things that others do which upset or bother you. List some of the things in the world that trouble you.

What assumptions are implicit in your dislikes? What is it as if you believed about yourself, others, the world, or existence? Take a moment to relax and settle deeply into yourself. When you remind yourself of all those things that bother you, what is it that you might hold to be true (if you couldadmit it to yourself without shame or guilt) about

* yourself
* others
* the world
* existence

d. Taken together do these beliefs presuppose other beliefs you haven't thought of yet? What underlying principle or assumptions seems to run through them all?

3. Do your conscious and unconscious beliefs match up? How true are they? Do your beliefs serve you well in your life now? Do you need to hold onto them? Is it time to revise them or let them go?

4. If there is a belief or assumption that seems unhelpful, ask yourself: How do I know this is true? What is my evidence for holding this belief? Then ask yourself whether the evidence really is enough to justify holding this belief.

5. If you would like to release this belief, check inside that all parts of you are ready to do so. If you experience any reluctance from any part of yourself, you will need to identify and take care of any concerns.

Identify what belief it is appropriate to hold now, check inside that all parts of you are ready to accept this new belief. Adjust the way you formulate it until it feels comfortable to all parts of you. Ask for the old belief to be released in all parts of body and mind. Allow your bodymind to welcome and accept the new belief.

(N.B. Step 5 is a delicate process, and you may need help from someone who is familiar and comfortable with this process.)

EXPLORING PERSONAL PATTERNS

Find some quiet time and space for yourself. Take a piece of paper to help track your thoughts.

1. Ask yourself: 'What is something that I do over and over again that I

like (e.g., a good habit)?' Note the answer that comes.

2. Ask: 'What are some other things in my life like that which I do?' Note these.

3. Ask yourself: 'What are these all examples of? What groups these together in my life?' Note your answer.

4. Ask yourself if there are other things in your life, like what you have just answered to the last question. Note down the first two or three that come to mind.

5. Ask what these are examples of. Note your answer.

6. Repeat steps 4 and 5, till you seem to be stuck or cycling round in the same area.

7. Consider the pattern implicit in what you explored. How has it manifested in the diverse aspects of your life — in your home, garden, eating habits, friendships, family relationships, work, hobbies, or play. How does this pattern express who you are?

8. Repeat the above process, taking something that you do repeatedly and dislike. When you reach step 7, notice how you feel in your body when you are aware of this new pattern. Notice how this pattern also expresses who you are.

9. How might you modify this pattern so that it expresses who you are congruently? What would be a more accurate truth? Allow yourself to give permission for the old pattern to be released in the bodymind, by quietly staying with any physical sensations connected to that pattern, till they begin to dissolve. When they have significantly lessened, identify a more appropriate pattern and slowly whisper it to yourself, allowing the bodymind to feel and absorb this new truth.

Revising Beliefs

Although beliefs are resistant to change — and the deeper the beliefs, the more resistant — we are constantly revising our beliefs in the light of experience. At periods of major inner change in our lives, a series of incremental challenges to our old beliefs resulting from positive or negative experience may culminate in a major shift in deeper values and beliefs, with consequences for behaviour. Sometimes this process is called growing up or maturing!

Many of the approaches to unfolding awareness that we have discussed in this book help bring about spontaneous shifts in our beliefs, as unwelcome patterns held in the bodymind dissolve. For instance, old beliefs can shift through deep rest and relaxation. Reduced metabolic states, such as those experienced in meditation, lead spontaneously to the release in the bodymind of old patterns. In the state of deep restful alertness, the body tends to eliminate the accumulated residue of stressful experience. Some of this residue results from the wear and tear of everyday life; some is due to the long-standing effects of past experience that has overloaded the bodymind. As such by-products are released in the body, mental patterns adjust themselves spontaneously. Unhelpful beliefs are gradually let go of and replaced by ones that are more in alignment with the deeper order of life. As a result behavioural patterns gradually become more in accord with the maintenance of well-being. The tendency to want to live in way that nourishes the body grows very naturally For instance, the desire to con-sume substances that weaken the body — such as drugs or alcohol — spontaneously lessens. And positive habits become stronger without any strain to live in a different way. We just feel different with different desires and needs.

Self-unfolding movement can also lead to the throwing off of old beliefs. Tension held in the body may dissolve, releasing an old pattern in the bodymind. Here the body again leads the process. As the tension and lim-iting holding patterns are activated and freed, they may be accompanied by mental images (pictures or words) that either symbolically or literally relate to the pattern that is being processed by the self-healing bodymind. Using other expressive media, as in the creative connection, can facilitate the unravelling of the full belief and its release and healing.

REVISITING THE DATABASE AND REVISING ASSUMPTIONS

Rather than tackling beliefs directly, it is generally easier to work with their underlying assumptions. When someone expresses a limitation about what they can do, one might ask: "How do you know that?" This question helps recover the original experience or evidence from which the belief was gen-eralized. It reveals some of the logic and assumptions that underlie the belief.

For instance, if I believe that 'I am bad'. I must have some evidence for that. By recovering the original evidence, I can determine whether the assumptions on which the belief rest are valid.[5] If someone says: "I can't learn new things", and I ask "How do you know that?", they might say, "Because, I was always slow as a child". We can explore how being slow as a child, doesn't mean that new things can't be learnt either then or more especially now. Speed of learning and ability to learn new things are two separate things. Once the old assumptions are known to be inaccurate, based on poor logic, the best evaluation possible at the time, the beliefs based on them often revise themselves quite naturally. The natural ten-dency is for the bodymind to evolve towards truth and wholeness, once this is known to be safe and desirable.

Releasing Old Patterns

When an unhelpful core belief of which we were unaware surfaces in our life, it is important to allow time to recognize, release, and revise it as appropriate. Here is a way to do this, based on some of the methods I use in Open Heart Learning.

ACCEPT THE OLD PATTERN

The first step is to be with the old pattern for a while, accepting that it has been at least partially true for ourselves, perhaps throughout life. Many of our core beliefs are both true and not true. A belief such as 'I don't deserve love', or 'I have no right to exist' may be so threatening or shameful that we may have both taken it on and rejected it vigorously in order to survive its life-denying threat. We function as if we both believed and rejected it at the same time, weaving a complex structure of thesis and anti-thesis, acceptance, rejection, and accommodation to find ways to function and survive We may be reluctant to admit it, even to ourselves. We may have been fighting all our life to prove this belief to be untrue to the world, to others in our life, and to ourselves. It is helpful to acknowledge this ambivalence inwardly and welcome this perhaps unwelcome truth. It may evoke strong feelings in the bodymind. It is very healing to sit quietly while any feelings, images, thoughts, and insights associated with this truth play themselves out. If the mind gets distracted to more surface concerns, gently bring it back to the old core belief.

We may experience a series of internal realizations, such as:. 'I'm not acceptable . . . I'm bad . . . When I'm bad, I'm me . . . I want to be accepted . . . I must be good to be accepted . . . When I'm good, I'm not me . . . I am not me [gesturing to left] . . . I am me [gesturing to right].' Such realizations are perhaps banal to the telling, but, when apprehended by the experiencer as newly recognized truths, stir tidal energies, as the beliefs re-enact consciously and physically the acceptance and rejection locked in the body.

It is important to recognize and accept such emergent realizations, so that the charge that held them in place and us in their thrall can loosen and dissolve. 'It is OK to be unacceptable.' In any case my deepest Self is neither acceptable or unacceptable. It is. It may be appropriate at times to be unacceptable to some people. It certainly makes it easier to be simple and direct if there is no conflicting counter thrust under the surface coming from a need for acceptance. By accepting fully the unacceptable in our beliefs we can break their spell. The beast in us recovers beauty.

ACKNOWLEDGE ITS IMPACT

Besides accepting the old belief, it is important to acknowledge how the belief has been influential in many aspects of life, from childhood onwards, in relationships and career. Notice how it may have functioned as both a limitation and a spur. For instance, in discovering a residual belief 'I am inadequate', I noticed that this had held me back in facing many challenges in life, I felt it in my sports life as a child and teenager (being forced to sit out several weeks of soccer as a 10-year old after contracting meningitis; not being a top notch miler), in my career, not really 'going for it' for many years, in my relationships, sometimes blaming myself for difficulties that weren't entirely my own making. At the same time, this belief was a stimulus to succeed academically, ultimately to get a PhD, about which I realize I have mixed feelings, like so much that is influenced by limiting beliefs (both valuing the intellectual training and rejecting it as almost a waste of time compared with living from the heart).

LET IT GO

Once you have acknowledged what is and what has been, you may well already have done much to let the belief go. Simply to name and own something we have in part denied or negated, to be with what is, already allows things to change. Because our bodymind is self-healing and naturally tends to be well, it will not hold onto outmoded beliefs unnecessarily. However, particularly with strongly held beliefs, it may be necessary to help the process of release and revision further. With beliefs about identity, it may be helpful to invite assistance from that higher ground of experience that transcends our identity.

Generally, updating old beliefs requires that something shift in the body as well as the mind. Where deep levels of the person are touched what Gene Gendlin the developer of 'focusing' calls a 'felt shift' — a feeling-shift in the body as well as our mind — is important.

Be attentive to where any residue of the belief is held in the bodymind. Notice any correspondence between the language and body used to sum up a pattern and blocks in the energy between head, heart, and viscera, as suggested towards the end of Chapter Ten. Allow blocks to dissolve by gently letting your attention be with any physical sensations in the body. If it helps, allow yourself to visualize the sensation and allow the image to recede or fade till it is gone. Imagine that part of the body being filled with healing light and energy. Ask that any learnings from this old belief be stored as appropriate for your benefit.

INTRODUCING A REVISED BELIEF

Once you have accepted, explored, and released the old belief or assumption, it is a good idea to entertain an updated alternative. This should specifically correct the old misperception. It should respect your personal truth and be in harmony with the deepest wisdom. For instance, the misperception 'I am wrong and out of place' could be replaced with a formula such as 'I am right and in place'. 'I am unacceptable' might be replaced with a revision that says 'I accept myself' or simply 'I am here', which jumps outside the dichotomy of acceptance or non-acceptance.

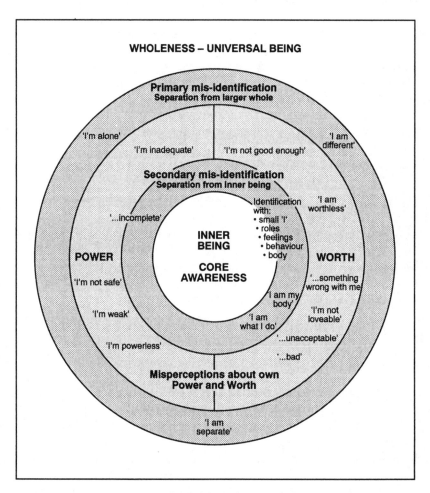

WHOLENESS – UNIVERSAL BEING

Primary mis-identification
Separation from larger whole

'I'm alone'   'I am different'

'I'm inadequate'   'I'm not good enough'

Secondary mis-identification
Separation from inner being

'...incomplete'   'I am worthless'

Identification with:
• small 'I'
• roles
• feelings
• behaviour
• body

INNER BEING

CORE AWARENESS

POWER   **WORTH**

'I'm not safe'   '...something wrong with me'

'I am my body'

'I'm weak'   'I am what I do'   'I'm not loveable'

'I'm powerless'   '...unacceptable'

'...bad'

Misperceptions about own Power and Worth

'I am separate'

KEY MISCONCEPTIONS

Trust your bodymind to guide you. Allow your bodymind to come up with an appropriate formulation. Allow it to check that yes, this is the new truth that feels whole and complete. Notice any jarring feelings or doubts and continue till you find a formula that is completely acceptable to the bodymind as a whole. If necessary explore the source of the doubts and make sure that any concerns that lie behind them are fully respected and met.

It may be that there is more than one formulation needed to update the old belief. Allow yourself to explore as many phrases as necessary and gently test them in the bodymind. When they feel right, whisper them slowly to yourself and allow yourself time to feel them resonating in the bodymind. Allow yourself to relax, deeply, letting their sound and meaning soothe and balance your whole system, particularly the centres of the head, heart, and viscera, so that you have an expanded and unified sense of your own being and your connection with the larger whole.

Acknowledge how you might find your life different in the future in those contexts where the old belief had been influencing you. Allow yourself to imagine in images and words a different future closer to this new truth.

Affirming the Wholeness of Life

Disruptive beliefs and patterns often manifest in nagging voices that remind us of the 'truth' about ourselves like outworn records stuck in some recurring groove, such as: 'You'll never amount to anything' or 'You can't do it'. People sometimes use positive affirmations to counteract these disabling messages. Affirmations presuppose that our primary errors are partly cognitive. They are designed to overwrite through repetition old patterns with a new more life-nurturing programme.

Affirmations can be helpful, shifting the bias from negative to positive patterns. Unfortunately, we easily reject affirmations that conflict with core beliefs. And while a particular affirmation may seem reasonable enough, such as 'I deserve to enjoy life's abundance', it may violate parts of our belief system that we are not even aware of. As a result, it may be rejected by the bodymind. Alternatively, we may create a new positive belief, without fully eradicating the old. This may create internal conflict.

Whether exploring core patterns and beliefs with a mentor or by oneself, it is important to emphasize that this is not a mental process. The verbal formulae picked up are not intellectualizations. They are felt truths that name what the body knows. They are the conceptual expression of something lived in the bodymind.

The most useful affirmations are thus those that come not from outside, but from the realization of deep truths about our own patterns. They then fit with our own awareness of our primary errors. When we have a profound insight that integrates every aspect of our life through time and in almost any context, our system is unusually open and attuned to recognizing and accepting its own truth. Affirmation of such truth needs no noisy repetition. Whispered gently into the bodymind, it seeps like healing balm into every pore of our being, because it is, quite simply, our truth.

I have suggested that the ultimate core pattern, the universal mistake of almost all minds is a confusion of the one and the many. Traditionally, in India, the master cements the student's enlightenment with the *mahavakyas*, simple affirmations of the nature of experience, such as 'Tat twam asi', 'Thou art that'. The *mahavakyas* in a sense do not affirm, they confirm. For it is only in a state of already knowing, that these phrases validate and illuminate. If the student isn't ready for them he or she understands intellectually, rather than viscerally. They need to be said at just the right moment, like a final piece of jigsaw completing and revealing a picture. The teacher artfully brings the student to the state of readiness in which such simple phrases penetrate deeply as undeniable yet long-ignored truths.

Just so with core patterns, in recognizing, not with the mind, but with the most pervasive and powerful pathways of our neurology that 'I have never been able to accept myself' or 'the more I open myself the more vulnerable I become', or whatever the pattern is, we create the space in which we can begin to recognize and choose to accept ourselves, to allow ourselves to discover indestructible strength in our openness. We realign the pattern so that we express who we are cogently and completely. We release boundaries and allow the being of core awareness to breathe through us, as we dance in the great rhythm of life.

Unravelling Beliefs and Patterns over Time

A number of interrelated beliefs generally shape our identity and our experience of the world. It is usually not enough to recognize and realign just one core belief. Often, we need to return a number of times to our deepest beliefs, recognizing and readjusting a number of core attributions, until the whole pattern of self permanently realigns itself.

An analogy might be with a tangled ball of coloured woollen threads. In one exploration, we may discover a knotted 'red' strand. We may release the knots in the red strand, but later find that there is a 'green' strand snarled up with it. This is in turn connected to a 'purple' strand, and so on. At first, it seems that just as we have got the ball sorted out, it returns again to something like its old pattern, just a little changed, but little by little it becomes more orderly or 'coherent'. And then finally, we unsnarl a strand and the whole ball settles into a new permanent pattern in which all the colours arrange themselves in an attractive and orderly way.

My own personal experience with this process may illustrate how we can gradually untangle some of our limiting beliefs and patterns. A few years ago, exploring a sense of insecurity I felt in my relationship, I saw a small beige medallion-sized image. Drawing this image and feeling with pastels, I found myself shaping a foetus surrounded by black space. I heard the words 'I am safe when I am alone'. This felt like an inner truth that was both comforting and sad to recognize. It felt familiar and yet mysterious and unknown. Exploring this belief, I sensed that it may well have come from when I was very small and vulnerable and might have found others threatening — perhaps my mother. I also realized that it implied that I was not safe with others. I recognized how I kept aloof from people to maintain inner security. Further exploration brought me to the realization that if I was safe when I am alone, I was in some way threatened by others. I sensed that this threat had to do with how I felt others evaluated me. I came to a very unwelcome and reluctant but inwardly resonating truth: 'I am unacceptable'. If I was unacceptable, to whom was this so? I wondered. To others and to myself, the answer came. If I am unacceptable, what am I? I queried, trying to get a felt-sense of self. The image came of a maggot and the words that fit this: 'I am vermin'. In entering into the image of maggot, my body began to wriggle, releasing muscular tension, and I found myself breathing heavily and eventually making some loud noises. Afterwards, my body felt healed with my energy freer.

A few months later, in doing some personal work, I found myself returning to this kind of movement and heard myself say 'I am not safe when I am alone'. I realized that this opposite truth was also true for me, that I had been neither safe alone nor with others, but vulnerable. Within a month, for the first time in my life, I took an extended retreat in solitude in nature.

During that retreat, I climbed to the head of a canyon and on a ridge beneath some ponderosa pines and oaks in Arizona, turned to the feelings of uncertainty I felt with regards to my career and to my then relationship. I realized that I was feeling a lack of fulfilment, a kind of restless neediness. I realized that I held the belief: 'I am needy'. Of what? I asked myself, seeking to supply the deleted object of this neediness. 'Of love and recognition', came the reply from within. It felt healing to name these feelings and recognize their hopeless nature. No amount of love from outside nor recognition could assuage a self that felt it was needy. I realized that I had to love and recognize myself and come to my own wholeness. Taking time to acknowledge the old truths, I then allowed myself to feel inwardly with gentle sincerity the words: 'I love myself', 'I recognize myself', 'I am full', 'I am complete'. This brought a sense of great peace and led to a more stable and settled feeling, which lasted for months after returning home, till I felt myself being called to a new level of challenge.

Later, in exploring some uncertain feelings before a workshop, I recognized that the feeling in my belly was one of fear. Recovering the deleted belief by asking: 'Who is afraid of what?', I realized that 'I am afraid of being judged'. Some days later, after feeling that again I was losing my sense of wholeness and centre, I found myself returning to the old belief, 'I am needy'. What does this presuppose, I asked myself and sensed a connection with the fear of being judged. At a deeper level, behind the fear of judgement and the neediness, I recognized a deep sense of being inadequate. Once again, to name and accept and let go of this belief, and gently introduce its complementary truth that I am whole and complete released energy and joy.

Some while later, setting up a new life in a new land, I found myself experiencing feelings of both neediness and lack of safety. Behind those feelings, I was afraid. Seeking the source of the fear, I realized that an some level I felt that I was 'just a drop in the ocean'. I realized that this was experiencing myself as small and separate from the overwhelming ocean of life. With this realization, I felt a physical release in my body, and a welling up of oceanic warmth and fullness. How much more comfortable to iden-tify with the ocean, rather than the drop.

The journey may not be over, all strands may not be unravelled, but the ball is less disorderly and becoming more coherent. In the process, I dis-cover a coherent self and deconstruct it, becoming, as Mallarmé put it, 'an aptitude that the spiritual universe has to see itself and express itself through what was me.'

NOTES

1. This definition is Robert Dilts', whose work — along with that of Gene Early and Chris Hall — inspired much of this chapter.

2. In the last chapter, we noted that every word is defined with, and by reference to, other words. Every word is a descriptive belief, equivalent to a network of meanings of which we may be more or less aware. The question: 'What do you mean by x?' is thus not only an important way of gathering information when a person's language is vague or problematic, but of identifying elements of what he or she holds to be true.

3. Daniel C. Dennett, *Consciousness Explained*, Little Brown, Boston, 1991, p.77.

4. M. Scott Peck, *The Road Less Traveled*, Simon and Schuster, New York, 1978, p.186. Peck cites the case of a client who believed himself to be an atheist but, as a result of childhood experiences, held an unconscious belief in an ugly and vengeful God.

5. Chris Hall calls this process, also used in Open Heart Learning, 'backing up'. Robert Dilts' 'Reimprinting' offers another approach where we trace feelings associated with a belief or a block back to the primary belief-forming experience, usually some early trauma. One then identifies the beliefs formed by the younger self. From the adult perspective, the conclusions drawn are not necessarily valid for all time. For instance, humiliation in front of a class of children when little, does not necessarily mean that people wanted to make you suffer, nor that groups in the future are out to get you, or that if you make a mistake you will be paralysed.

In Reimprinting, we bring resources to the younger self — such as confidence or the ability to speak up and express discomfort, in the above example — and to significant others such as parents or teachers. This allows the bodymind to experience a positive alternative to the original trauma. New responses become possible. These can be brought forward into the present and future, allowing new beliefs to generalize, opening possi-bilities in contexts where they were limited before.

CHAPTER TWELVE

Role, Identity and Personal Purpose

Summary
In the last chapter, we considered how to identify and update restrictive beliefs about self and world. Here we delve into the nature of self. Our assumptions about who we are overlay the inner knower with particular qualities and characteristics. We find identity, acting through different roles, to be both real and unreal, according to our perspective. It is something to go beyond and to fulfil. Uncovering our purpose and aligning our life with it helps to do both. In fulfilling our purpose we unfold our relation to the larger whole. This restoration of wholeness gathers pace as we identify, accept, and accommodate disowned parts of ourselves.

> *each hung bell's*
> *Bow swung finds tongue to fling out broad its name:*
> *Each mortal thing does one thing and the same:*
> *Deals out that being indoors each one dwells;*
> *Selves — goes itself; myself it speaks and spells,*
> *Crying What I do is me: for that I came.*
>
> G. M. Hopkins

Somewhere a thought is ripening. I don't know if this is it. It seems to rest in the folds of the sea, carried like salt-spray on the tart breeze. Awareness carries shape and form as the sea the spume. Oh salty drop, how much sea is in you?

'I' and Identity

Our sense of self has been the subject of philosophical, psychological, and spiritual enquiry down the ages. Some say there is no real self, only an apparent self masking an impersonal void. Others pretend that individuality is a recent historical construct. They point to cultures, such as those of the Third World and the East, where the individual differentiates himself far less from the social. Others claim that identity is a makeshift aggregate of hopes, desires, and expressions. Others say that our 'I' inhabits a series of glove puppets which each hold centre stage for a while and may even squabble amongst themselves. Still others maintain that our individuality is a fragment of some larger identity.

There is some truth in all such views. The reality shifts according to where one views the self from, according to what we identify with. As we saw in Chapter Three, in maturing, our sense of who and what we are evolves. We eventually recognize that the self is both real and unreal depending on our perspective. Our habits, feelings, and skills, our values and beliefs are not our identity, but what we identify with — accretions to a subtler and more elusive sense of 'I'. They are clothes our simple self puts on to become Peter, Paul, or Mary, while concealing who and what it truly is. The 'I' has no name or race or creed. Identity is our particular and mutable coloration of this non-specific I-hood or *ahamkara*.

The 'I' is two-faced, like Janus. In one direction it is the organizing principle that harnesses the different facets of our internal world — loves, loathings, tastes, tendencies, fears, gifts, habits — into the unity of a particular and unique 'me'. In the other direction, it offers the possibility of perceiving, as we realize what we are, that our individual life is none of these, but wave to the ocean of awareness. We can experience our 'I' as an 'I', as *the* 'I' and, beyond that, even as 'It'. We recognize that the undifferentiated Knower that we are enacts in our own awareness a drama which is repeated everywhere. Assuming a separateness and distinctness, our 'I' is really the one 'I' masquerading in us and in others as an infinity of separate knowers. My 'I' wakes up to know it is the one 'I Am' playing hide and seek in us and others, too. As Hopkins put it: "Christ plays in ten thousand places,/Lovely in limbs, lovely in eyes not his".

Just as an actor may become momentarily absorbed in playing a 'part' (that is, something that is not the whole), so we become absorbed in our identities. We become so taken with our present parts in the supreme fiction of daily life that we focus on our unique individual flavour, scent, and storyline. We take ourselves to be fixed and frozen into one way of being, instead of a phial of fluid possibilities. And we perceive ourselves as separate from other identities and forget the animating awareness that gives to both life and being.

Pivotal between the 'one' and the 'many', identity is both prison and release, enemy of awareness and pathway to its awakening. In identifying with a particular one — 'me' — and forgetting that awareness which is the simple witness of all experience, we become vulnerable to suffering. In holding fast to our personal self, we lose the radiant sustenance of universal awareness. As identity is consumed in its contracts and accretions — job, home, mortgage, friends — and these become more important than what we really are, we do disservice to our identity. And it no longer serves us. Life shrinks. We lose our true Self. As a result, knowing that to live in the One, inspired and animated by it, is to experience joy and fulfilment and release identity into a larger pasture, sages and saints have taught sacrifice, surrender, even annihilation of self.

At the same time, others, recognizing that identity serves as a conduit for powerful life energies, have emphasized an apparently opposite approach — unfolding and fulfilling self. There is sense to this view too. Our identity branches out into the fronds and fringes of our outer life, has roots down into the deeper soil of the bodymind, where our unique genetic fingerprint is woven from the particles and energies of all things. When our identity is fully engaged, we feel more vital and alive. We vibrate with the pulse of our existence. The river of our life flows deep, broad, and rich with precious alluvia. The heart beats to the rhythm of our being and our blood flows with each cell pulsing to the tune of who we are. Our horizons and vistas open up to embrace much more of life. To fulfil identity is to surpass it in some way.

Living awareness involves recognizing both truths: the importance of fulfilling identity and of transcending it. This involves becoming aware of who and what we are both temporarily and ultimately, of how we veil our true nature and what that true nature is, and how, as we fulfil our personal purpose, we naturally move deeper into alignment with the larger whole of which our individual identity is part.

Role

Role reflects on a small scale the same kind of reduction that universal awareness has in taking on individual identity. We assume a kind of second self, an identity within our identity. We become mother, father, engine driver or manager, reducing the total possibilities of our self to meet the needs of a particular context.

This reduction is dangerous if we lose identity and a role becomes our only identity. A mother whose children have grown may lose her life's meaning if overly identified with her role. And when role pinions reluctant identity to something alien to ourselves — the wrong profession, for instance — the result can be life-denying. So many people work where they find no room to express very much of who they are.

Yet role does have a place. It simplifies relations in practical contexts. It helps to know how an assistant in a shop, or a policeman, is likely to respond to our requests. We know where we stand and so do those that interact with us.

Investiture of identity into role allows both ease and excellence. The carpenter or chiropractor who can say at the appropriate time "I am a carpenter" or "I am a chiropractor" is more comfortable and competent, learns faster and inspires others more than the person who says, "I make things with wood" or "I adjust people's bodies". The one describes identity and the other, behaviour. When what we do is part of who we are, there is no separation between self and action: we move from managing to mastery.

Role liberates when we can genuinely put much of ourselves into it. It becomes a conduit for discovering and expressing who we are. Such a role is both us and not us. It is animated by our life energy, but we remain more than it. A strong sense of our individuality transcends and transforms it with its animating energies, making it rich, full, and satisfying — a validation of deeper levels of life.

From Role to Awareness

Switching roles offers a moment in which we can recover pure awareness. As we switch roles, say from professor to parent, there is a shift of self, like a rapid costume change in a theatre piece. We put aside one outfit and don another. The point at which we subtly shift our inner frame, as we drop one set of beliefs, attitudes, and even patterns of posture and voice — how different talking to one's child or partner than to a customer, boss, or employee — offers a chance to recognize the inner 'I' that becomes these different 'I's. If the required change is unexpected or out of context — your children appear in the middle of a company meeting — there may be a moment of confusion or hesitation in which role is no longer an unnoticed habit, but something we become aware of. We can sense the dropping of one role and the taking on of another, with the words, images, feelings, and body postures that accompany it. The shifting from one 'I' to another offers a moment in which we can glimpse the 'I' that is common to our different selves. This offers a chance of recognizing and identifying with the one we truly are. It may be true that, as Ozimandias puts it in Wallace Stevens' poem,

> the spouse, the bride
> Is never naked. A fictive covering
> Weaves always glistening from the heart and mind.

But we begin to recognize that fictive covering as just that, a residual covering that allows us to be our wider being and yet to function freely, yet lightly, in our particular evolving identity with the roles it assumes to perform practically in the world.

ACTIVITY: UNPACKING ROLE'S ROLE

1. Identify the different roles you play. Jot them down in your journal or on a piece of paper. Which roles are most comfortable? Which ones least comfortable? Which release and which restrict you?

2. Choose at least three of these roles. Assume each of these roles in turn, allowing enough time to sense each one. What shifts take place in
   * your sense of self
   * your beliefs

* your values,
* how you feel
* your capabilities
* what you say or do
* how you say or do it, and
* your posture and gesture

Take time to respond to each of the above facets of experience. Consider noting your responses or sharing them with a friend. How does your response to others change in each role? How does their response to you change? How much are these roles an expression of who or what you truly are?

3. Now practise switching roles. Slow down the process of dropping or taking up a particular role. Can you identify the point at which you are no longer in a particular role? Can you identify the point at which you assume a new role? What is common to all roles and to the transition between them? What happens when you speed up the transition from one role to another and switch quickly among a number of roles?

Purpose

A sense of purpose helps ensure we choose appropriate roles, ones that liberate rather than bind. A strong sense of our purpose serves as an inner lodestone that orients us in any avenue. We become attuned to what is and isn't aligned with who we are. That makes it easier to select roles that suit, and drop them as our sense of purpose is fulfilled.

Roles through which we fulfil our purpose and become who we truly are unfold inner awareness. We enter such roles from choice, consciously and freely, and easily grow and find fulfilment through them. And we are less likely to become over-identified with them. The role is vehicle, not destination. Should circumstances hijack a dear role — a job disappears; a function is fulfilled — we are not bereft.

ULTIMATE PURPOSE

Purpose answers the question 'Why am I here?' In recognizing our purpose we realize the in-born connection between our individual self and the larger whole, on the one hand, and its practical expression through activity in daily life, on the other.

Purpose is multi-levelled. It involves the relation between our personal identity and that which surpasses it. At the deepest level it commits us to a whole greater than our usual selves. My work has shown me repeatedly that we are as if pre-programmed to unfold our identity with the larger field of being in which we occur. This programming is often deeply buried amidst our daily desires and preoccupations, but enquiry reveals it as the motive behind all our motives. In spite of differences in temperament or belief, we discover when we explore our often unconscious values that individual life is designed for a greater reality than that encompassed by a narrowly defined personal self. To find purpose is to recognize that we are called in some way to ground our identity in a state or quality of life that transcends and imbues it. This fulfils identity; it explodes all boundaries to release it into that which is larger than the largest, smaller than the smallest, the brimming ocean of conscious being.

Our purpose, then, anchors us in the harbour of wholeness. It helps us balance the needs of self and other in everyday life. Wholeness is both individuality and relationship, or it would be less than whole. Our purpose transcends these dichotomies, so that we are both self-sufficient in this world and contribute to its richness in our own way. This development of our relationship with the larger whole — both as that which transcends our identity and that in which we behold and uphold other identities — is our *ultimate* purpose. It is a common purpose, shared by all, although we each have our ways to fulfil it.[1]

Fulfilment is an integral part of purpose. Wittingly or unwittingly, we all seek it in some form. Fulfilment resides not in the people, places, and activities and things we usually associate with it, but in the fullness we experience within. Lesser fulfilments lead towards greater ones. Such fullness is complete when our self surrenders itself, expanding into all-embracing inner awareness. That is one way of describing our ultimate purpose, though each person may conceive or phrase it differently.

Purpose is something that we know with the heart and with our whole body, rather than with the mind alone. It is a felt-sense of what ultimately orients the whole of myself. Like our important beliefs, it is something that is part cognitive and part feeling. We know it because our whole being recognizes and resonates with it, says 'yes' to it without hesitation.

Some people seem always to have known their purpose. Others find that it gradually emerges from some deeper level of awareness. Others come to a point in life when they recognize that their first priority is to find it. For these the sense of personal purpose needs to be dug for. Yet purpose is something we uncover rather than something we invent for ourselves. No-one can tell us our purpose. Nor can we find it in books. External sources can point the way, offer opinions and suggestions. But it is up to each one to ask the question, 'Why am I here? What is my purpose?' And only we can know if an answer, whether from without or from within, resonates with the truth of our own being. The activities in this chapter are designed to support this process.

FROM ULTIMATE TO PERSONAL PURPOSE

Ultimate purpose sets the context for *personal* purpose — the particular way we express our relationship with the larger whole in daily life — perhaps through an emphasis on some way of being, becoming, living, loving, learning, or knowing. Such deep, universal tendencies of human life, picked up uniquely by each of us, shape the personal expression of our ultimate purpose.

Our personal purpose resides in a sense of what motivates us profoundly in almost any given context. We fulfil our purpose as we discover ways to channel that sense of purpose through our particular temperament, tendencies, and talents into some specific course of action over time. Purpose creates a direction, which eventually manifests in a sense of calling or vision.

PURPOSE AND CALLING

If purpose connects personal identity to the transpersonal whole, calling propels purpose towards practical expression in the wider world. Calling is akin to what is popularly termed mission. I prefer the word 'calling', because it is more modest. Mission, when interpreted on the wrong level as specific outcomes in the world — such as, 'convert the heathen' or 'become the biggest conglomerate in the world' — can lead to the release of fantastic but fanatic energies, personal and collective, murdering conquistadors, enslaving inquisitors, blinded by self-righteousness and oblivious to the wisdom of others or the wider whole.

A deep sense of our ultimate purpose ordinarily reminds us that we are in a context greater than our personal selves. It helps ensure that any calling or mission we adopt is pursued in a spirit of humility. It reduces the risk of the person with a mission becoming a missionary in the worst sense of the word.

Calling, like purpose, is not invented; it is revealed or uncovered. We discover the best way for us to fulfil our personal purpose in the world. For instance, Christians might define their purpose as being 'to know, love, and serve God', but all are not called to do so in the same way. Only a few are called to monastic life or to the priesthood, and fewer still are called so literally and clearly as Saint Francis in the dilapidated chapel to 'rebuild my Church'.

In bringing a sense of purpose and calling to our work and home life, we choose well and commit to them. We approach them with awareness, putting a great deal into them, without being consumed by them.

PURPOSE AND VISION

With vision we conjure a compelling, idealized image of future possibilities. Vision is closely linked to both purpose and calling. Purpose propels us forward like an inner source of power; vision attracts like a magnet or beacon.

Typically, we perceive a vision-image centrally in the visual field, slightly higher than straight ahead. When we have vision, wherever we turn, it is always potentially before us. The image is compelling, because it is connected to positive feelings. What it represents fits with our values and appeals to us to manifest it. The image may not be detailed. It may be a symbol or icon of many things. For instance one of the developers of NLP (Todd Epstein) described himself as motivated by an image of the earth seen from space, like a 'blue ball', representing the harmony and well-being of the planet. He sensed his purpose was to contribute to this well-being. He described his commitment to NLP as the best way he knew of fulfilling it at that time.

Vision, like purpose, simply offers a direction, realizable in a number of specific ways. We may change direction in order to fulfil our vision. On the other hand, within the frame of a general vision, we may discover other visions that indicate ways of accomplishing our ultimate vision. For instance, Todd envisioned the way forward for NLP through the creation of a university, and was committed to creating this up to his death in 1995.

To some extent, a vision may be shared with others, like purpose and calling. The members of a training institute in a large state industry I consulted for shared a vision of their organization as an island with many linking causeways bringing people to and from the island, lighting up those who came to it and sending a stream of light to the different places linked to the central island. This metaphor fitted closely with the practical service offered by this industry — bringing electricity to the public.

Purpose also precedes vision, enabling one to recognize and fulfil vision from a place of surrender and humility. Vision, without a prior sense of ultimate purpose may lead to imbalance. If our vision is too fixed or over-defined we may become focused on the vision and forget the larger purpose it serves. I know of couples who have had a vision for their family and children. This helped them bond and move forward together through difficult times, but created hell for their children when they started to fulfil dreams of their own.

PURPOSE AND GOALS

With purpose comes quiet confidence from a sense of knowing who one is and what one is about. Calling and vision mobilize our energies and talents towards a sphere of action or accomplishment. Vision scapes a master goal that helps us create something specific within that sphere of action.

Between them purpose, calling, and vision involve our principal senses and the key levels of our psyche. Purpose is more feeling; calling more auditory; vision, more visual. Purpose connects us with that which is beyond our identity. Calling and vision direct our identity towards the fulfilment of deep beliefs and values through the full use of our abilities within the environment we find ourselves in.

If purpose answers the question 'why?', calling and vision connect the 'how' and the 'what'. Calling indicates how to fulfil our purpose, while vision shows us what to create. Alternatively calling suggests what to aim for, and vision shows how. Goals provide the practical small steps leading to our outcomes.

Purpose functions as our identity's 'goal', although identity does not consciously create it. It's already 'there' when we discover it. And we remain in a constantly evolving relationship with it. It is much less concrete than an ordinary goal. It is so general it can embrace all aspects of our life and in doing so sets the tenor of our personal existence.

Goals tend to be specific outcomes for the future, and generally involve the levels of environment, behaviour, or capabilities — like obtaining a piece of property, winning a trophy, attaining professional qualifications, even getting married and raising a family. Such goals may be expressions of who we are; they may be ways in which we fulfil our purpose, but they are not our purpose in themselves.

As with vision and calling, one can mistakenly find one's purpose in a goal and this can be very powerful. A goal held as one's purpose earns total commitment, and we put all of ourselves into it. And sometimes for a short time this is necessary. Mountains are moved this way — fortunes made, wars won, impossible deadlines met.

But just as mistaking role for identity has a price, so mistaking goals for purpose costs. Goals taken as personal purpose can leave us purposeless when achieved. Fulfilment comes fleetingly in achieving the goal — then, what? Select any other goal? If we have such a pattern, we may be driven from achievement to achievement, but not necessarily achieve the things that truly matter to us.

In short, being aware of purpose helps us choose appropriate goals or outcomes and to pursue them with commitment, without getting lost in them. Goals shape specific intentions, which we realize through action. Our attention helps us monitor and adjust our pathway to particular outcomes, and the sense of fulfilment (or lack of it) punctuates achievement, orienting us towards a sense of alignment with our purpose or divergence from it.

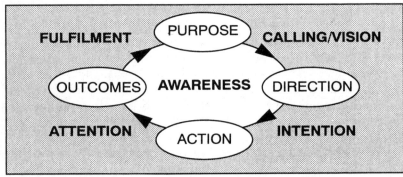

PURPOSEFUL ACHIEVEMENT

ACTIVITY: HEROES AND VILLAINS

Think of three people who approached life with great conviction, but had a destructive impact on the world around them. What was peculiar to each one? What was common to them? What made them destructive? Think of three people you admire with a sense of purpose, calling, or vision and seemingly positive effects on their world. What was unique to each one? What was common to all three? What distinguishes them from the other three people you selected?

Did their lives reflect balance — emotional, intellectual, spiritual? Were their private and public lives in balance? What did you learn from both groups that can guide you in realizing your own purpose? What did you learn that can inspire you to greater balance in your life?

Finding and Fulfulling Personal Purpose

Finding personal purpose is an intimate part of unfolding who we are. And it can take a time of reflection and discovery. Take your time for this process, particularly if you feel far from knowing your sense of purpose. Allow the process to ripen in you and come back to it till a sense of certainty emerges. If you can, take a period of retreat, alone and where you will not be disturbed, even if only for a day or two, ideally for longer. In many cultures, a period of retreat precedes the transition to adult life or the undertaking of life-tasks and challenges. Whether called a time in the wilderness, 'vision quest', or vigil, a time of quiet and reflection allows us to surrender to the sacred, be receptive and open, and engage in quiet relationship with that which surpasses us. It lets the deeper currents of life teach us, as we become open to learn, not with the mind or intellect, but with our whole being.

A wise and experienced guide at such a time can be a great help, but is not essential. If we approach this process with patience and humility and sensitivity to our own rhythms, needs, and capabilities, guidance comes readily from inside. Time spent alone in forest and mountain has taught me that nature supports the unfolding of our own nature, if our heart and senses are receptive. Away from the trappings of 'civilization', it is often easier to attune to that deeper current of life which pulses in all things.

The distinctions between purpose, calling, vision, and goals made here are somewhat arbitrary. They map gradations from ultimate purpose to specific action in the world — from what is most inward to outer expression. As such, they fracture a dynamic process into somewhat artificial portions. You may find that some parts of the distinctions I have made more helpful than others. Allow the exercises to highlight what seems most meaningful to you without trying to get a perfect match to these distinctions. If you prefer example before explanation, you might care to read the section "Finding purpose and direction — an example" before attempting the activities.

FROM VALUES TO PURPOSE

Personal purpose is a kind of core pattern, like those we discussed in Chapter Nine, one that, as we come into alignment with it, allows us to function coherently in our life as a whole. As such, one way to find our purpose is in scrutinizing the patterns of fulfilment and enjoyment, ecstasy and aliveness, preferences and talents running through our lives. What is the pattern that connects the things that mean a lot to us and to which we gravitate? To find this pattern, our values are important, because our purpose is closely connected to that which is of ultimate importance to us.

This first part of the process covers some of the same ground as the hierarchy of values activity in Chapter Eight. But its focus is slightly different. Identify three things in your life that are of great importance to you. Jot them down. Take one of these, and ask 'What's important to me about that? What does it give me?' Ask this question again of each answer you come up with, until you feel 'That's it, there's nothing beyond this' or until your answers seem to cycle back to an earlier one. Both events indicate that you have reached the top of the hierarchy.

Repeat for the other two of the original three most important values. Consider the value or values that have resulted from your questioning. Do you have three different ones or are they the same? What value seems to underlie all your values? Is there just one, or one with one or two closely connected ones? How does this value or value-group subtly drive your behaviour? How has it been implicit in the different hopes, desires, activities that have been present in your life — either because it was there as a driving force or because it was absent?

Take your time to relax and quietly explore the implications of this value inwardly: How is it to recognize this value as a central expression of who you are? How is is related to the theme of this book: living awareness? How is this value connected to your sense of purpose?

IDENTIFYING PATTERNS IN WHAT ANIMATES AND ENGAGES

Identifying what inspires, interests, or engages you also helps reveal a sense of personal purpose and direction.

Think back over your life as a whole. What were two or three of the really special experiences that stand out in your first decade of life? In the second decade? Jot these down on a piece of paper and repeat this for every decade of your life since.

Then note down also what has grabbed you and made you feel passionate, alive, and intense. What has compelled your attention, fascinated you, or held you riveted? What does so now?

Finally, what are your skills, talents, and gifts? What are the areas where you are easily creative or effective, where do your abilities naturally flow and give results? What are the areas where people recognize your competence and ease? Jot these down on a piece of paper and sit back and relax for a moment.

Reread your notes listing your key values, the things that make your feel more vital, and your gifts. What is the pattern that runs through all the things that speak to you personally and heighten your sense of who you are? Take your time. Ask your unconscious to reveal the pattern that connects. What is it as if your purpose is? Allow a few words to formulate inside you that seem to capture the essence of what you respond to deeply or express in many different ways.

Write this down in your journal and come back to it from time to time over the next few days, allowing yourself to respond to it. Does it capture the essence of who you are? Does it need a little refining or adjusting? Does it subsume all the important strands in your life? Does it include both self and other?

If it is very oriented towards others, what do *you* get from serving others? How is this part of your purpose?

FORMING AN IMAGE–METAPHOR FOR YOUR PURPOSE

Words often speak to us profoundly, but it can be helpful to represent purpose in other ways, such as through image and movement.

Take your sense of personal purpose from the previous exercise, even if it has not crystallized completely into words. Review the multitude of contexts and experiences that engage you most fully. Relax and close your eyes, allowing yourself to keep a loose sense of what your purpose seems to be. When you are nicely relaxed, so your mind is beginning to function in a slower, more floaty way, ask your unconscious to give you an image or metaphor that captures the essence of your personal purpose.

Your unconscious may offer you one simple image or even a series of images, letting you sense which one seems to fit best. Take the image that seems to express your sense of purpose, and note it down.

It can be helpful to explore and develop the image. Take some crayons and make a drawing or sketch of it. Don't worry about pictorial or aesthetic accuracy, allow yourself to focus on the feeling that goes with the image.

Freewrite for five or ten minutes just from the image and associated feelings or from the verbal formulation that came up.

Explore the image from different perceptual positions. Become the image and move it. Allow your body to move freely in the room or wherever you are, as if you are the image. How does it express itself through you in spontaneous dance? How do you feel as you literally embody this image?

Dialogue with the image, ask it questions. What does it tell or suggest to you?

Consider the image from third position. What's striking about it? Is it active or passive? Does it involve self or others or both and in what relationship? What are the apparent strengths suggested by the image? What might be possible weaknesses? How does the image express who you are?

FROM PURPOSE TO CALLING

How does your purpose seek to express itself in your life? Considering your overarching personal purpose, what pathway seems to best suit your particular mesh of talents and tendencies?

Go back to the sheet with your list of what makes you feel vital and happier and the areas in which you are talented. Ask yourself: how can I fulfil my purpose? What pathway would engage most of me? What channel includes opportunities to do things that make me feel vital and happier and uses or develops the skills I am drawn to use?

Is it what I am already doing or something else? Relax and ask yourself, if my purpose is to (and mention your purpose), what is my calling? How am I uniquely called to fulfil my purpose at this time?

FROM CALLING TO VISION

When a satisfying answer comes to this last question, you may like to ask your inner self to let a vision-image form representing the fulfilment of your calling. Explore this image as you did your purpose-metaphor.

Allow the elements of purpose, calling, and vision to unfold and evolve as you do. Come back to these processes from time to time and update them as you change and develop. You can use them as a touchstone for evaluating your life's undertakings and for guiding important choices and decisions. At major turning points check what you are about, ask 'Does this fit with my purpose and sense of who I am?'

FINDING PURPOSE AND DIRECTION — AN EXAMPLE

This is how an MBA student from the Caribbean began discovering a sense of purpose, when she was unsure how to apply her talents and was experiencing conflict between the expectations she felt family and potential partners might have of her to be a traditional wife, mother, or daughter, and her deep need to fulfil her own unique pathway.

This student cited three important values for her as: 'the happiness of those close to me', 'achieving academic and career success', and 'finding my niche'. We explored the values behind each of these values in turn, by asking questions such as 'What's important about that for you?' and 'What does that get you?'

The value of academic and career success led eventually to a sense of 'self worth' and 'making a contribution'. These in turn led to a sense of 'satisfaction' and thence to 'peace'.

When those close to her were happy, she felt she was 'free to focus on my own needs'. And this eventually gave her 'satisfaction' and 'peace' again.

'Finding my niche' was important because it enabled her to 'commit to something that involved me fully'. The importance of committing to something fully was that it enabled her to have 'ultimate satisfaction' and 'ultimate peace'. With ultimate peace she had the possibility of becoming a 'free spirit'. Beyond this, words and experience began to fail her. She had a sense of entering some spiritual reality and becoming 'selfless'. This seemed new and somewhat unfamiliar territory.

In the model we have presented here, becoming 'selfless' is an important aspect of her ultimate purpose. She is sensing her relationship with the larger whole. Becoming a 'free spirit' is part of her personal purpose. The vision-image that came to her initially for this purpose was of a cat that confidently wandered the world and was itself, without compromising its integrity in any way.

When it came to considering her personal pathway for becoming a free-spirit and ultimately selfless, we looked at some of the animating experiences from her childhood, teens, and twenties. These included playing with brothers and sisters and friends in nature by a stream, being together with her family, and being loved and made to feel special by her father. Later she remembered the delight of winning academic prizes and achieving career goals. More recently she was fascinated by what made people tick and by the whole area of organizational change and development.

Taken together the experiences that engaged her, her core values, and her ultimate and personal purposes suggested a possible calling to work as an independent consultant to help organizations become places in which free spirits could flourish in a climate of greater togetherness and community, thereby easing the accomplishment of organizational goals and ultimately the integration and development of her region. Her next step or action would be to complete the MBA which opened up this pathway.

FROM PURPOSE, CALLING, AND VISION TO ACTION

A wild oncologist from the Balkans used to look at me in despair and then intone loudly like some exasperated prophet, as he tilted his head heavenwards and shook his open hands extended skyward, "Not just Vision", adding with great drawn-out emphasis — as he dropped his arms and gestured vigorously open handed at knee level — "Action!" Then he would repeat the ritual in reverse, "Not just Action, Vision!"

There is a danger of getting lost in vision or in action. We need both and the awareness to pass back and forth between the two.

Take some quiet time, sitting poised on a firm chair (feet on the floor, torso balanced so that you feel your sitting bones on the chair). Relax into a state in which you are both inwardly settled and quietly alert. Notice whether this is easier with eyes closed or open. As you become more settled, yet remain vitally present, acknowledge your sense of purpose and your alignment with it throughout your whole body. Recall the channel of activity that best enables you to fulfil your purpose, your particular calling. Allow yourself to feel your sense of calling and to see the vision that this calling invites you to manifest, let yourself see this before you and a little above the ordinary straight forward line of vision. And ask, "What are the best next steps to fulfil my purpose at this time?" Jot down what comes up as a guidance for action.

Or take a few minutes each morning to ask the highest and deepest aspect of your inner life how best to fulfil your purpose today. Let your attention settle inwardly, so that the answer can come from as quiet and whole a place as possible within you. Listen and watch inwardly for a sense of what is needed for your well-being and the greater whole on this day. When you return to full waking, check that your inner guidance is congruent with your whole being. If you are not already doing this as a part of your daily routine, try it for a two weeks and continue thereafter, if you find it helpful.

These inner questions also help orient attention towards fulfilling purpose:

From time to time:

What's my purpose?

What lets me know I am fulfilling it?

And more often:

What is the best way of fulfilling my purpose right now?

Is what is happening serving my purpose?

Healing and Transcending Identity

Our identity often serves us inadequately when aspects of ourselves are unacceptable to us. Whenever we reject, deny, or split off parts of who we are, we fracture our wholeness and dam up part of our creative intelligence, making it unavailable for effective action. We turn parts of ourselves into rebel selves, marginalized outlaws, armed terrorists waiting to sabotage our other aims and activities. Still more of our energy goes to counter-terrorist activities — sand-bag defences, inhibitions, no-go areas — to prevent the insurrection of the unwanted in everyday life. Many of these measures are ineffective. We find ourselves flagging in energy for the things we truly want and the secret or unwanted self finds ways to remind us of its existence through illness, accidents, and all kinds of unloving or antisocial behaviour.

Delinquent identities can be persistent offenders. The aberrant self may sabotage attempts to transcend it — with wandering thoughts or drifting dullness in meditation or stony hearts frozen to prayer. Irksome identities may require remedial attention in their own right, if we are to progress from the personal to transpersonal levels of develpment. Counselling and therapy can help. But we can also turn our own attention to the maverick portions of ourselves, to investigate, honour, and own our prodigal shadow-selves. We may need to open the beam of awareness to ask who or what is fluttering at the edges of our conscious life, like a bird beating against an imprisoning window.

For Arnie Mindell, our 'primary process' — the portion of our experience with which we consciously identify in the moment — often competes with a 'secondary process' — the unsatisfied needs of parts of ourselves we may be ignoring.

Our secondary process is nature's way of enabling life to flow. Ideally, we give ourselves to the moment (primary process), yet remain sensitive to our other needs (secondary process) to eat, sleep, play, be creative, work, and relate to others. These then become primary process at the appropriate time . . . and so on. In reality we often block our other needs — sometimes for decades — and build a backlog of frustration and resentment from unsatisfied aspects of our wholeness.

If we find ourselves inwardly sabotaged when pursuing our conscious intention (primary process) — perhaps we are unable to concentrate on a chosen task or behave in ways that contradict our self-image, being impatient when we would be loving, restless when we would be at peace — a question inwardly asked, such as "Who is this 'I' that does not want to work right now?" Or "Who is this 'I' that resists my desires for rest?" can help us. These questions allow us to expand the space of our self-centred self to include a wider horizon of our inner needs. We can then seek a way to balance and incorporate the conflicting energies so that we accept all of us. This process allows our separated selflets to coalesce increasingly into an orchestrated and open sense of self, which lives dynamically in the now, flowing naturally from moment to moment.

This is maturity — grounded in a secure sense of self, responsible for oneself, but also responsive, ready to learn, grow, and change. This is living with awareness.

Short, rough-cut bleached hair, pink baseball cap in hand, black headphones, a white carnation in the pocket of her leather jacket. She rocks to the rhythm of her music. Big-bodied, she is never still, cutting sheet metal, drinking tea, dismantling a miniature carpet sweeper, smoking, waving to passers-by. She puts a green chair on the pavement, sits, stands again, walks off, comes back, staccato gestures, like a one-man play by Beckett or Ionesco.

When I look up in thought, my resting gaze half takes her in, caressing her clowning contrast to my serious words. As I watch the letters emerge on my com-

puter screen, she's there in my peripheral vision, up to some new antic, leaning the rootless, leafless remnant of a bush against her apartment porch, or singing to an empty oil drum.

But what if I open the window? Her voice wafts in with the March air, and my word-work falters, competing with songs, sounds, and chit-chat.

I've watched her for weeks, appreciating her eccentric shadow-presence in this stuffed-shirt street, but only today does she find her way into this book. Only today, I recognize her as a second self, at times aligned, at times jangled divergence from my primary process.

ACTIVITY: THIS IS ME; THIS IS NOT ME

Whenever we make judgements about ourselves, we separate and split our wholeness. Identity involves selecting from the infinite possible ways of being. This makes life practicable, but impoverishes it. In this activity we use creative expression to explore and integrate aspects of self and non-self into a larger whole, and to experience something of an expanded sense of self.

You will need some space, art materials (oil pastels or pastels), two sheets of drawing paper (preferably A3 or larger) and notepaper. You may like to share this process with a friend or partner. Allow about an hour and a quarter if you are alone; two hours if you are a pair.

1. Allow yourself to explore some of your many ways of being. Assume a role from your life, such as 'this is me as mother/father/daughter/son'. Feel what that is like and walk around the room as if in that role for a minute or two. Then switch to one or two other roles, moving about the room with some sense of how each one feels in body and mind. Repeat the process for one or two emotional states — such as happiness or sadness.

2. Get a sense of how you are at your best. Imagine you are at your best right now. Walk about your room or be still and really get some sense of what it feels like to be you, when you're at your best. When you have a felt-sense of what this is like, take a piece of drawing paper and starting with the feeling allow yourself to draw on the paper for about 10 minutes. Don't try to produce art; let the feelings guide your hand and draw from them or from any image that came up for you as important. Consider using the hand you don't normally use for writing or drawing. Let this hand choose the colours.

3. Now, put this drawing and this state to one side. As you walk about the room allow your body mind to find a state which is 'not me'. This may be some aspect of yourself that you reject or simply a way of being that is utterly unlike anything you know or expect of you. Don't try to find this intellectually. Suspend judgement and let your imagination find this and express it in your body as you move about the room. When you have a felt-

sense of something that is 'not me'. Take this feeling into a second drawing, also with your non-dominant hand.

4. Now place the two drawings where you can see both.

a. Look at the 'this is me' drawing and imagine that you have taken it inside you or that you have gone into it. Allow the drawing and the feelings it evokes to begin to move your body, in whatever way it takes you. Trust the process. If it seems to dry up or stop, come back to the drawing and the feelings it evokes in you as you become it, and let a   further   phase of movement begin. Do this for about 5 minutes.
If you try this process with another person, have them sit and watch your movement, giving you their full and undivided attention. This amplifies a space of awareness in which you move.

b. After about five minutes, give your attention to the second drawing, 'this is not me'. Move this second drawing in the same way, allowing all the feelings of 'this is not me' to express themselves in your movement. Again, this is not an analytic process; allow your innate bodywisdom to unfold itself in its way, trusting the impulses to come up. There are no rights and wrongs here; allow this process to be one of learning and discovery.

c. After about five minutes moving 'this is not me', allow yourself to alternate quickly between moving each of the two drawings. Switch quickly between the two feeling-movements, allowing yourself to find a way of moving that seems to fuse and integrate the two .

5. After moving, freewrite for 5-10 minutes, letting whatever words come to you flow onto the page.
If you have a witnessing partner, share your experience for a while verbally, the one who moved speaking first. Then repeat steps 4-5, with the witnessing partner now the mover and you witnessing them. Again finish by sharing what came up for you both. What was different about the sense of 'me' and 'not me'? What happened in the movement integrating these?[2]

Beyond integrating the unacceptable, we ultimately balance and heal ego and identity by transcending them altogether. Spiritual pathways are predicated on this assumption. Many such approaches dismiss our finite self as a distraction. Or they may simply uphold our higher Self, as Swami Nisargadatta and many others do, as infinitely more valuable than its pale personal reflection. For most people the notion of loss of personal self is unappealing. The middle way suggested here recognizes the value of fulfilling the self and discovering its essence, which has both personal and transpersonal dimensions.[3]

In interviewing those who value aware and authentic living — people like Douglas Harding, Natalie Rogers, pioneer of Person Centred Therapy, and Tony Crisp explorer of 'inner directed movement' — I discovered a common edge for these otherwise different people. They all recognize the importance of being true to self and of surrendering it to something larger than themselves — of honouring the self and of letting go of it, so that it could be an instrument of unfolding the greater whole. Yet such surrender, although desirable and necessary, was an elusive mystery for them, both product of, and means to, a state of grace.

Surrender cannot be forced. It already presupposes some loosening of personal confines, a lessening of fear-bound separateness, and an ease and comfort with the larger whole. Premature renunciation of self may postpone fulfilment of personal needs that eventually reassert themselves. One visit to the cinema by entertainer Tony Monopoly was enough to end seven years of Carmelite austerity. If we perceive the need for surrender and move towards it, we may need to do so with sensitive attentiveness to the swings of life. These may invite us to surrender a chosen form of surrendering, lest we become attached (and thus unsurrendered) to our very surrendering. Monopoly did not waste seven years; they contributed to his personal unfolding. Flowing with life's current meant a phase of silence and a phase of sharing himself and his talents, but from a place of greater centredness than might otherwise have been possible.

Surrender thus does not consist of a simple once-and-for-all act of renunciation, but a continual checking of personal impulses against deeper and broader levels of inner truth that include, but are not limited to, our immediate personal self. This process does not weaken self, but gives our personal pilot the support of the ship of living awareness and puts its course in alignment with the great currents of life.

The best way to surrender self is to enter into it fully, to know it by delving deep into the lived experience of 'I am'. As such, meditation and prayer, in many forms, are powerful ways of repeatedly aligning self with what transcends it. They generate self-healing processes that weld fractured identity. They dissolve unwanted barricades in the bodymind and enfold our frightened separateness in the security of that which surpasses it. We bypass our personal problems and transfuse our struggling self with its larger essence.

NOTES

1.   This point is beautifully made by Richard N. Bolles in his excellent little book, *How to Find Your Mission In Life*, Ten Speed Press, Berkeley, 1991.

2.   This activity is based on a process used at N. Rogers' Person Centred Expressive Therapy Institute.

3.   See Almaas, *The Pearl Beyond Price.*

CHAPTER THIRTEEN

Living Awareness in Groups

Summary
Groups are like living beings, with their own patterns of behaviour, skills, values, identity, and a shared ground of awareness. As individual members become more coherent and begin to live with awareness, so does the group. An aware person can raise the quality and performance of a group or team. Conversely, a group that begins to live closely to pure awareness helps unfold awareness in the individual. It also positively influences the wider environment of which it is part. Discovering what supports or disrupts coherence — for example, by participating in small awareness groups — can help us unfold this shared quality of awareness in ourselves and in the groups of which we are part.

A true community does not need a police force Malidoma Patrice Somé

Introduction — The Coherent Group [1]

As the old paradigm of separate minds breaks down in fields as diverse as semiotics, cybernetics, ecology, physics, and economics, a new paradigm of wholeness, unity, and interconnectedness is emerging. From that perspective, consciousness appears both individual and shared, an unlimited field resonating with what happens within it. As Rilke put it, we are like pyramids, with separate summits and a common base in the great matrix of existence. This base we experience as our own awareness in its simplest form. When we operate — either individually or as a group — from this base or closer to it, we influence the whole. We are more effective in our actions and a life-nourishing influence on those around us.

Many people find they are more aware when alone, without the distracting call of others and their needs. The challenge is to be aware, both alone and with others. Relationships, whether domestic, social, or professional, can test our ability to remain centred and aware, but they can also help our awareness to unfold. Here we consider how to support the unfolding of awareness through its shared aspect, so that our own growth is enhanced and the groups we are in function better.

Coherence is the key to healthy functioning in groups. We are coherent when congruent and centred in our awareness, when all aspects of ourselves are balanced and aligned. At such times, our speech and actions

197

communicate coherently. We have a positive influence on others, simply from our way of being in the world. Like vibrating tuning forks, we offer a pure note whose resonance entrains others. (Conversely, we create dissonance when we are incoherent and conflicted.) Coherence is thus also a shared phenomenon. We experience it in groups, when we feel balanced and aligned, not only with ourselves, but with those whom we are in relationship. In group coherence, our awareness resonates harmoniously with that of others, in a single lively and enjoyable field.

Almost everyone has experienced coherence in relationships. We sense it in groups in the periods of synergy, the delight in being together, the unity of atmosphere, the infectious influence of discovery or achievement, the moments of magic when an impasse resolves to satisfy and uplift all. Creativity, co-operation, truth, insight, energy, conviction, well-being — these are the kinds of qualities enjoyed and expressed at such times. Such qualities appear together with a deep sense of the pulse of existence itself, the very essence of our being alive. When this often fragile sense of being is present in a group and its members, it guides its thought and action impeccably. Although such groups may seem the result of happy chance, the principles involved are simple and easily applied. Anyone can learn how to become more aware in groups and to support coherence.

Coherence in Organizational Settings

Many of us spend a great deal of time in groups within organizations. Coherent team functioning (and the problems and losses associated with dysfunctional groups) are familiar to most businesses. Coherent groups can transform organizations. Their unity of purpose, depth of mutual understanding, and influence on the collective atmosphere can quietly galvanize the wider group to greater things.

Many of those who founded the large companies which straddle our planet were highly coherent people. They displayed in their lives a high degree of creativity and organizing power. Even after their departure something of their core patterns characterizes the corporate cultures they founded. The patterns of the coherent are simple and clear, both to themselves and to others. But the founder's coherence alone is generally insufficient to accommodate all the diverse people who eventually work in an expanding organization, nor to shape it indefinitely. Organizational coherence depends upon the presence of a measure of coherent individuals and teams. These depend in turn on the extent to which an organization supports the unfolding of personal coherence and grounds its teams in the processes which initiate and sustain it.

Many organizations have attempted to promote coherence in working groups. Most have proceeded from the outside in. For instance, difficulties in group formation or functioning may be handled by relocating an ill-fitting person or bringing in someone to balance or complete an existing mix. Attempts have also been made to engineer successful groups by analysing the balance of qualities or capabilities needed for a successful team and then bringing people together with the appropriate profile.[2]

Unfortunately, although changing personnel may improve the team environment by removing obstructing behaviours or melding a better balance of skills, the group may still function below its best. Our model of the different levels of human experience suggests why such approaches have limited success. Attempts to affect the group by addressing outer behavioural or environmental factors tend to neglect the impact of the subtler, less evident levels of belief, attitude, and identity.

Our capabilities crystallize around beliefs and values which support them. But the belief system which sustains one set of skills may clash with the beliefs and values of others with a different profile. For instance, Kolb's Learning Styles Inventory shows how people with a bent towards 'convergent' thinking may function in a way that is antithetical and even unpleasant to those with strongly 'divergent' tendencies.[3] Similarly people strong in abstract thinking may prefer to process the world through the written word and be poles apart from those with a preference for concrete learning or interaction with others. People often do not appreciate or understand those different to themselves. Hence the carping between departments in a company, the ill-will between accountants and others, between the DP department and the data users, or between engineers and those in, say, sales.

Instruments such as Kolb's or Belbin's help people to understand their differences, and to recognize that these have practical value. The levels of beliefs and identity are addressed indirectly, with the implicit recognition that a person's skills are an expression of his or her uniqueness. We are different and our differences are inevitable, but they contribute to our particular qualities. These we bring, with the rest of our person, to the larger whole where our shared contributions make possible things that we could not achieve alone.

Such approaches, however, are best complemented by methods that directly support the unfolding of coherence and awareness. In particular, a shared sense of purpose is a key to coherence. A group needs to be clear about its *raison d'être*, and members aware of their relation to it. But sensitivity to process is also important if shifting individual and relational needs are to be accommodated in the thrust for task and achievement. It helps to practice being more open and flexible, more aware of the powerful patterns present in individual and group behaviour, recognizing and responding to what is actually happening in the individuals and in the group as a whole. For many groups, this means taking time outside the task-oriented setting of work to review current patterns and discover what happens, delightfully, in simply being together.

Building Coherence In Groups

Groups function much like individuals. A group's internal 'map' of reality may contain conflicts, with one part of the group's desires or values clashing with something of importance to another member of the group. For instance, part wants to commit to action and achievement, and part needs to deepen relationship.

Such conflicts within a group are not unlike those between different parts of an individual. Internal conflicts manifest in incoherent behaviour, roughness, harshness, frustration, and difficulty in completing tasks and achieving goals. In the group, there may be surface issues — disputes about boundaries, responsibilities, rewards, communication — but these are a symptom not a cause. Treating the symptoms may relieve them, but while the deeper causes have not been addressed, the roots of conflict remain. These deeper causes ultimately have to do with our ability to accommodate and manage differences in the larger whole.

Maintenance of internal conflicts within the individual or within a group requires energy, as does *trying* not to have conflict. No army stands strong divided against itself. In rejecting what is not wanted (consciously or unconsciously) individuals and groups sabotage themselves. Sometimes a group member may fail to express a personal concern for fear of rocking the group boat. But the desire for consensus can only be fulfilled if it is freely reached.

The first step is for everybody to attend more fully to what *is*. By creating a climate in which we acknowledge and appreciate what is happening, conflicts can be recognized and resolved more easily.

Unfortunately, social conditioning and pressure to fit into what Charles Tart calls the 'consensus trance' distorts our ability to tune in accurately to what is happening in or around us.[4] Sometimes we do not even notice our own reaction, as we block off something which, if acknowledged, would lead to our questioning an apparent consensus. We may require a considerable period of new learning and unlearning to recover an accurate ability to recognize what is happening. And yet it is highly rewarding.

To acknowledge even incoherent patterns in the group is like using the opponent's energy in certain martial arts. Energy that is being used to force or resist expression is freed and can be redirected. The destructive force of incoherent patterns is neutralized and the energy becomes available for creative use. This is a natural process. Ultimately our strongest impulse is towards wholeness and unity.

How do we enhance this acknowledgement of what is? First, a group needs a shared sense of what coherence is like. This provides a yardstick for evaluating the quality of experience. Discussing as a group, at some point, the qualities of such experience helps build a shared representation and vocabulary for recognizing the presence or absence of coherence.

Second, attentiveness to the present rather than what has been or has not yet happened is essential. Nothing is negated. Simple questions, such as 'What is happening now?' or 'How are we doing?' draw attention directly to the present. Such questions may be used externally at first. After a while they are internalized as group members develop a natural attentiveness to individual and group functioning. The individual or group learns to go 'outside' itself to a perceptual position, in which there is more objectivity and distance for evaluating and understanding what is happening.

In another way, group coherence, like individual coherence, results from turning the attention to group functioning. Human awareness is self-referring; we can be aware of our thoughts, feelings, and actions and even aware of being aware. In bringing awareness to the group process, our awareness of what is happening becomes the object of attention, the knower becomes its own object of knowledge. This closes the usual gap between knower and known, promoting a sense of wholeness and oneness, from whence appreciation and constructive co-operation are almost inevitable.

Usually people attend only to the surface content or event. For instance, someone in a group might say 'I think feelings are running a bit high here!' 'Or we seem to be a bit tired, how about a break.' Here we are suggesting going to a deeper level and attending to the underlying patterns involved, and beyond them to sensing the feeling-quality of the group field. This requires a deeper level of self-reflexivity. And it rewards us with a deeper level of group coherence. Questions again reorient awareness, such as 'How is what is happening an expression of the group? What pattern or patterns keep happening in this group? How are these patterns happening now?'

These questions guide the group members and the group as a whole towards 'truth'. In accurately naming what is happening, there is a release, bringing what is, fully to consciousness. When the group as a whole recognizes that the pattern or issue involved has been accurately identified, the group field unites in a feeling of 'Yes, this is it'. That united feeling allows the group to resolve differences in a way that meets everybody's needs.

Readiness to respond truthfully depends upon a climate of honesty and trust. Without these, it may be difficult for people to say out loud what they sense is happening. Often people's feelings of insecurity or lack of safety will need to be addressed as part of 'what is happening now'. Such an approach fits ill with highly authoritarian or repressive leadership. The leader of a group with such a past may need to be quite courageous to open up more honest exchange. Members who might want things to change, but fear the consequences of speaking up, may also need to take risks if they want their groups to become more coherent.

Coherent group functioning depends on the group accommodating the needs of all involved. When it follows a line that alienates or excludes even one member, coherence drops. Conversely, when one individual disregards the needs and priorities of others, group coherence suffers. This manifests in a lowering of the energy or synergy within the group, and dullness, restlessness, or even disruptive behaviour.

A lowered level of coherence is an important signal. In recognizing it, group members notice that the group is in some way not addressing what needs to be addressed. Our senses (both outer and inner) let us know that we are on the 'wrong' level. When a group is finding its way to coherence, this may mean openly admitting that things are not working. This self-reflexive gesture already begins to restore coherence, even if a fuller recognition of group patterns may be required. As the group becomes more aware of its rhythms and patterns, the loss of coherence is less frequent and the return to coherence more automatic.

For full coherence, then, differences have to be more than accommodated. They need to be fully appreciated. On a deep level divergent values and views have to be acknowledged and even welcomed. This may mean that the coherent group will obey different more intuitive rhythms. With coherence things develop with an organic logic. They happen at 'the right time'. Ripeness is all. At times, a coherent group may find itself unable to match externally imposed deadlines. Its creativity depends on all members having the space to move towards the solution which is collectively recognized as expressing the truth of the whole group. Conversely, the coherent group may accomplish things in less time than would be expected, as there is less friction, less ego-display and greater harmony. Then that flush of recognition that, 'Yes, this is the solution', arrives much faster.

Appreciation and constructive cooperation are enhanced by greater self-knowledge and understanding of others. If awareness of the richness of our own map is one avenue to personal coherence, awareness of the variety and qualities of the maps of others helps open collective coherence. Misperceptions are less likely to arise when we are sensitive to differences and aware of how others function. The questions outlined in Chapter Eleven, for instance, help us understand odd patterns in others, and hence to appreciate their uniqueness. This helps our groups flourish.

The approach outlined here balances idealism and practicality. It provides a model that fulfils our desire for relationships of the highest quality possible, while allowing us to make mistakes and to learn all the way. Group coherence is lovely to experience. A group could think that it is failing if it became incoherent, but such failure is always a potential success. Incoherence offers us the opportunity to return to what is happening without judgement. In returning to the present, we instantly enliven coherence.

Activities Supporting Coherence

To honour our own needs, those of others, and those of the group as a whole, presupposes open awareness. We need to be in a state where we are sensitive to what is happening inside ourselves, in others, and in the group as a whole. Attention is finely poised, resting in inner awareness, but broadly including the 'field' around us in which the group is.

OPEN AWARENESS

1. Before a meeting, or in its early stages, take a moment to experience awareness in your own body. Resting on the breath, breathing a little more slowly and fully than usual, allow yourself to sense awareness in your head, in your heart, and your belly. In each place, allow your awareness to expand to include the whole body, so that you have a sense of yourself as a poised, aware, being.

2. Then allow your field of awareness to expand and include the whole space around where you are. Allow yourself to have 'soft' visual focus, so that your field of vision is wide; allow yourself to hear the full range of sounds around you, while continuing to feel whatever you are feeling inside. Don't try to hold on to this state while you are actively engaged in the group, but come back to it from time to time, when you are less actively involved in the meeting, as a state in which you are readily aware of 'I', the other(s), and 'we', shifting the focus of your attention amongst these, as necessary.

MULTIPLE PERCEPTUAL POSITIONS

Open awareness develops with our ability to take different perceptual positions. When we are comfortable in these positions and can use them flexibly, we can rest in that state of open awareness, shifting subtly among the different positions — staying with ourselves, while monitoring the whole.

1. Take some time to review some of your experiences, both pleasant and unpleasant (four or five of each), in relationships and in groups. Notice the perceptual positions which you seem to favour.

2. Review each experience from different perceptual positions, so that you experience each situation from first, second (with key members of the group), third observer position, and as the 'we' you create together. What new realizations do you make from the perspective of these four positions?

3. Project yourself into six or seven future contexts in relationships and groups, imagine yourself in each context taking some time in the various percep-tual positions:
Notice yourself taking time in first position to check what is happening in

your own awareness. Imagine taking second position with key individuals whose behaviour or response you are unsure of.

Imagine making use of cues — such as feelings of discomfort, a decline in the quality of exchange in the group, or simple boredom — to trigger a shift to third position or to sensing the group field as a whole. Notice opening your awareness to what is happening in the group and asking yourself: 'What is happening now? What pattern is occurring? What may need to happen for the group? For myself?'

4. When you are actually in groups, take some moments to explore the various perceptual positions — your own fully associated first position, second position with key members, the third observer position, and the fourth 'we' position.

PATTERNS

1. Consider three or four groups of which you are, or have been, a member. What recurrent patterns in your outward behaviour or internal responses do you display in each of the groups? Are the patterns that you identify in yourself present when you attend any group or only in some of the groups? Are they present all the time or only occasionally? Who or what triggers these patterns in you? What deeper beliefs and patterns are implicit in the patterns that you identify in yourself?

2. What patterns do you notice recurring in the behaviour of individual members? What patterns were these patterns themselves examples of?

3. What patterns do you or did you notice in the relationships among specific individuals (e.g., behaviour initiated by one member of the group and taken up and responded to by one or more other members of the group in a repeating sequence)?

4. What patterns do you notice in the group as a whole?

KEY PRINCIPLES

* Self-referral: being with what's happening
* Whatever is happening is right
* Recognizing what is happening frees blocks to allow change
* Appropriate balance of task and relationship
* Everyone is essential
* Everyone's input is relevant to the whole
* Consensus:
> There is a right solution.
> It must be right for all.
> Everyone will/must recognize it.

ATTITUDES/INTERNAL STATE:

Awareness (clear and open) ; intention (to increase coherence); attention (on present)

Honesty

Attending to both self and others.

Attention to the fine level of feeling

Acknowledging, accepting, and appreciating the present

Trusting inner knowingness/truth

WAYS IN:

Allowing pace to slow. Royal pace. Luxuriating. Soft focus.

PROCESS QUESTIONS:
* What level are we on?
* Are we on the right level?
* What's happening?
* Where are we now?
* What pattern(s) keep happening?

AWARENESS QUESTIONS:
* How am I an expression of this group?
* How is this group an expression of who I am?
* How are the members of the group an expression of it?
* How is what is happening an expression of the group?

LEADERSHIP
Leading from the non-leading position; leadership present throughout the group

Attention to the larger frame (without neglecting the small): 'What's happening to the whole?'

KEYS TO COHERENT AND AWARE GROUPS

Creating an Awareness Group

Awareness Groups are small groups of people with a shared interest in awareness, meeting from time to time to simply be together. Awareness Groups
offer occasions for learning more about how the magic of coherence occurs,
and for enjoying it, as members becomes more sensitive to the collective
dimension of awareness. Awareness Groups offer a special kind of support
group.

SIZE AND COMPOSITION OF THE GROUP

For an Awareness Group, you first need sympathetic members. It helps if
potential members are already committed to becoming more aware in their
own lives and are taking steps towards personal coherence by unfolding
their own awareness in ways suggested earlier in this book — for instance,
by opening the bodymind through movement and meditation or by recognizing and resolving negative patterns and beliefs in their lives.

Although you can experience coherence as a pair, it is more powerful in
a group. Three is probably the minimum, four better. A group of 5-7 people
seems to work best. If your group grows to about a dozen, consider splitting
into two groups. Larger groups can also function coherently, but need smaller
'cells', so that everyone can be heard in a way that is not possible in a big
group. If you introduce a new member to an established Awareness Group,
it is important that the new member be fully acceptable to all.

Being in an Awareness Group means learning how your own experience
relates to the group field — is part of it but separate. It means recognizing
how to accommodate your own needs and those of others. As members
attend to what is happening, they settle more and more deeply into their
own being-awareness. As such for periods less and less may be expressed.
Awareness Groups may lapse for extensive periods into silence. This can be
strange or difficult to people unused to it. Strong feelings may also come up
in a group context. It is important to be able to sort out different perceptual
positions: one's own feelings, those of others, and patterns happening among
members of the group. Having some prior experience and understanding of
the nature of Awareness Groups is desirable. One way to gain this experience and understanding is to invite someone who is experienced in this
approach to start your group off. Alternatively, attend a workshop or another group and then share what you have learned with the other members.

FREQUENCY AND LENGTH OF MEETINGS

How often and how long you meet for will be determined by the members
themselves. Where people live further away from each other, less frequently
and for longer, makes sense. My original group met about every six to eight
weeks, usually for an evening and a day. We found that if we hadn't met for

a while, it took a fair amount of time to catch up with each other before the group really settled down to simply being together. If you do live close by each other, you may need to check out what works best, so that you don't just go through the preliminaries, but have time to settle to the being level. If you don't meet very often, you may find that you also need longer meetings.

MEETING GUIDELINES

The key principle for ensuring the success of an Awareness Group is willingness to settle into deeper levels of being and simply be with what is happening, both as an individual and as a group. That means, there is no agenda or procedure, except to be aware of what is happening to you as an individual, to other members of the group, and to the group as a whole. This is not something to worry about or strain to achieve. Being with what is happening means also accepting that you will often forget to be with what is happening! When you notice that you have not been present with what is happening, gently return to noticing what is happening now.

As members are likely to be interested in exploring and unfolding awareness both in themselves as individuals and in the group as a whole, awareness provides a focalizing theme recurring in different ways in the discussions, experience, and exchange of the group. But it is not a narrow focus. Everything in our lives touches awareness in some way, so almost anything that comes up can be a vehicle for self and group unfolding.

If you or any member of the group has strong needs to do something different from usual, express it. If it's something the group picks up strongly, then it's a coherent expression of where the group is now. If people respond indifferently or negatively, then, you may need to jump a level to recognizing that different parts of the group are experiencing different needs.

It can help both the individual and the group to use the awareness and process questions in the summary chart. These questions bring the attention back to our own individual and collective experience. That self-referral curving back of the awareness on itself is the key to coherence. In a new group, you may need to use these questions more often, in an established group less often, as the patterns of awareness that underlie them will be installed in the group. It's worth coming back to the questions from time to time, particularly if you are unsure about what is happening in the group.

In an Awareness Group, it is helpful for all participants to be familiar with and able to take different perceptual positions. Notice patterns recurring in the group. If you discuss patterns in the group, what patterns occur in the way you discuss what is happening?

CHECK-IN AND PROJECTS

Early on in a meeting, it is useful to give people some time to check in with what is happening in their lives, particularly if the group hasn't met for a while. It is very helpful to individuals to have the attention of a coherent group simply focused on them, without any judgement. This often helps problems to clarify and issues to shift, without any trying whatsoever. As the group simply listens, sometimes nothing need be said. As members stay with what is happening, they will sense whether they need to ask some questions to aid understanding or to respond in some other way.

It also helps for members of the group to have some kind of project. This could be anything that the individual wants to achieve or change in their life. But if the project relates to deeper concerns of personal purpose and direction, so much the better. Projects that are connected to our deeper sense of purpose are more deeply part of who we are. To identify and share these projects is one way to activate the being level, both in ourselves and in others. Again simply describing the project to the group, allowing the group to listen and respond with questions and comments (to clarify and share experience rather than to judge, criticize, or even to advise) is very powerful. It is as if group coherence helps to clarify the project for the individual and have it sink to a deeper level of being. Projects brought to the group in this way accomplish themselves effortlessly almost without a lot of conscious input from the individual. It is as if the projects are supported and accomplished from the being level, rather than from the level of striving and doing.

CONNECTING	Establishing relationship; update of surface events, etc.
SETTLING	Group settling into being together; greater awareness of process
SLOW FLOW	Increasing silence, with desultory exchange
DEEP COHERENCE	Deep silence and awareness building up
BUBBLING	Creative group process arising from the silence
ACTIVE COHERENCE	Follow-through and exploration of theme/action that has arisen
LOW COHERENCE	Gap between quality of what's happening and past experience of what's possible. (Can appear in almost any phase)
PEACEFUL ACCEPTANCE	Relaxing and enjoying being together in the after glow of deep coherence
CLOSING	Tying up loose ends and ending

SOME IMPORTANT PHASES IN THE MEETING OF AN AWARENESS GROUP

AWARENESS GROUPS — A PERSONAL ACCOUNT

For several years, I was part of an Awareness Group that met from time to time, largely to just be together in a simple and enjoyable way.[5] Our meetings followed a typical pattern:

Typically, the group meets for supper at the house of one of the members. At first the tempo is quite fast and the energy high. We are delighted to see one another again. We exchange news. The conversation ranges widely across work, mutual acquaintances, recent interesting experiences, what's happening in the world, and so on. It's as if there is a need to connect, and clear any 'noise' arising from the different worlds we have been in.

Then at some point, it happens, perhaps during or just after the meal, or when we have settled ourselves physically in another room. Suddenly, activity settles. It's as if a hole appears in the clouds of casual conversation and the sun shines through. Everyone notices the shift. Awareness is almost palpable in the silence, like an inaudible resonance inside and around each of us.

During this settling phase, such moments may last just briefly before a fresh wave of conversation arises. But the active waves lessen, like they do at sea, when the wind drops. The group may pick up a thread introduced by a member of the group, play with it for a bit, embroider upon it, or follow some interesting association, before falling back into the silence of just being together.

Everyone recognizes the drift, luxuriating in the quiet, perhaps exchanging glances or acknowledging this invisible visitation from inner depths. But no-one tries to force it or suppress any desire to talk. It's just that, inside each of us, the stream of thoughts is slowing, and the urgency to cross the threshold into expression drops. Less and less seems really necessary to share, but what does is taken up and explored or quietly acknowledged like a little gift from someone close. It is allowed to reverberate and leave eddies in the pool of being. Some things disappear entirely. Some re-emerge instants or minutes later, transformed with fresh insight or energized into new directions.

The flow slows. Interventions are fewer and farther between. Directions start but are not taken up. The silence thickens and congeals. The coherence becomes so rich and dense, it can almost be spread with a knife, like rich clotted cream. The room rings with a vibrant and potent stillness. It's strange to feel so in everything, like floating in an enormous warm bath of being. At times I feel like a crease in the seamless fabric of eternity. I am a living flame in the bonfire of being. I feel present in a medium which contains everything around me, the fabric of walls, the carpet and crystals, or even the sunlight casting slow but perceptibly moving shadows through the fronds of plants. At times it is as if I am an unwitting co-generator of an enormously powerful force-field. At other times, it's as if we've merely helped each other to align ourselves with a quietness in which we at last listen to the unheard song of the world of things, and to our own silent song. In the quiet a sweetness tinctures each heart with a note, at once one's own and a fusion of all within the silence.

In its own time, the silence ripens. A few words, which moments before would have vanished like stones into the vast emptiness of space stir echoes and recognition in the group. The unformed energies around and within us seem to coalesce and align in a lively, bubbling dance. The group is suddenly active and involved, taking a direction, as if propelled from its self-reflexive shared silence into expressing creative possibilities. The energy ripples round the group, like a shower of sparks. The baton is passed effortlessly and engagingly from one side of the room to the other. The silence is more muted but remains like a sparkling edge to everything said, etching its clarity upon all.

As the group becomes more active, content begins to seize centre stage. The feeling of being fades and the self-reflexive curving of group consciousness on itself drops. The group gets engaged in a course of action and, the sense of coherence lessens. Suddenly there is a gap between our unexpressed expectations of that special quality of being together and what is happening in the group. It's as if the cohesive magic of even moments before has lost its spell. As one or more members of the group recognize this, and they remind everyone: 'What's happening? We seem to have lost "it". We're not on that level anymore.' The group gets back on track, settling once more into itself, maybe returning to slow flow or deep coherence, or into a new active phase.

Perhaps its time to break and simply be together over lunch or tea, reconnecting on surface levels of daily exchange, but now with peaceful acceptance of one another or whatever is happening. Maybe after lunch, peaceful acceptance means that instead of deep coherence, the group drifts into a brief peaceful sleep. It is another way of simply being with what is, as some level of fatigue surfaces and we surrender to it. It is what is happening now, until it passes and the group with it to some other state, some other way of being together.

And then perhaps it's time to go. Clearing loose ends, completing, and taking farewells and taxis. But with us goes a warmth of awareness, a ring of renewal, a softness and sensitivity to others, a recognition of the rhythm and harmony of all things, to which it is now much easier to harmonize oneself. Droplets of coherence bedewing others in so many different places as we depart to different parts of the country.

As I write the above, I glow inwardly. Cobwebs dissolve and vistas of inner space open out. Warm bubbles rise inside. I step lightly. I am fulfilled. I feel it on my face.

Beyond the Coherent Group

Any coherent group is a delight to be part of. Such groups influence larger structures within an organization or culture, and by extension the culture as a whole. The coherent culture is harmonious and stress-free in its internal functioning and effective in its external relations. It responds appropriately to what is, becoming a centre of coherence in the larger environment in which it finds itself. It is a positive influence on society as a whole. It influences the wider world positively and is secure from hostile influences without. It is the cornerstone of a more creative and peaceful world, a world of wisdom and awareness, such as we would wish for our children and theirs in the coming millennium. Everything starts with coherent and aware individuals and groups. In the next chapter, we consider the options for accelerating the unfolding of such individuals and groups for a better world.

NOTES

1.   This chapter owes much to Gene Early, who did much to launch NLP in Europe. Gene's 'Structural Coherence Model' broke new ground in the understanding and refinement of individual and group functioning.

2.   See, for instance, Meredith Belbin, *Management Teams — Why They Succeed or Fail*, Heinemann, London, 1981.

3.   David A. Kolb, *Experiential Learning*, Prentice Hall, New York, 1984

4.   Charles T. Tart, *Waking Up*, Element Books, Shaftesbury, 1988.

5.   Many of the points made in these sections are the fruit of our exchanges.

CHAPTER FOURTEEN

From Personal to Planetary Transformation

Summary
Accelerated unfolding of awareness among the individuals and groups that make up the global mind is a priority for the future of our planet. It is the key to the greater wisdom we need. Here, we examine the main highways to this enlivening of awareness: commitment to awakening inner essence on one's own; apprenticeship to a teacher or teaching; and participation in a shared pathway, such as a spiritual or religious group. Each option has distinct pros and cons, challenging us to find ways of supporting the maturing of planetary consciousness while respecting individual integrity.

> *All of a sudden I saw seven mirrors with seven reflected candles.*
> *The real candle was not visible. A voice said:*
> *There is only one real candle. You can never see it.*
> *You can see only its reflections.* Hasan Askari

Awareness, Spirituality, and Global Consciouness

Our sense of self unites the different elements of our experience. It connects our actions, thoughts, feelings, abilities, and beliefs to an inner 'I'. But our 'I' exists within a greater awareness beyond identity. Opening to this transpersonal awareness connects us with a wholeness beyond our individual selves. This subtle experience is essentially spiritual; it is the deepest essence of our encounters with both the sacred and the mundane. It not only connects the diverse strands of our personal experience, but holds our universe. Without this awareness there is no experience. It is the arena in which electrons and quarks are conceived and in which the galaxies spiral to the edges of outer space. Wherever we turn our attention, like some multi-directional radar, whatever we perceive or conceive, we do so in this infinitely tolerant, generous, and flexible receptor. Like a gentle mother with myriad children, it perceives everything and judges nothing.

We recognize, as we know it more deeply, that, besides holding our universe, this awareness is the inner essence of all things. We sense that it passes far beyond our personal sphere. It is not only the container of our particular set of thoughts, feelings, and perceptions, but the liveliness sensed within whatever we perceive. We find the contents of consciousness shot through with a subtle glue that seals the individuality of flower or stone, accentuating their particular qualities, while linking them to everything else. Not only is our awareness the inner witness of our experience, it is the animating essence unifying all things. We glimpse it in the beauty of moss and cloud, of wind and rain, and in our sense of being part of a larger whole.

Our awareness, then, is ultimately a universal consciousness that in some sense is experiencing us as well as all things. It is as if we discover that we are not just beings with awareness, but that our awareness holds us and all else, so that we move within universal awareness, like some sea creature that knows it is water, buoyed within water, swimming in an ocean in which there is an enormous variety of wonderful creatures all sustained by and structured out of that same universal water.

Our individual awareness is thus intimately connected with what appears to pass beyond the boundaries of personal existence. It is intimately related to the awareness of others. In its qualitiless simplicity it is ultimately what we have most in common with one another. The Being of each being is a shared ground. We may watch different movies and hear different melodies, but we share a common screen and a common silence. Stripped of all the contents of consciousness, the inner knower is simply a subtle and self-existent knowingness with nothing to differentiate it from the knowingness that any other knower finds as the ground of his or her experience.

This shared awareness is the subtlest element of the collective consciousness that so easily forms in a group. Although the collective awareness created in any social context functions on many levels — group behaviour, group thinking and feeling, group identity and so on — it depends ultimately on that silent awareness, which is present within and beyond all the more active phases of consciousness.

Our social groups intertwine with each other in a complex set of relationships. Some social groups are more fixed and long-lasting than others — nations generally are quite enduring, businesses and large organizations and families, too, though their shape may be quite mobile. Other social groups form and dissolve over a short span of time, as with a seminar or party. Most of us are part of more than one social grouping and may be involved in many different groups even in a single week. The threads spun as we participate in various groups create rich patterns, weaving all the groups in the world into a vast multi-dimensional network of networks.

Just as individual consciousness transcends the life of the cells and organs that make up our physical bodies, so global consciousness transcends the many individual and collective awarenesses that exist in it. The web of planetary interrelationship is supported by a complex network of global communication systems, but at a deeper level our shared awareness is its unifying foundation. A truly global consciousness is emerging. And as the cells which form our physical bodies may work together harmoniously or conflict with one another, depending upon the degree of balance in our own consciousness, so the groupings that form the larger collective consciousness may function in a harmonious or conflictual way, depending upon the degree of grounding in that shared unifying awareness.

Global consciousness fluctuates in its grosser manifestations. We notice this in the world currents reflected in fashions and fads and political and economic trends that sweep across the planet. We have instant access to graphic information about what is happening anywhere — whether a cause for celebration or mourning. News flashes send ripples through the global mind, which responds instantly to events in its parts. We are particularly aware of this global sensitivity at times of rising hope — as when the barriers to human rights and world peace began to crumble in the old Communist block — and at times of rising fear or tension, as during the Cuba missile crisis or the 1991 Gulf war.

At a time of rising expectations for more material ease and diminishing resources, with pressures of rising population and threats to the physical fabric of our planetary home, global consciousness is delicately poised. Our problems are multifold, but their solution does not so much depend upon our intelligence and capabilities, as our collective wisdom and maturity. What frustrates those concerned for the welfare of the planet, whether at the social, political, economic, or environmental levels, is that many of the measures that could secure the future of our world and the life on it appear self-evident, but short-termism and vested interests resist them.

In a sense, this frustration is both a healthy sign and part of the problem. Our individual bodymind is a self-regulating, self-organizing system whose natural tendency is towards balance. Problems arise within it when the needs of a part override or conflict with those of other parts or the whole. Because awareness unifies and grounds all parts of the bodymind, when we live with pure awareness, all expressions of ourselves come into balance. Groups function in a similar way. When they are coherent and aware, they become balanced self-regulating systems. The global bodymind is potentially the same. It already functions as a complex self-regulating system. Unfortunately, like most individual bodyminds, the living with awareness is so patchy that the system is easily out of balance, and the restoration of balance often delayed and violent.

Wars are one way in which tensions in the global system manifest and are released. They are the sociological equivalent of stress-related sickness in the body or an argument in the family. They have a positive function. However, they are a last-recourse release and reflect a failure of intelligence in the global bodymind. If we wish to survive as a species, we need a more supple way of soothing the global psycho-physiology than a mix of primeval aggression and modern technology.

We cannot solve problems with partial thinking that separates and fractures wholeness. Complex societal problems surpass the capacity of the mind to consciously compute. Such problems require solutions from that subtle field sustaining the complex balance of nature as a whole. More than clever answers to our questions, we need greater wisdom. Wisdom comes from being grounded in that state of consciousness from which everything is known. It comes from that wholeness which is both knower and known and the process of knowing, source of the multiple perspectives we can take, of time, and the different levels of life, source too of answers that resonate with wholeness.

Pathways to Transformation

Ultimately, then, our problems reduce to one: insufficient grounding in that larger wholeness which underpins, permeates, and permits all our more active phases of feeling, intelligence, and action. Our times challenge us to live closer to this awareness, so that global consciousness can naturally function with self-regulating wisdom and wholeness. Given the urgency of change in our times, the question of how to support that unfolding on a large scale is a vital one. There are three broad ways to the unfolding of consciousness, each with its own promises and pitfalls:
  * following one's own inner guidance
  * apprenticeship to a spiritual teacher or teaching
  * membership of a collective pathway, such as a spiritual or religious group.

SELF-DIRECTED INNER UNFOLDING
Ultimately each person is responsible for himself. Inner awareness is the touchstone of personal truth. By referring to that truth, each person can find his or her way to do what is necessary to release that deeper level of awareness. Where the individual can commit whole-heartedly to discovering and living his or her own personal truth, progress towards wider wisdom can be rapid. The individual can become an influential, authentic, creative, and self-reliant voice, speaking from hard-won personal truth, rather than collective cliché. However, few are at present geared to finding their own way from within. To function in this self-referral way already presupposes a degree of inner-directedness, awareness, and wholeness. Not everyone is ready to take this kind of responsibility for themselves.

The difficulty in following one's inner truth is compounded by our patterns of parenting and education. These encourage children (often with good reason) to listen to others as the primary source of evidence and authority. Our judgements about what is right and wrong for children, together with their relative immaturity, mean we approach child-rearing in ways that weaken their ability to gauge what is right for themselves. It can take many years to recover the ability to guide ourselves reliably with our inner knowingness.

A totally self-reliant pathway of personal unfolding can be limiting in other ways. It can be lonely, without the company and support of others in dry times. It can leave the individual vulnerable to distraction by the many side-shows of life, particularly if the process of referring to what is right is neglected. Our society exerts enormous collective pressure to follow the crowd, keep our heads down, do what everyone else is doing — marry, have children, a 'good' job, holidays in the right places, the latest gadgets, and so on — even if this is not what we truly need.

Moreover, it can be time-consuming and inefficient for each individual to reinvent the spiritual equivalent of the wheel, when appropriate guidance might lead to shortcuts. We might have difficulty discovering for ourselves where and how to start, or how to continue if stuck.

Excessive self-reliance may also conceal relational issues that can impede entering into a wider wisdom. We may follow our inner truth and have an excellent relationship with ourselves, but still avoid resolving those issues that arise from rubbing shoulders with others — whether with other individuals, such as family members, or with groups. Certain obstacles to awareness may only be dealt with if we place ourselves in contexts where they insist on our attention.

Living awareness involves a curious mix of commitment to openness and surrender to it. Sometimes the commitment is easy and the surrender difficult. Contact with others — partner, children, and groups in and outside of work — may provide the force that rounds off our personal edges and engenders the necessary surrender and humility.

But the ultimate difficulty for those who attempt to be self-directed is that we may be self-directed on many levels. We may follow the call of our senses, and become trapped in hedonism. We may follow the rule of logic and obey our own rationalizations to make personal but partial choices. We may be swayed this way and that by strong feelings. Or we may be guided by the deepest level of our own awareness where all parts of our personal well-being are harmonized and our needs aligned with the larger whole. That is the level from which true inner direction arises.

So while our pathway must ultimately become self-directed, it may be helpful, particularly in the early stages, to learn from others, perhaps in some kind of spiritual apprenticeship or partnership. Using the self-guiding qualities of our own awareness, in any case, means recognizing what, when, where, and how we might need to learn from others.

APPRENTICESHIP TO A TEACHER

Finding a teacher or teachers can shorten the pathway to personal unfolding. The teacher has ideally already trod the path and reached the destination of living with awareness. As such, he or she can offer suggestions and shortcuts based on the experience of what helped and hindered progress. If in good relationship with pure awareness, he or she will also have ready and profound intuitions of what to say or do to shift stuck states in others.

A good teacher teaches simply by being. We are all as tuning forks that resonate to universal awareness wherever it is enlivened within the amplifier of human neurology. When we are in a state of integrated awareness, even for a short time, we create an influence that is felt and shared by those around. Similarly, we feel our own awareness enlivened when we are in the presence of someone enjoying a state of grace. It feels good to be around such people.

This is the appeal of the true teacher, although such are rare. We are naturally attracted to the organizing energy of living awareness. We enjoy the peace and delight we experience as we sense the other's being silently influencing and aligning the different aspects of our world, like iron filings in a strong magnetic field. That delight is nothing but our own awareness becoming lively within us, perhaps after being submerged by the preoccupations of day to day living.

The delight that the teacher can bring, simply by being who he or she is, and by conveying a sense of greater wholeness, can awaken a great deal of love and devotion. This loving response is extremely valuable in unfolding the channels of awareness in the student. These are not just cerebral, but heartfelt and whole bodied. This opening of the heart should not be dismissed as psychological transference to an idealized parent, though that may be part of it. Such opening lays the foundation for true maturity in which life is lived from a place of inner security, love, and acceptance.

The idea of deep commitment to a teacher can be extremely threatening to Westerners. We are very aware that not all teachers match their teachings and the expectations they create. But our suspicions pass beyond anxieties about spiritual charlatans. We may also be motivated by a less conscious and more suspect form of self-preservation. We deeply fear the loss of self that is necessary for full spiritual awakening into wider awareness. We have, since the Courtly Romances of the Middle Ages, been enculturated with metaphors of individuation, exalting the self. This for Joseph Campbell is the significance of the Tristram and Isolde and Grail myths: drinking from the cup of individual experience. Having drunk of it, Tristram says he would choose it, even if it meant death or hell. And now our cultural expectations of individualism grip us so deeply that we collectively fear the surrender of self, even to that living awareness which animates and contains us.

Yet, our very emphasis on the individual and finding our own way can be a trap. Our esteemed self-reliance becomes a way for the unregenerate 'I' to run riot through life, heading in every direction except that which leads towards the nodes of fear that create and sustain this dubious yet tenacious concept of a separate I-thing.

Our individuality is precariously constructed from secondary responses and reflexes set in motion, whose reason for being is then forgotten. Like a Gothic cathedral held up by flying buttresses without which the whole edifice would collapse, the sense of 'I' is sustained by well-constructed responses in the bodymind that surround the core truth, but are not central to it. The 'I' is really an altogether simpler thing. In some sense, it is nothing at all, but a local variation on the great emptiness of all things. To really flow in this emptiness requires a giving up of self and a yielding to a greater fullness and abundance which nurtures and sustains not only this flimsy scarecrow self, but the whole fabric of existence. A teacher can help this subtle process.

Learning in the context of awareness is primarily experiential, rather than conceptual. Experiential learning comes from moving through the world or withdrawing quietly into ourselves. It also results from 'modelling' others. By being open and receptive to an appropriate model, willing to learn by imitation and association into a different world, we can expand and enrich our own. This kind of vicarious learning — so natural to a child — can be particularly helpful in accelerating the comfort and appreciation of our own awareness, where our model has a rich and deep quality of awareness that permeates everything that they do. By aligning ourselves with an inspired teacher, we can surpass ourselves.

But we can lose momentum in the stagnant waters of imitation. We may find ourselves following empty rituals and ignoring the rich vein of our own life impulses, particularly if our focus is half-hearted. Deep learning requires that we make our learning our own, test it, explore it, interact with, question it, take it in new directions. We may expect so much of the model that we fail to do this. The teacher can then be a limitation.

Unfortunately, the master is generally innovative, and the disciples derivative. The master stays in the fresh, the now, the unexplored, channelling uprushes of the unforeseen from the empty present moment. For this reason he is exciting to be around. He is an intersection of time and the timeless. He is a hole through the frozen ice flows of custom and limited thinking to the krill-rich ocean below. Things happen, outside of boundaries, he is unbound, breaks boundaries, has a fresh take on reality, goes in unexpected directions. He makes untrod tracks in the sand. It's exhilarating to follow in his fresh, foaming, ionized wake.

But his followers follow. He tells, they repeat; he thinks, they do. They can be loyal, douty, but rarely inspiring. They don't originate, they imitate, picking up and reiterating his first thoughts. This they may do extraordinarily well. They may to some extent do so in their own way; but this personalizing is that of a chorist bringing a personal tone to the composer's melody. They may even get to the point where his message becomes theirs, and they have it. But there can be quite a time of personal stripping away and focus on the other before their self is regenerate and their thoughts are no longer second thoughts of the master, but their own first thoughts. For all must eventually own their own reality. Life will accept nothing less.

It can be useful to follow an apprenticeship, to learn from those who have trod the path and negotiated some of its obstacles, perhaps even reaching the destination. It is helpful to associate with the wise. But at some point, because the path is one of self-reference, we must follow our own music. Although Eastern paths often emphasize surrender, this point is also acknowledged, perhaps a little brutally, in Zen Buddhism. It is suggested that if we meet the Buddha, we are to slay him. We must eventually take the master's mantle, if we are to come into our own.

The question is: When is it appropriate to do that? The answer differs for different people. If we feel called to a long apprenticeship in imitation, it is important to honour that calling, if we are to be truly inner-directed. And it is vital to listen quietly and make sure that it is indeed our call and to recognize when our deepest Self calls us to something different.

UNFOLDING AWARENESS THROUGH AN ORGANIZATION OR GROUP

Besides self-directed unfolding of awareness and apprenticeship to a teacher, membership of a personal development, spiritual, or religious group can help awaken awareness. Such groups may range from loose and informal gatherings of fellow explorers to the monolithic structures of the world's great spiritual traditions. Spiritual groups are potentially both help and hindrance, both enlightening and stultifying.

On the positive side, established groups, such as the old religions, offer a rich tradition stretching back in time. They provide a sense of continuity to inspiring models of saints and sages. They may possess a wealth of routines and rituals for raising awareness. They may furnish inspired accounts of both the pathway and the destination, texts offering wisdom and instruction for daily life. They may also offer an organizational structure through which individuals with special gifts, deep experience, and training can share a wealth of knowledge and guidance with those on an inner journey.

Groups offer the promise of certainty in a world whose dominant paradigm is one of scepticism. This is particularly important in the spiritual context, where the subtle essence of inner life is easily obscured by the mists of habit and the pressure to conform to our era's predominant hallucination — that only the tangible world exists and is worthy of attention. Belonging to a spiritual group supports the kind of commitment that brings results, since what we place at the centre of our energies and attention tends to grow and develop. The greater the commitment, the more rapid and complete the alignment of the bodymind that must accompany it. Warm and supportive company eases the lonely pilgrimage towards heightened consciousness during some of its more tedious phases. Encouragement and inspiration help awareness to open to itself. Spiritual groups offer a community of like-thinking and like-practising people, speaking a common dialect of the language of spirit and sharing a framework for interpreting reality and experiences. And, naturally, sharing special experiences of awareness inspires and awakens more of such experience.

Yet membership of a group can also dampen the unfolding of awareness. Spiritual groups may focus on the wrong logical level. Prescribed and proscribed beliefs and behaviours remove responsibility from individuals to think for themselves. Organizations also exercise forms of persuasion, sometimes subtle, sometimes unbelievably crude, to maintain a uniformity that suppresses people's right and duty to know their own truth for themselves. Individual thinking that is in any way deviant or simply different may be crushed, stifling personal unfolding. This can lead to automatic responses, ritualized behaviour devoid of lived meaning and mouthed platitudes that do not engage the whole person. Some of the received beliefs may ossify as dogma that is untrue and potentially harmful if held at a given state of growth. People may be persuaded that their only hope and security is within the framework of the organization and that to leave the nest is to lose all they have gained within it. When this happens, the group may be more a hindrance than a help.

Groups offer a further difficulty. In unifying the differences that the various members bring to them, they can create an extended sense of self, a kind of greater 'we' that gives a feeling of security and a glimpse of the extended unity of expanded awareness. While this unity supports the opening of awareness, it also carries a price. Such unity is often reinforced by emblems, symbols, rituals, and shared habits of speech and thought. The outer distinctions — Hasidic Jewish ringlets, Christian crosses, Islamic veils, and so on — ease identification of members with their own grouping, but may also visibly accentuate distinctions to non-members. The group then, while uniting within, divides from those without. Group unity then becomes a localized affair that compromises our universality. We meet our fellow human beings, not directly in our shared essence, nor even in our common humanity, but through the group persona we have identified with or which they have bundled us into. This is impoverishing, because we cease to communicate deeply, relating instead through cliché. The greater unity of life is riven until our unity includes all beings and things.

Pseudo-unity is also potentially lethal. For spiritual groups unleash powerful energies. Devotion to a greater being than ourselves in prayer opens the heart to intense and expansive feelings. To conceive that being we must surpass or surrender ourselves. We open to the oceanic; awareness is suffused with its own excess. The dry walls of ordinary awareness dissolve or dance to a deeper pulse. But when such experience of the transpersonal releases intense energies that flow back through an immature mind or unresolved identity, we may take our truths for the truth. Divine love deviated through our imperfections can then discover diabolical energies embodied in those that differ from us. When our truth denies all others, we can maim and kill in God's name. That is the shadow of fundamentalism.

Yet, cohesion is possible without exacerbating differences. It depends on the kind of 'we' we create in our groups, and how we frame this 'we' in relation to the still larger 'we' of our shared humanity. That is partly a function of attitudes shaped by our beliefs and values. It also depends on our awakening to pure awareness, the witness of all experience and ground of openness and understanding.

As with allegiance to oneself or to a teacher, adhesion to a group or tradition needs careful attentiveness for it to remain useful. Shifting perceptual positions from time to time to evaluate what is happening to self, to others, and to the group as a whole is an important way of checking that participation in the group continues to be both healthy and helpful.

Another Way

Unfolding awareness, then, is an essential ingredient not only for a life of quality, but for the flourishing of that self-balancing wisdom implicit in healthy global consciousness. Yet, the three broad pathways to wisdom — taking responsibility for one's own development, learning through apprenticeship to a teacher, and participation in some kind of organized spiritual pathway — each offer rewards and pitfalls.

In the face of these mixed benefits, it would seem we must either continue haphazardly as we have been doing or seek a complementary fourth approach to help make the best of the three principal pathways. (These, in any case, are not mutually exclusive. Most people find any quest for quality means an evolving mix of methods. Anyone seeking to unfold the deeper meaning of their existence at times follows their own judgement, at times seeks the guidance of a teacher, and at times draws on the fellowship of a group.)

Any new approach to the wise pursuit of greater awareness requires certain qualities if it is to be effective. For instance, it needs to support both distance and engagement — distance so that we can draw back from our own process and from any particular pathway to take stock of strengths and weaknesses; engagement so that real passion and commitment inspire the unfolding of awareness. For such distance and engagement, we need a broad view that suggests how the various paths and options relate to each other. At the same time, this wider view must translate into specific practical ways to awaken awareness, suitable for our temperament and phase of development. As such, our fourth way ideally addresses both understanding and experience. Understanding helps us make sense of experience. It helps the mind and heart work together. Experience ensures that concepts become practice and lead to maturity not just in ideas, but in how we live and breathe. Finally, our fourth way needs both depth and simplicity. It needs sufficient depth and complexity to satisfy those for whom the mind is important and to give confidence to those who lead and influence others, whatever their preferred pathway. It needs simplicity so that it's key principles can be easily understood and hence widely accessible. In this book, we have the rudiments of such a fourth way. I call it the Way in Wisdom. The final chapter outlines its key elements.

Activity

Review your life-teachers, from childhood through to the present. On paper, list the key influential
   * figures in your life
   * books, images, films, theatre, places
   * groups, communities, and traditions

To what extent have these influences lit up the unfolding of inner awareness? To what extent have they led to long fallow periods of resting on past experiences and answers?

To what extent have you learned from others? To what extent have you learned from following your own truth?

Take your time for the next phase and allow yourself to be somewhere where nobody will disturb you for a while. Relax and centre yourself, breathing deeply and allowing your awareness to be in the body. In this comfortable state of wakeful rest, allow four beings who for you resonate with your inner being to come to your awareness one by one. Just ask quietly within that they may come to your attention, then wait for them to appear.

From a detached 'third person' observer perspective, notice their qualities, their atmosphere, their way of being in the world.

Go to second position with each in turn. Imagine being them with those qualities and behaviours.

Return to your own 'first position' and imagine them around you supporting, protecting, and guiding you. Imagine them as image, sound, light, and qualities of energy and feeling, which are at once around you and infusing you.

Let yourself experience a sense of harmony, fullness, and light growing within you, spreading from you to include all races, creeds, and communities on the planet, and from there into the solar system and beyond, out into the cosmos, returning thence to enrich the fabric of life everywhere.

They say the Virgin was appearing for most of the eighties to a group of young people in Medjugorje, Bosnia, guiding them with messages and teaching both for themselves and for the world. Who can say what really was happening there? The place before the wars felt like a world-navel, heavenly energies permeating that Mediterranean hill valley, with palpable peace and the magic of miracle, which touched and transformed the hearts of all who visited there. Once the Virgin re-ferred to a certain villager as the most devout in the community. "But she's a Muslim", people protested. "Man makes divisions", the Virgin responded.

I like this story. Sadly, the message was lost on the people of the Balkans. Let us not forget that all around, and even within us, are differences. Life is difference. But integrating and suffusing that difference is that which is both loving and indifferent, the One. The nameless current carrying the oscillating charge of life. This we all share.

CHAPTER FIFTEEN

The Way in Wisdom

Summary
The Way in Wisdom offers a simple synthesis of the diverse ways to awaken awareness. It helps us manage the relationship among the three primary approaches to unfolding awareness in a way that makes them more effective and in harmony with each other. It also provides a simple pathway to living awareness in its own right.

Knowledge comes, but wisdom lingers. Tennyson

The Way in Wisdom

The Way in Wisdom is the way we tread as we align ourselves with our own unique course. It provides a framework that supports the unfolding of aware-ness, no matter which way attracts us — alone, with a teacher, or as part of a group. It suggests an integrated approach to awakening that is sufficiently comprehensive to include the major facets of life, but open enough for us to explore them in diverse ways. It complements our choice of a particular teaching, while offering a pathway in its own right in which we can explore with others the questions and answers we encounter on our journey.

The Way in Wisdom offers a meta-perspective on the various approaches for unfolding awareness, helping us understand how they relate to each other, and thus how we can negotiate a path among them. The notion of multiple perceptual positions (Chapter Three), for instance, helps us have both distance and engagement, allowing us to take a comprehensive and detached third or meta position, a committed first position, and to identify with any group or with humanity as a whole as an expanded 'we'. This supports both tolerance and engagement.

The Way in Wisdom rests on a seven simple postulates:
  * human experience includes a dimension of awareness beyond iden-
    tity
  * personal and planetary well-being depend on this essentially spir-
    itual dimension
  * awakening to it is both desirable and possible
  * there are many ways to bring about such awakening
  * the various maps and pathways to it are not the awakening itself
  * ultimately our knowing is within ourselves, but we can also learn

from one another
* people have a right to pursue any way that does not impinge unduly
on others

In the notion of levels of development (Chapter Three), the Way in Wisdom offers a general account of how our consciousness unfolds through a number of discernible levels or phases. Levels of development explain the mixed results of the three primary pathways to personal unfolding. At the early levels of development (levels one to three), we may need the help and support of a group and of a teacher or teaching. It is difficult to be truly inner directed while we are still enmeshed in the co-operative social frames (level three) and before we attain an integrated sense of self (level four). We are simply not ready. But as we individuate, the group may become distracting. Similarly, while we are dealing with the issues of the instinctual, power and control, or the pressure to conform, our groups will have a measure of irrationality and unresolved shadow. Their relation to the individual will be ambiguous, sometimes supportive, sometimes oppressive. The Way in Wisdom indicates that we may need to adjust our relationship to the three basic pathways over time, according to the phases of development we pass through. It helps us perceive that we are not mistaken or misguided at such times of adjustment, but called to be sensitive to the deeper currents of our life.

The Way in Wisdom emphasizes both understanding and experience. It offers a global vision of heightened consciousness, while suggesting practical ways to accede to it. A simple mandala graphically summarizes the key elements, with eight petals around an empty centre. This unlabelled centre represents being or pure awareness itself. It stands for the implicit, but often unstated, goal of any path to a life of quality, the indescribable sacred core of each of us and of all things. The petals represent key ways of returning to that centre. Through knowing it, we enjoy increasing balance and quality in the active parts of our lives.

In gravitating towards a life of quality, we discover that any activity can open a window to greater enlightenment. Even driving a car or washing up can hasten awakening. But sooner or later we need understanding to guide action. Understanding is almost always provisional, but it orients us in the journey through life. The understanding of who and what we are — through studying the structure and dynamics of experience — is represented by the top right segment of the mandala showing the outline of a human head and shoulders, with a smaller version of itself inside it.

Although 'the map is not the territory', a map helps any journey, especially the journey to discover who you are. The opening chapters of this book (One to Five) offer one such map. However, in the Way in Wisdom, everyone is a cartographer in their own right, checking and modifying any maps used, and charting new pathways as they research and explore new territories. The Way in Wisdom is not about dogma, but about a shared context for exploration and discovery.

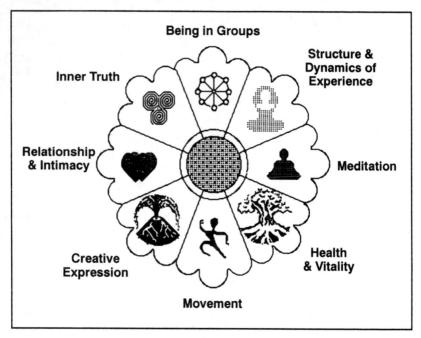

THE WAY IN WISDOM

Insight into the structure and dynamics of experience naturally illuminates the experiences provided by the other aspects of the Way in Wisdom. It helps us recognize what happens through meditation or movement, for instance. Conversely, the experiences arising with the practice of the various methods for unfolding awareness extend our understanding of the structure and dynamics of experience. Self-study — through asking important questions, keeping journals, introspection, and through 'modelling' others — supports the refinement of our maps of reality. It helps us make more accurate distinctions in our experience and to recognize blind spots we might otherwise ignore.

Meditation, withdrawing from daily activity to contact that being-awareness underlying all forms of mental activity, is a key part of the Way in Wisdom. This is symbolized by the seated Buddha figure to the left of the mandala. In Chapter Six, we considered approaches to meditation that involve gently allowing mental activity to be transcended. The Way in Wisdom also honours other types of practice, such as techniques emphasizing 'mindfulness' — attending to what is present in the field of consciousness — or devotional practices such as the 'prayer of the heart'. Personal preference naturally determines our choice of meditation. Ideally, we become more sensitive to the feedback provided by our own body, heart, and mind, fa-vouring approaches in which the process is comfortable and the result life-enhancing.

Wisdom involves taking care of the body, as how we treat it affects aware-ness enormously. The tree symbol in the next section of the mandala represents the importance of life-enhancing healthy habits, such as eating nourishing food in appropriate quantities, or exercising and sleeping ad-equately. We have not emphasized this aspect in this book, as it is easy to be prescriptive in a way that is insensitive to individual needs. But if we be-come more sensitive to the feedback our own bodymind provides, we know when and what to eat and how much, similarly for other aspects of daily life, such as sleep. As awareness opens, we naturally make healthier choices. The Way in Wisdom encourages this process.

Taking care of the body also involves ensuring simple and satisfying sen-sory enjoyment, as discussed in Chapter Eight. Body-oriented therapies such as deep massage or physical manipulation also help, freeing blocks in the body and bringing awareness to the body as a whole. When we select envi-ronments for living and working where we flourish and feel good, we also support health and vitality.

Besides meditation and care of the body, self-unfolding movement dis-cussed in Chapter Seven also enlivens inner awareness. The bottom part of the mandala uses a dancing figure to represent this. As we saw in that chapter, dance and gentle forms of structured movement, such as *tai chi* or *yoga* can also refresh the body and open awareness.

Open and easy emotional expression is a prerequisite for, and means to, the unfolding of awareness. The symbol of a volcano (bottom left) points to the opening of awareness through the freeing of the emotions. We have suggested (Chapter Nine) that the free use of the expressive arts (including the voice) in the 'creative connection' can greatly help this process. This part of the mandala also acknowledges the importance of more conven-tional art in heightening awareness, both for the creator and the appreciator.

In the Way in Wisdom our relationships, described by one Indian teacher as 'the yoga of the West', also provide a context that stretches our aware-ness. While our relationships can be a minefield, in which habit and negativity send us in a downward spiral, one-to-one relationships, repre-sented by the two hearts, can help us open consciously to a shared ground. Such opportunities exist in our relationships with our partner, close friends, and family. Appropriately awakened with a partner, our sexuality can also support the freeing of intimate loving awareness.

Besides general understanding of the structure and dynamics of human experience, the Way in Wisdom suggests that we may need to explore our own patterns to discover the mistaken conclusions we may have made, divorcing ourselves from our own being and from the larger whole. The little triple maze in the top left segment symbolizes the inner journey to unravel *pragyaparad,* the mistake of the intellect, which separates us from inner Being. Open Heart Learning, described in Chapters Ten and Eleven, offers one such approach.

The Way in Wisdom also acknowledges the importance of short solution-oriented therapy to resolve certain life-challenges. For instance, unhelpful habits that we find hard to change, whether ways of responding to others, or destructive behaviour, such as excessive smoking or drinking, may benefit from simple focused attention.

The maze symbol also reminds us of the importance in the Way of Wisdom of knowing our heart's desire, of having a sense of purpose, giving direction and meaning to our journey through life (Chapter Twelve).

Lastly, the Way in Wisdom recognizes that groups play an important part in our daily experience, both helping and hindering the unfolding of pure awareness (Chapter Thirteen). Our culture subtly influences us and it is important to become more aware of its power and pull. Our ability to be ourselves when with others is an important part of the journey to wholeness. The wheel-like symbol at the top of the mandala represents the challenge of groups. Awareness Groups described in Chapter Thirteen help master this dimension of the Way in Wisdom. This sector also acknowledges the importance of ritual and ceremony in building coherence among people and supporting the awakening of deeper levels of group consciousness.

The Way in Wisdom, then, offers a comprehensive approach to personal development that addresses the key aspects of life. It helps us be inner-directed, whether as individuals or as groups, by making it easier to notice where we are naturally strong and where we might need to give attention. It offers the elements of a pathway in its own right. Yet, at the same time, it serves as a kind of spiritual 'meta-model' that helps us situate and understand the emphasis of a particular teacher or teaching, so that we can identify strengths and weakness — for instance is mind emphasized and body or emotions neglected? The Way in Wisdom does not impose certainties, but sets a context in which we can explore what works. Then progress can be not only towards wisdom, but in wisdom.

The wise transcend the boundaries of their own systems and speak with a universal voice. They straddle the extremes of surrender and commitment. They trust in both silence and action at appropriate times. Their response to smaller minds — like that of Jesus to those who tried to trick and test him — is to jump out of the limited mental and emotional space offered to them, to point with a conviction and logic that has the compelling force of deeper truth, to the larger frame beyond. It is this larger frame that we ultimately need in order to accommodate and harmonize our differences in a spirit of respect. Our passion and conviction can then ignite the world with complementary but caring flames, as pure awareness harmonizes our personal dance with that of the planet, within the one ineffable and intrinsically loving and living awareness that we share.

The mist lifts to reveal a row of spiderwebs beaded with dew. Minute watery crystals tremble almost imperceptibly on silken strands. Placed strategically at geometric points and sparkling in the diffuse light of the sun, they accentuate structure. The webs are utterly invisible at certain angles and against certain backgrounds. They need the contrast of dark tree-tops to reveal the fragile artistry of their one-morning magic. The irradiation from the central circles is uniformly irregular. In the middle is a round nebula of gossamer. Then there is a gap in which both the outward and the crosswise strands are fewer, till the main web resumes. From this hollow hub-surround, lacy, trembling spokes reach out to the edge, encrusted periodically with light-refracting dew, like a miniature sun or star. The spiders are nowhere to be seen.

A Personal Quest

EARLY INFLUENCES

From an early age, awareness has fascinated me, although I did not have the words to name it then. I was curious in quiet moments about a subtle 'something' that I sensed somehow present within all my experience, but which I ordinarily missed while caught in the rush of play. This subtle awareness, which makes it possible to experience whatever we do experience, is the quiet ground of all our delights. It is the essential and unassuming ingredient of a fine quality of life, and has been a compelling, if sometimes interrupted, focus of exploration, discovery, and enjoyment throughout my life.

Periods of enforced rests on sunny afternoons in darkened rooms in north Norfolk, England, form some of my earliest memories. Adults made themselves the arbiters of my needs. I knew I wanted to rush and play. They thought that I needed to rest or sleep. Perhaps, I would be compelled to settle on a sofa in a front room at my grandmother's bungalow, with a stuffed toy or two. Or maybe I was placed in a bed in a little upstairs room of the terraced cottage in Holt, the small market town where we lived.

At first frustrated, hurt, and bitter at being incarcerated so unjustly, I became resigned, and then genuinely quiet, though still awake. I didn't sleep, but settled into an inward place. I watched the folds of the curtains, shifting occasionally just a little in the breeze. I became fascinated by the rounded shapes of the curtain and the muted afternoon light coming through them silhouetting the geometric patterns of little emblematic birds and animals, arranged like Egyptian hieroglyphs. I became absorbed in discovering the shapes made by the interwoven patterns, now looking at the geometric shapes, now dwelling in the spaces between them, now resting in the more organic forms of the folds in the fabric. On another level I became aware of my own existence as a distinct being, a centre of consciousness. This experiencing self was both involved in what it was experiencing, and not involved, as if simply experiencing the experience. I was aware of my own being, aware of the curtains, and aware of my own exploring of the curtains. Later, I don't know if I slept, but I would wistfully rejoin the late afternoon sun, running up the garden pathways in a jungle of mauve and pink flowers, golden rod, red hot poker, and carnations as tall or taller than me, sensing that I had missed an important part of the day's fire, but that the garden was full, full of itself, full of secret messages to my rested and opened soul.

My next important opening of awareness was the first of many in which images and ideas played an important role. When I was about four or five, sitting in the child-sized chairs at the low desks of my first primary school, my teacher Miss Goffe, a firm, but soft spoken middle-aged woman, introduced me to the idea of God. This notion catapulted my young mind into places it had never been, as it tried to understand a Being who has no limits, is in everything, sees and hears whatever you do, including when you tell a little lie or steal a biscuit from the tin, or think some angry thought about your new little brother. This Being is a kind of person, but doesn't live down the road. It's as if he or she has a face and a beard, but is everywhere. Somehow the boundaries of my young mind were stretched. The image engenders a sense of endlessness, omnipotence, omniscience. Suddenly just in conceiving it, my world is enlarged, boundaries stretched and shifted. And we are being watched!

When I was eight, I made my first Holy Communion, dressed in white with a group of other children. We were well drilled, and I remember kneeling on the dark blue padded pew, saying my prayers devoutly and wondering why the heavens did not seem to be opening. I was trapped in the church, uncomfortable, fidgeting involuntarily, wondering if I had failed because my mind would so easily wander off to thinking about walking down to the sea with Granny afterwards or why the service seemed to take forever. I wondered about this God-person, to whom I was taught to talk, but who never seemed to reply, at least not in words.

I looked up to the black and white chevrons painted on the roof-beams of St Joseph's in Sheringham, noticing the patterns, and again finding that half-dreamy, half-wakeful state as with the curtains. I watched the other children taking communion in white dresses and trousers, wondering if they were communing with God more successfully. Then it was my turn, nervously receiving the wafer, returning to my pew, wondering whether eating God was having the effect the teachers had promised and wondering if I was worthy enough to know. I was so disappointed, due to unmet childish expectations, that I failed to notice that this context of quiet devotion and restraining inwardness had taken me to a place where I again sensed, not only the sky and trees reflected in the stream of my life, but the flowing transparent current of consciousness as well. I almost missed the sacrament of communion with my own being.

Around this time I wanted to be a priest. With ritual robes, curling wisps of incense, inspirational words and devotional chants, in noble arched buildings with stained glass, priests used the mind and senses to help one imagine and attune to an ineffable Being beyond the edges of our own. I could glimpse another and delectable realm and thought that priests were those people who knew about it. They were professionals of the sacred. To become one of them was to put one's attention on what is most important, unlocking the door to the secrets behind our earthly exile and making them available to others.

An annual holiday in the country opened me to another aspect of aware-ness. Every summer I used to stay in a small rose-trellised cottage with a devout lady in the small village of Walsingham, home since the eleventh century to an important Marian shrine. I would also camp in a field by a shallow stream for a week or so with two pilgrims with gentle northern burrs. Each day with the early morning mists still swathing the ground and the grass dripping with beads of dew, we would walk to the small shrine chapel for mass. In those days it was still in the centuries-old Latin, the daily ritual connected like a silvery thread to the beginning of history. This whispered mystery transformed the present moment into a gateway to the timeless, connected magically to the past. Tudors, Plantagenets, Saxons, floated in and out of the stones of that ancient village, and from Miss Jelf's lips, as she roamed through history with stories always involving some per-sonal connection-the mysterious plesiosaurus washed up on Blakeney Point, the archaeological dig in the grounds of the old Abbey, travels through the Himalayas as a young woman . . . .

The stay stimulated my young mind intellectually and nurtured me spir-itually. Each year, I was aware that the kinds of activities in which I was engaged, the talks of God, the periods of silence, the quiet confidence in another realm, had transformed something deep within me that spread to my life as a whole and continued to be present long afterwards. I felt differ-ent. The whole quality of my life had been raised. I was aware of something quintessentially true, real, and vital, if quite fragile, animating me. I felt a better person.

Unfortunately, as the year wore on, this sense of personal transformation declined. I seemed to get sullied, hardened, desensitized, coarsened, as the boundaries of reality thickened and set once more, depriving me of a fine joy and awareness of the soft sparkle of life. I knew that renewal was possi-ble as summer approached, but each year, as I grew older, it seemed harder to recapture that purity of spirit. And each year, it seemed to disappear more quickly. The contrasts of heightened and coarsened consciousness convinced me that life could be lived in different ways. And some were better than others.

At age 11 or 12, I discovered that other, more secular concepts could also awaken awareness. We were asked to research a topic and present it to the class in a short five-minute speech. I chose Einstein who was a revela-tion. I didn't understand the mathematics, but the concepts were a continuation of the areas opened up by Miss Goffe. Space and time were connected. Energy and matter were two facets of the same reality. Here was

a spirit grappling with eternal verities and attempting to explain this enig-
matic world in which we find ourselves. And his successors such as Niels
Bohr and Werner Heisenberg continued this exploration of the frontiers of
reality, taking me with them as they plumbed the nature of matter, energy,
space, and time. (What a contrast with the numbing physics of pumps and
pressures we were drilled with subsequently.)

About the same time, I discovered science fiction and after 'lights out'
spent hours spent under the bedcovers reading with a torch. My selections
from the library were made indiscriminately-anything whose cover bore
the library's code for science fiction, an X. Voyages to impossible planets,
travels through time, beings with other bodies and other realities than mine
expanded my world and filled it with wonder.

I used to imagine what it would be like to be a creature from another
corner of our universe, forged in different circumstances. What would things
be like perceived through other senses? Supposing our windows to the world
gave us not reality as we so easily assume but a distorted substitute. If so
what is reality? Do we have any chance of apprehending it?

And there was no need to go to other planets. Gazing into the eyes of my
grandmother's spaniel and half-wild tabby cat, I wondered what reality was
like for them. What really happens in a feline or canine mind or heart?
What do they experience as they look back at me?

At school, my teachers and classmates of Irish, Polish, Italian, Indian,
and Chinese extraction offered glimpses of different human worlds. I wondered about the inner reality of the Malay, Johnny Yap who saw "The Sound
of Music" eighteen times, about 'Fingers' Dowling the compulsive shop-
lifter, and about my friend Amrit who had flown coloured kites on dusty
Indian hillsides. I almost made the jump to perceiving that my own
enculturation already created a set of filters subtly determining what I paid
attention to.

And here also were those minds from the past-Racine and Corneille,
Shakespeare and Milton, Cicero and Caesar-whose works we read. If they
could travel through time, I wondered what they would make of the 20th
century. Somehow I knew that automobiles and aircraft, televisions and
telephones were only part of transformations that meant communication
across time and space would be even more hazardous than it is with our
contemporaries. Each of us, as Louis L'Amour puts it, 'perceives the world
in the light of his own experience'.

LATER ON
Dimly I recognized that Catholicism offered me a world view which clashed
with two incongruities. One was the dominant spirit of society all around
me. Playing football in Christchurch Park with sundry friends and fellow
Ipswichians propelled me into a different universe than that suggested by

the church, breathless, sweaty, earthbound, confined to the here and now, scrambling to control a small leather ball. That ball symbolized the tunnel vision most people seemed to display in life. I discovered, as I mixed with townsfolk in holiday jobs at the Post Office, seaside restaurants, and building sites that I was rubbing shoulders with those for whom the Holy Trinity had no meaning, particularly compared with the pay-packet, Friday night at the pub, or pin-ups and related matters.

The other incongruity was more subtle. About half my teachers wore black robes to the ground and white dog-collars with a kind of small forked, white bib. These people had taken vows of poverty, chastity, and obedience, and dedicated themselves to service to the Almighty through teaching. While they were clearly good people, their message of the all-importance in a secular society of Divine Life did not quite shine through into daily life. They seemed much like everybody else in their strengths and weakness, foibles and failings. Whatever the words, the quality of life irradiated did not make us respond naturally with a confident trust that 'These people have something we must have.' The message was strangely hollow. Its main potency for me lay in raising a 2000-year-old standard with the message 'there is more than meets the eye' to which thousands of great minds had rallied. I could not dismiss it lightly as not true. But what had happened to the transforming inspiration that had sent the martyrs to joyful deaths and so impressed a jaundiced empire that the Old Gods had been abandoned and forgotten? Had the message of the Saints been somehow disconnected from well-springs that were there, waiting for rediscovery?

I had no map and no guides, but a ferment of renewal and discovery was in the air as anyone who grew up in the West during the 60s will remember. Years later I remembered watching Malcolm Muggeridge interview an Abbot and a Yogi on TV when I was fourteen. I remembered recognizing the voice of theory and mind in the Abbot and knowledge through lived experience in the Yogi. I could tell that this silk-clad long-haired man from the East had a deeper lived experience of God than the man of God from the West. I had no idea at the time how or why this should be, nor that this Yogi would later become my spiritual teacher.

In the meantime, as I moved on through my schooling, I began to sort what I had been told from what I knew for sure from my own experience. Three things stood out:

* My internal state varied. I sometimes felt clearer, better than at other times.
* It was possible to influence that state by what I did, the company I kept, and even what I ate, drank, or smoked.
* My normal state was often far from what I perceived to be optimum either in myself or in others.

I concluded from the above that it ought to be possible to find a way of influencing my state in a positive direction, that accounts of illumination, ecstasy, and integration ought not to be rejected out of hand — for who knew where the boundary would be? — and that the ideal ways would be 'natural' without the damaging side-effects of the chemical utopias then being explored.

Already by the end of the 1960s many meditative alternatives jostled for attention. A couple of chance encounters led me to Transcendental Meditation (TM), then of recent popular fame due to the patronage of the Beatles. I had met a wistful young woman in Durham whose boyfriend disappeared for several days to London to 'see his guru', who turned out to be a teacher of Transcendental Meditation. She followed in his footsteps and wrote to inform me of her progress. Her brief and shakily written note claimed that "TM was great". Six months later I received a similar epistle. But this time the handwriting was neater and firmer. Something had changed.

About the same time a friend told me that he would visit a TM teacher, who lived in Suffolk a few miles from us. We caught a double-decker bus out to the still green fields near Woodbridge, where a well-spoken and enthusiastic artist-cum-farmer's wife collected us. Impressed by the vivacious manner of the telling, and attracted by, yet sceptical of, the enormous claims made, we decided we had nothing to lose and possibly much to gain by starting. The clincher for me was the claimed naturalness of the practice. Anything that worked with nature rather than forced or strained against it must be good, I thought, sensing that if grass and cows grew naturally then so ought we.

A few days later we returned with fruit and flowers for a short ceremony and our first plunge into inner depths. The experience was a revelation for me. Already at 20 I felt the world too much with me, my powers wasted in a thirst for novelty that had left me dry and wondering how I was to nourish my later years. In just a few seconds I felt as if reconnected to what I can best describe as a well-spring of healing gentleness within, as sweet as the daffodils I had brought with me. I recognized that that source was really always there, part of my true being, inviolate and inviolable, whatever encrustations I allowed to accumulate on the surface of life. The following days enriched and rounded out this discovery, reminding me that this was something I could take wherever I went, even on buses and trains. And it spilled over into every aspect of waking life, scaling away the accumulated crud to reveal clearer colours, sharper sounds, and a happiness, freshness and delight in whatever I was doing.

A week later I returned to Liverpool University, where my studies had gone dry, interest withered by a young tutor's response to my first essay: "If you've come here to be stimulated, you have come to the wrong place." This had installed a self-fulfilling prophesy which had lasted for the following eightteen months. Then fresh from my inner renewal I happened upon this passage from Rousseau:

The ebb and flow of this water, its sound, continuous but swollen at intervals, striking my ears and my eyes without interruption, replaced the inner movements that reverie was extinguishing within me and were sufficient to make me feel with pleasure my existence, without taking the trouble to think . . . What does one enjoy in such a situation? Nothing outside of oneself, nothing but oneself and one's own existence, and so long as this state lasts one is self-sufficient, as God is . . . Without movement, life is mere lethargy. If the movement is uneven or too strong, it arouses us, bringing us back to the objects surrounding us.[1]

I recognized that this passage described something similar to what I had encountered in meditation. I sensed too that the pattern of the experience indicated universal principles governing the mind's functioning. Gradual reduction of inner activity, while alertness is maintained, reveals a greater awareness that transforms and irradiates the humdrum.

I also sensed that Rousseau's experience was intimately connected with the creative process, and the creative process in both artists and scientists intimately linked to expansion of awareness. These two experiences set in motion a journey that has continued to this day, but whose main lines for the next 14 years were the exploration of the role of states of heightened consciousness in the creative process in artists and writers, in the shaping of their work, and in its anticipated impact on the perceiver.

During this period of research a poster on a breeze-block wall at the University of East Anglia, 'Learn How to Study', caught my eye. I had studied for many years, but had been told virtually nothing of how to do so. The course matched my intuitions of vast untapped riches to the human mind. It also offered practical ways to draw upon it, such that my intractable academic work started maturing into shape and the mountains of reading became more manageable and better managed. Before long, I was working with Tony Buzan's Learning Methods Group while completing my thesis, offering courses in learning skills to students, teachers, and business people in schools, colleges, and company training departments in the United Kingdom and overseas.

It soon struck me that even such universally useful techniques as Mind Maps (a visual noting technique) eluded some souls. Others would love visual notes for planning essays and projects but loathe them for noting from books or lectures and meetings. Once again I was being reminded of the differences in the way each of us organizes our world and of the tremendous power of our beliefs and deep feelings to make or mar our performance in any field.

Eager to understand the mysteries of the world of the learner, I began to explore a brash new discipline, Neuro-Linguistic Programming (NLP), a self-styled 'study of subjective experience', that offered tools for 'modelling' how our patterns of perception and thought determined both our successes and our failures.

I was by now thoroughly embued with an Eastern approach, which emphasized the primary importance of a long-overlooked dimension of life, our consciousness-the inner essence that illuminates all else. Both intellectually and experientially this was my habitual reference point. From there, I engaged in the exploration of more manifest layers of life, latticed, like a interwoven webs emanating from a central source.

NLP in contrast had developed from the outside in, and at times made me wonder if it would ever adequately probe our elusive core. Its founders saw that the senses filter all that enters in or out, and grounded their approach in the sensory nature of almost all our experience. They also took the utterances of everyday speech and tried to trace the deeper, fuller structures, from which the deletions, distortions, and generalizations of workaday words arise. But they seemed to have no conception of the subtle screen of awareness upon which the contents of experience are projected.

Later pioneers in the field dug deeper to unearth the buried layers of beliefs and values, and thence the organizing principle of our identity. More recently, practitioners of this young discipline have begun to map whatever may lie beyond. This book makes a further contribution to that process.

Makers of models and maps, mappers of metamaps and metamodels, some of the key explorers and developers of NLP, inspired by the visionary thinking of Bateson, seeker of 'the pattern that connects', began in the late 1980s to outline a unifying model. They sought something that would not only integrate the multitude of principles, patterns, and practices that have mushroomed in less than two decades from NLP itself, but in a much wider sense could provide a 'meta-model' for the multifarious principles and practices, arising from the quest of Freud, Jung, Rogers, Perls, and so many others for a new and practical science of mind.

That caught my imagination for I have always liked and distrusted maps: revealers of relationships, diviners of distance, guides and companions for journeys, yet reductive simplifications, deceitful selectors and omitters. Maps have helped me make a pathway through life. But I've always felt a need to imbibe them and use them, and then discard them to face the irreducible freshness of what is. In time, I've enjoyed returning to old maps and renewing them. I've enjoyed discovering new maps and comparing, contrasting, and combining them with old ones to create fresh ones.

Within and beyond them, something subtle and exciting has always drawn me like a migratory bird seeking its place of birth — the sense of approaching closer the perilous place that no map reaches, yet to which all maps ultimately point, the territory that is most map-worthy and most unmappable, in the inner sanctuary of our being, the essence that defies categorization, which bubbles like a life-salving spring from elusive regions that words seek to secure, like nectar in a sieve.

Maps have edged me there again and again, only to split and tear, from overuse and alteration. A map is a means and not an end, an aid to the journey, but not the destination. This work patches together the beginnings of a map of maps. But it also raises signposts that point beyond itself to the irreducible ever sparkling territory that is our inner essence, our birthright and our beauty.

AND YOU?

What special moments of awareness did you experience as a child? How have they continued to influence you since?

NOTE

1. J.J.Rousseau, *Les Rêveries du promeneur solitaire*, Oeuvres Complètes, Gallimard, 1959, pp.1045-47. My translation.

APPENDIX

Living Awareness in Practice

DAILY ROUTINE

What we attend to grows. Awareness needs time and attention. Here are some activities that help turn attention back to that source of quality which contains all experience:

* Take at least one, ideally two, periods of silent meditation each day

* Listen to inner Being beyond the 'I' for your direction each day

* Give time to the body for free-movement, dancing, stretching, yoga, etc.

* Use 'dead-time' — moments of waiting in queues, travelling, showering, in the toilet, cleaning-teeth, walking,   even eating alone — to settle into the bodymind. Allow breathing to be a little fuller and deeper, and feel the flow of awareness with the breath. Notice what is happening and be aware of that which is experiencing.
From that place, gently appreciate the contents of consciousness

* Allow yourself to function with attention directed gently to 'the edge of the beam' in the 'twilight zone' between the conscious and unconscious

* Balance activity with rest and relaxation

* Eat moderately what enhances your well-being

* Minimize the intake of toxins and stimulants

* Gently savour moments of transition, such as those from sleep to waking. Allow them, if possible, to lead you naturally to the moment of readiness to rise. Seek a tranquil state of bodymind as the pathway to deep and peaceful sleep

* Keep some kind of journal. Record little and large moments of happiness or awareness from the day. Record small milestones in the miraculous journey of self-discovery. Freewrite, starting from anything; let your story unfold by itself

* Identify and incorporate into daily life your own activities and rituals for enhancing the quality of life and unfolding awareness.

KNOW AND FOLLOW YOUR PURPOSE

If you don't already have a strong sense of personal purpose, make discovering it a priority. Once you have it, check that it aligns all aspects of yourself.

If it does, trust and follow it.

CLEAR PAST HISTORY

If unhelpful patterns of living and behaviour persist, probe them gently, either with the tools we have outlined here, or with the help of someone skilled with whom you have rapport and feel comfortable. Clearing unhelpful patterns may include:

* Neutralizing past traumas and associated beliefs
* Reintegrating split off or conflicting parts of the psyche
* Releasing tension and old holding patterns in the body
* Revising core mistakes about ourselves, others, or the world.

HELPFUL COMPANY

Although each is responsibile for his or her own journey to living awareness, we may lose the threads of personal progress. Keeping company with like-minded people can help, as we explore possibilities and share progress together. Awareness Groups are one vehicle for this; books, another.

AWARENESS EVENTS

Extra days, weekends, or weeks — alone or with others — given over to unfolding awareness give impetus to this remarkable adventure. The benefits are often long-lasting.

Enjoy the destination with each step of the path!

SOME KEY TERMS

Allowing: Allowing what happens in the bodymind to happen.

Accepting: Welcoming what is happening in awareness without attempts to stop or change it.

Acknowledging: Indicating to deeper aspects of the bodymind that one recognizes what is happening in awareness.

Appreciating: Accepting in a loving way what we experience so that deeper aspects of it emerge.

Asking: Checking inside for a deeper sense of meaning or direction.

Attending To: Allowing ourselves to remain aware of some experiential content.

Attention: Directed awareness.

Awareness: That consciousness which is ready to become conscious or aware of something.

Awareness Groups: Groups that meet to be together, and to explore, and enjoy awareness as an individual and group phenomenon.

Awareness-in-the-Body: Awareness which is grounded in the body and in which the body participates.

Awareness-in-the-Head: Like awareness of; awareness that is cerebral and cognitive. The awareness enjoyed by the seeing, hearing 'I'.

Awareness-in-the-Universe, Awareness-in-the-All: Awareness which is not only grounded in the body, but experiences itself as a local event in the larger field of awareness in which everything occurs.

'Awareness of': Being aware of some particular content; noticing content, but not necessarily the knower or that which contains the content.

Being: That which simply and dynamically is, our ground.

Belief: A decision about self or world that shapes future patterns of response in the bodymind.

Body Awareness: Awareness of the body. Also that awareness which the body has, through touch, etc.

Bodymind: The body and mind as a single entity in which subjective events have a physiological aspect and *vice versa*.

Coherence: Conflict-free balance and alignment in the bodymind that unifies and harmonizes differences in the individual or group, allowing them to have a powerful unspoken influence on the environment.

Conflict: When part of the bodymind wants or attempts something in opposition to another part, either simultaneously or sequentially.

Congruence: When all parts of the bodymind are aligned, supporting and agreeing with the conscious direction being taken or expressed.

Consciousness: That which enables us to be aware.

Core Awareness: Awareness of our own inner being.

Core Mistake (or Misperception): An influential belief about ourself or existence that has been true for the individual and has affected their life radically, but is not fundamentally true, e.g. 'I am unworthy'.

Core Pattern: A pattern that is part of identity and organizes many patterns on more manifest levels of experience, such as the behavioural level.

Directing: Turning, focusing, and holding the attention to enable us to be a aware of some content (as opposed to allowing the awareness to flow freely how and where it will).

Energy: Energy is our inner experience of our bodies in excitation. Energy is neither as material as the physical body nor as subtle as consciousness, it is the body moved and moving.

Energy Lock: Part of the bodymind where the energy flow is interrupted, restricted, or bottled up.

Excluding: Suppressing or holding something out of our conscious awareness. May be a deliberate (conscious) or unconscious process.

Focus: Hard/Soft, Wide/Narrow, Foveal/Peripheral vision, Foreground/Background, Figure/Ground; these terms cover a similar terrain. Awareness can be relatively 'open' or 'closed', narrowed down or containing more. We may be more or less aware of what else is potentially there besides what is at the centre of our attention.

Holding Pattern: A pattern in the bodymind which leads us to hold our bodies and hence its energies in a certain way, thus creating an energy lock. Freeing an energy lock is temporary until the holding pattern is itself dissolved. This requires belief change at the level of the bodymind (i.e. cognitive, affective, and physical).

Imprint: The residue in the bodymind of a marking experience or experiences. An imprint is a kind of learning that continues to shape and drive beliefs long after it may have been consciously forgotten.

Intention: Awareness consciously or unconsciously oriented towards an outcome.

Living Awareness: That awareness which is the life to our life.

Noticing: Becoming aware of something, registering some content.

Pattern: Some configuration in the bodymind that recurs. Patterns may be on almost any level of experience (postural, gestural, verbal, behavioural, emotional, etc.) and may encompass many levels and contexts.

Pure Awareness: That level of awareness which simply is, but can contain all active forms and contents of awareness.

Primary Stress: An overload to the bodymind that leaves a physical holding pattern and core beliefs which will influence or determine responses to subsequent stressors.

Resisting: The act of holding back some natural urge or desire, resulting in internal conflict, disruption in our internal energy flow, and incongruence in the bodymind.

Self Unfolding: The process of allowing the self to open to itself through undirected movement, sound, art, etc.

Shutting Down: The result of resisting or holding back — a giving up by key parts of the bodymind and with that the suppression of natural energy and vitality.

Techniques: Methods to awaken and re-educate the bodymind to full awareness. Life is better lived spontaneously than in or through techniques. However, the effects of techniques, used in their own time, can seep through automatically into everyday life. Examples: Freewriting, Meditation, Self-unfolding (through movement, sound, etc.)

Trauma: A shock to the bodymind that creates holding patterns and influencing beliefs.

Unconscious (The): That which is not conscious at any moment. That which is not conscious may become so, and may need to do so before we can enjoy living awareness. Some parts of the unconscious may be closer and more accessible to consciousness than others. Much feared, the unconscious can be our ally, both in unfolding inner awareness and in manifesting the creative potential that goes with living awareness.

Reading Around Living Awareness

A H Almaas, *Essence: The Diamond Approach to Inner Realization*, Weiser, York Beach, ME, 1986.
Diamond Heart, Diamond Books, Berkeley, CA, 1987-90.
The Pearl Beyond Price, Integration of Personality into Being: An Object Relations Approach, Diamond Books, Berkeley, 1990.
Hasan Askari, *Spiritual Quest: An Inter-religious Dimension*, Seven Mirrors, Leeds, 1991.
Alone to Alone, Seven Mirrors, Leeds, 1991.
H Benoit, *The Supreme Doctrine*, RKP, London, 1955.
Itzhak Bentov, *Stalking the Wild Pendulum*, Destiny, Rochester, NY, 1988.
Morris Berman, *The Reenchantment of the World*, Bantam, NY, 1984.
Coming to our Senses: Body and Spirit in the Hidden History of the West, Bantam, New York, 1990.
Richard N. Bolles, *How to Find Your Mission in Life*, Ten Speed Press, Berkeley, CA, 1991.
Richard M Bucke, *Cosmic Consciousness*, Dutton, NY, 1901.
Linda Cappachione, *The Creative Journal: The Art of Finding Yourself*, Swallow, Athens, OH, 1979.
Leslie Cameron-Bandler & Michael Lebeau, *The Emotional Hostage: Rescuing Your Emotional Life*, Future Pace, San Rafael, 1986.
Anthony Campbell, *The Mechanics of Enlightenment*, Gollancz, London, 1975.
Seven States of Consciousness, Gollancz, London, 1973.
Ken Carey, *Starseed: The Third Millenium*, HarperCollins, San Francisco, 1991
Richard D. Carson, *Taming Your Gremlin: A Guide to Enjoying Yourself*, Harper, New York, 1983.
Forrest Carter, *The Education of Little Tree*, U of NM, Albuquerque, 1991.
Deepak Chopra, *Quantum Healing: Exploring the Frontiers of the Mind/Body Medicine*, Bantam, New York, 1989.
Perfect Health, Bantam, London, 1990.
Unconditional Life: Mastering the Forces that Shape Personal Reality, Bantam, London 1991.
Paulo Coelho, *L'Alchimiste*, Carriére, Paris, 1994.
James Cowan, *Letters from a Wild State: an Aboriginal Perspective*, Element, Shaftesbury, 1991.
Tony Crisp, *Mind and Movement: The Practice of Coex*, Daniel, Saffron Walden, 1987.
Liberating the Body: Movements that Awaken the Inner Self, Aquarian, London, 1992.
Mihaly Csikszentmihaly, *Flow: The Psychology of Optimal Experience*, Harper, New York, 1991.
Anthony de Mello, *Awareness*, Doubleday, New York, 1990.
Joanna Field, *A Life of One's Own*, Virago, London, 1986.
Eugene Gendlin, *Focusing*, Bantam, New York, 1981.
Natalie Goldberg, *Writing Down the Bones: Freeing the Writer Within*, Shambhala, Boston, 1986.
Amit Goswami, *The Self-Aware Universe: How Consciousness Creates the Material World*, Simon and Schuster, London, 1993.
Nicholas Hagger, *The Fire and the Stones: A Grand Unified Theory of World History and Religion*, Element, Shaftesbury, 1991.
Douglas Harding, *On Having No Head - Zen and the Rediscovery of the Obvious*, Arkana,

London, 1986.

The Little Book of Life and Death, Arkana, London, 1988.

Head Off Stress, Arkana, London, 1990.

Andrew Harvey, *Hidden Journey*, Arkana, London, 1991.

John Heider, *The Tao of Leadership*, Wildwood, Aldershot, 1985.

Jean Klein, *Transmission of the Flame*, 3rd Millenium, Guernsey, 1990.

Jeffrey Kottler, *Private Moments, Secret Selves, Enriching Our Time Alone*, Ballantine, New York, 1991.

Brian Lancaster, *Mind, Brain, and Human Potential: The Quest for an Understanding of Self*, Element, Shaftesbury, 1991.

Ellen Langer, *Mindfulness*, Harper, London, 1991.

Anne Morrow Lindbergh, *Gift from the Sea*, Hogarth, London, 1985.

Maharishi Mahesh Yogi, *The Science of Being and Art of Living*, SRM, London, 1966.

The Bhagavad Gita, A New Translation and Commentary, Chaps I-VI, Penguin, Harmondsworth, 1967.

Franklin Merrell-Wolff, *The Philosophy of Consciousness Without an Object*, New York, 1973.

Dan Millman, *The Way of the Peaceful Warrior: A Book that Changes Lives*, Kramer, Tiburon, CA, 1984.

Arnie Mindell, *Working on Yourself Alone: Inner Dreambody Work*, Arkana, Harmondsworth, 1990.

Richard Moss, *The I that is We*, Celestial Arts, Berkeley, 1981.

The Black Butterfly, An Invitation to Radical Aliveness, Celestial Arts, Berkeley, 1987.

Sri Nisargadatta Maharaj, *I Am That*, Acorn, Durham, NC, 1988.

Eva Pierrakos, *The Pathwork of Self-Transformation*, Bantam, New York, 1990.

James Redfield, *The Celestine Prophecy*, Sartori, Hoover, Alabama, 1993.

Sogyal Rinpoche, *The Tibetan Book of Living and Dying*, Rider, London, 1992.

Natalie Rogers, *The Creative Connection: Expressive Arts as Healing*, Science and Behavior, Palo Alto, 1993.

Gabrielle Roth, *Maps to Ecstasy: Teachings of an Urban Shaman*, New World, San Rafael, 1989.

Winifred Rushforth, *Something is Happening*, Gateway Books, Bath, 1983.

Peter Russell, *The White Hole in Time*, Aquarian, London, 1992.

Martin E P Seligman, *Learned Optimism*, Knopf, New York, 1990.

Alistair Shearer, *Effortless Being, The Yoga Sutras of Patanjali, A New Translation*, Wildwood, London, 1982.

John O Stevens, *Awareness, Exploring, Experimenting, Experiencing*, Eden Grove, London, 1989.

Charles T Tart, *Waking Up: Overcoming Obstacles to Human Potential*, Element, Shaftesbury, 1988.

Michael Washburn, *The Ego and the Dynamic Ground*, Suny, Albany, 1988.

Ken Wilber, *The Spectrum of Consciousness*, Quest Books, Wheaton, Ill, 1993.

Peter Wrycza, *Higher States of Consciousness and Literary Creativity*, unpublished doctoral dissertation, U. East Anglia, Norwich, 1983.

& Luh Ketut Suryani, *Moksha: A New Way of Life — Practical Wisdom for Our Times*, Bali Post, Denpasar, 1996.

Nelson Zink, *The Structure of Delight*, Mind Matters, Santa Fe, 1992.

TO CONTACT THE AUTHOR

Peter can be contacted by *e-mail* at
100410.1423@compuserve.com

by mail at
Pos Restan, Sidemen, Karangasam, Bali 80864, Indonesia

In Europe,
c/o NLP World, Les 3 Chasseurs, 1413 Orzens, Switzerland
Fax: +41.21.88.777.21

INDEX

[Note: **the references in bold** with *ff* (and pages following) are the principal entries for the subject]

acceptance 171
acknowledging 55, 171, 174, 200, 202
Adler, Janet 92
Al Huang 84
alertness 65
Alexander Technique 85
Aquinas, St Thomas 107
attention **3***ff*, 57, 65, 109, 127, 138, 143, 212
  body 147
  broad 201
  edge of the beam 109
  and senses 5
awareness **11***ff*, 212, 230
  balancing opposites **72***ff*
  body 55, 80, 87
  core awareness 54, 64, 175, 180, 203
  edge of the beam 9, 193
  flat or lively 31
  ground of language 129
  heightened 58, 128
  and heightened language 4
  as knower, knowing, and known 98, 121
  and language 133
  'of' 13, 15, 24, 30, 54, 63
  and patterns of nature 66
  pure 12, 15, 17, **20***ff*, 24, 27, 39, 57, **62***ff*, 71, 98, 115, 127, 163, 181, 225
  and purpose 183
  and senses 101
  and time **53***ff*

Balinese 55
Balzac, Honoré de 46
Bateson, Gregory 8, 42, 107, 237
beliefs (see also levels of life) 26, 130, **153***ff*, 199, 237
  absorbed from others 220
  affirmations, caution with 174
  core beliefs 157, 159
  definition and function 155
  descriptive 155
  exploring 167
  formation 157
  about identity 172
  injunctive 156
  interrelated patterns 175

language and head, heart, viscera 172
  letting go 172, 206
  opinions 157
  part cognitive, part affective 158
  presuppositions 156, 161
  secondary 159
  structure 159
  unconscious 157
  underlying assumptions 170
  updating 169, 172
body 25, 171
  awareness, (see 'awareness-in-body')
  centres 146
  time 83
  wisdom 82
  two sides and language 147
bodymind 158, 169, 173, 215
Bohr, Niels 233
boredom 54
breathing 77, 102
Bucke, Richard 62
Buddha 218
Buzan, Tony 236

Caddy, Eileen 42
Campbell, Joseph 217
capabilities 26, 199
coherence, group 154, 165, 197
commitment 216-7
congruence 122, 144, 192
conscious mind 7
consciousness 57
  and awareness 12
  collective 213
  contents of 13
  group 228
  heightened 220, 225
  witnessing 41, 51
creative gap 14, 17
creative connection 118, 122, 170
creativity 11, 54, 65, 121, 168
  and language 129
Crisp, Tony 92, 161, 196

dance **85***ff*, 117
Dante 30, 39

De Niro, Robert 46
Derrida, Jacques 133
differences and unity 65
Dilts, Robert 52, 70, 156, 177
dissociation 47
dualism 66

early warning signals 11
Einstein, Albert 232
Eliot, T.S. 13
emotions 80, 116, 227
environment 25
Epstein, Todd 185
exercise 72, (also see movement) 86ff, 227
expressive arts 117

feelings, finest 26, 115ff
Feldenkreis Method 85
food 227
freedom 148
freewriting 57, 123
fulfilment 183

Gendlin, Gene 172
goals (see intention)
God 29, 160, 232
   transcendent or immanent 97
groups 197ff, 205, 228
   awareness 228, 240

Hall, Chris 135, 177
Harding, Douglas 24, 31, 89, 101, 104, 195
Hatha Yoga 84
Heisenberg, Werner 233
Heraclitus 62
higher states of consciousness 100
Hopkins, Gerard Manley 46, 102, 142, 149, 179

'I', the 30, 65, 80, 147, 158, 179, 196, 212, 217
identification 61
identity 27, 178, 182, 192, 194
incongruence 144
individuality 38
intellect 26, 106ff, 115
   and fine feeling 106
   and mental grouping 108, 154, 162
   mistake of 133-4, 161
   noticing presence/absence 109
intention 6ff, 11, 15, 54, 68, 185
   conscious 193
   goals 185
   intuition 9
   prayer 7
   setting 9
   ultimate 61

intuition 11, 15-6, 85, 92, 115

John of the Cross, St 42, 97
journal 33ff, 57, 123
Jung, Carl Gustav 39, 237

Keats, John 46
Ki Aikido 84
knower, knowing, and known 98, 131, 215
   and perception 201
Kolb, David 199

language 36, 126ff
   appreciation 142
   and bodymind 143, 147
   and communication 136
   as meta-language 132
   mirror of self 129
   miscategorization 134
   and nature 130
   and personal maps 136
   subject-verb-object structure 131
   two sides 146
leadership 19
learning 17, 218
letting go 56
levels of development 36ff, 225
levels of life & experience 25ff, 63, 98
   transfiguration/natural world 29
life of quality 1, 10-1, 225
love 41
   divine 221

Maharishi Mahesh Yogi 100
Mallarmé, Stéphane 127, 177
maps of reality 225
Maslow, Abraham 39
massage 105
maturation 35
meditation 74, 78, 83, 93, 117, 163, 206, 226, 239
memory 54, 57
mentors 46
mind 26, 106
Mindell, Arnie 92, 193
mission (see purpose)
Monroe, Marilyn 126
movement 71, 83ff, 131, 206, 226
   Self-unfolding movement 227
   structured 84
   unstructured 87
Muggeridge, Malcolm 234

nervous system 62
Nisargadatta, Swami 30, 41, 195
NLP 236

Open Heart Learning 150, 154, 163-4, 228

pathways to transformation 215
  apprenticeship to a teacher 216
  spiritual/religious group membership 218
patterns 66-7, 127, 227
  core 163, 174
  exploring 165
  in groups 204
  in language 138, 151
  personal 161-2
  ultimate core pattern (see Intellect, mistake
  of)
  uncovering 162
perception 98
  heightened (see senses)
perceptual positions 37-8, 45ff, 64, 132, 203,
  207, 215, 221-2
  switching among 50
Perls, Fritz 237
Proust, Marcel 13, 46, 57, 102
psi 29
purpose **182**ff
  and action 191
  and calling 184, 190
  finding one's 187, 228
  and goals 185
  personal 183, 187, 239
  ultimate 182
  and vision 184, 190

Ramana Maharshi 101
relationships 18, 35, 49, 198, 216, 227
representations 3, 98, 127
rest 72, 117, 169
Rilke, Rainer Maria 46, 77, 102, 197
Rogers, Natalie 92, 118, 195, 237
roles 180
Roth, Gabrielle 88, 92
Rousseau, Jean Jacques 236
Rumi 42

Sacks, Oliver 46
Self (higher) 44, 57, 117, 119, 132, 171, 179
self (personal) 7, 27, 47, 55, 120, 127, 178,
  183, 196, 212, 217
loss/surrender of 196
self-reflexivity 201, 207
self-transcendence 78
Self-unfolding 87, **89**ff, 215, 239
  and creative connection 120
  movement 117, 170
senses 25, 96, 185, 227
  heightened perception 98
  personal bias 103
  responses to 99
sensory systems 137

shadow 39
Sign of the Cross 148
sleep 83
  between waking and 32
Sogyal Rinpoche 13
sound 94
space 6
Stevens, Wallace 181
stillness 71, 131
supernatural 29
surrender 216, 218

Tai Chi 84
Tart, Charles 200
Tennyson, Alfred Lord 13, 58
time 12-3, **53**ff
  future 4
  past 4
  present 4, 55
time line 57
timeless moments 58
Traherne, Thomas 97
Transcendental Meditation (TM) 74, 235
transpersonal 29, 39, 212

unconscious 7, 11, 27, 83, 119, 137, 160
unified field theory of awareness 68, 132
unity 42, 61, 65, 197
  and differences 62, 134

Valéry, Paul 13, 15, 75, 101, 127
values 26, **109**ff, 237
  core values 110
  and finding personal purpose 188
values mandala 112

walking 6, 94
Way in Wisdom 221, **224**ff
wholeness 144, 148, 160, 162, 183, 194, 197,
  212, 215
Williams, Robin 46
wisdom 134, 150, 211, 221
witness (see consciousness, witnessing) 213, 221